D1644907

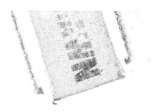

THE ENGLISHMAN

'Gypsy Life'.

REGINALD POUND

THE ENGLISHMAN

A Biography of Sir Alfred Munnings

HEINEMANN

LONDON   MELBOURNE   TORONTO

William Heinemann Ltd

LONDON MELBOURNE TORONTO

CAPE TOWN AUCKLAND

THE HAGUE

First published 1962

© REGINALD POUND, 1962

Printed in Great Britain
by The Windmill Press Ltd
Kingswood, Surrey

Contents

Illustrations

Author's Note

To LADY MUNNINGS I owe thanks for help in acquiring essential material for this biography and permission to use it; particularly for giving me access to letters in which Sir Alfred Munnings revealed himself often more intimately than he felt able to do in his autobiographical books, *An Artist's Life*, *The Second Burst* and *The Finish*. I thank the publishers, Museum Press Ltd, for allowing me to quote from those volumes. Except where otherwise stated, quotations in the text are from Sir Alfred's letters, by courtesy of Lady Munnings.

I have been fortunate in being able to call on the experience and guidance of Mr Humphrey Brooke, Secretary of the Royal Academy, who allowed me also to draw freely on his time and patience. His suggestions have been invaluable. He gave me the opportunity to see many letters written to him by Sir Alfred Munnings. In regard to parts of the book, I have had the advantage also of recourse to the President of the Royal Academy, Sir Charles Wheeler K.C.V.O., C.B.E.

Despite the suggestion in a leading article in *The Times* of 1 November 1958, that there are bounds to the necessity of acknowledging one's sources in writing history and biography, I cannot forbear recording my thanks to others who have helped with generous contributions of reminiscence and good will. In printing their names below no order of priority is followed. If there is any omission it is accidental and deplored.

Sir Gerald Kelly P.P.R.A., Dame Laura Knight R.A., Mr Charles Simpson R.I. and Mrs Ruth Simpson, Mrs Dod Procter R.A., Mr Henry Rushbury R.A., Mr James Gunn R.A., Sir William Hutchison P.P.R.S.A., Mr W. E. Plumstead, Major R. Macdonald-Buchanan, Mr Stanley Wade (Messrs Frost & Reed), Mr Oscar Johnson (Messrs Leggatt Bros), Mr James Green (formerly of the Bond Street Galleries) and Messrs John and Richard Green, Major Thomas Bouch, Lady Diana Cooper, Mr E. J. Rousuck and Mr A. W. Rawlinson (Messrs Wildenstein), Mr A. Egerton Cooper, Mr Anton Lock, Mr Adrian Bury A.R.W.S., Mr Guy Schofield, Mr Garnet Wolseley A.R.W.S., Mr Frank Law F.R.C.S., Mr Ian MacNicol, Professor John Mavrogordato, Sir Kenneth Clark, Mr John Booth, Mrs Dorothy Jones, Mr Pierre Jeannerat, Miss Emily Draper, Miss Rosemary Hancock, Mr Collie Knox, Mr Nevile Wallis, Mrs E. Porter, Mrs Evelyn Noel, Mr Jack I. Straus, Mr Marshall Sisson C.B.E., A.R.A., F.R.I.B.A. and Mrs Sisson, Mr Walter P. Starmer, Mr William Munnings, Mrs Marie Strube, Mr B. J. Waterhouse F.R.I.B.A., Mr John Young, Mrs John Read, Major-General R. D. Inskip, Mr Anthony Gray, Mr R. H. C. Callaby, Mr H. M. Bateman, Dr C. F. Bunting, the Hon. David Astor, Mr Donald Fraser, Mrs D. Grapes, the editor of *The Cornishman*, Lord Mottistone, Mr R. H. Mottram, Miss Patricia Potter, Mrs H. Rodwell, Mr E. Johnson Taylor, Miss A. M. Toulmin, Mr Walter Spradbury, Mr Dudley Down, Mr P. Welham-Clarke, Mr Tom D. Copeman, Mrs M. Fowler-Dixon, Mr Oliver Brown (the Leicester Galleries), Mr Fred Butters, the Secretary, City Club, Norwich, Sir Colin Coote, Mr George Bell, Mrs Phyllis Read, Mr Owen G. Bales, Miss G. M. Cason, Mrs Clare Collas, Mr Eric Entwisle, Mr R. J. Minney, Sister Henrietta Mills, Mr J. M. Woolf, Mr F. Hubbocks, Mr L. G. Ramsay, editor of *The Connoisseur*, Mr. J. P. Kennedy, Los Angeles Turf Club, Mr Ruskin Spear, Mr Sebastian Earl, Mr J. H. Martin, Mrs Jo. Collings, Mr Michael MacCarthy, Mr Victor Bridges and Mr H. A. Bush.

For facilities provided, practical help given, and suggestions made by Mr H. Watson Vince, Librarian, Eastern Daily Press Ltd, Norwich, I have reason to be specially grateful. Thanks are also due to the Librarian of the Royal Society of Medicine, the Librarian of the Central Library, Norwich, to the London editors of the *Melbourne Herald* and *Sydney Morning Herald* and to the B.B.C. Publicity Department.

CHAPTER 1

Tragedy in the Fields

(1)

FOR the young artist walking that afternoon in the East Anglian fields there was more than the wind on the heath to make life sweet. Soon to be twenty-one, he had already tasted the wine of success and the satisfactions of independence. He owned the studio he painted in, part of the carpenter's shop in his native village of Mendham, on the Suffolk side of the Waveney Valley. He had bought it freehold for £50, out of his earnings. At eighteen, he had exhibited at the Royal Institute of Painters in Water-colours. At twenty, he had two pictures in the Royal Academy, the first of the three hundred and more which he was to exhibit there, often with resounding success, in the coming years. He had won the gold medal at the Poster Academy held at the Crystal Palace. The future beckoned him with alluring visions of fulfilment beyond the pale of the Norwich School, in whose gentle traditions he had been trained and whose leaders, Crome and Cotman, held his deferential respect.

The Norwich art-dealers, who mostly sold antique furniture too, were ready with cash and encouragement. They were headed by the Boswell brothers, Jim and Sam, whose family business was founded in the eighteenth century. Sam, 'thoughtful and refined', would counsel him: 'Don't do pot-boilers.' Jim, the true dealer, would be at him with the demand: 'Sell it – and paint another!' Shaw Tomkins, director of the local chocolate and mineral-water firm of Caley – 'the kindest, gayest, most happy and optimistic friend a youth ever had', the young man afterwards wrote – gave him commissions to do designs for Christmas-cracker box-lids. Payment was in gold sovereigns. Their jingle in his pocket was one of the artist's abiding memories, a symbol of good times to be recalled with boisterous poignancy in the years that lay ahead. 'There was I, a provincial, youthful artist, with good patrons and jolly dealers who gave me lunch, made us all merry, and bought pictures and took them away in a waggonette, smoking large cigars and waving good-bye. It is unbelievable, yet it happened again and again'.

It was not only the last year of the nineteenth century. It was the end of an exciting, perhaps the most exciting, decade in modern British art. George Moore had proclaimed the gospel and the blue-smocked cherubims of the art schools were intoning it: 'Art is the praise of life and it is only through art that we can praise life.' The air was loud with art controversy. The long supremacy of the Royal Academy was being challenged.

Strife with convention gained the day so far as to allow the triumphant impressionism of the '80s to be tempered by the personal and, if need be, idiosyncratic vision. A new *raison d'être* was acknowledged, seeing through the eyes rather than with them, art as a source of spiritual enrichment. The New English Art Club and the still newer Glasgow School indicated vitality and produced variety. Nothing like it had been known before in British art history.

Not that the art philosophies much interested young Alfred James Munnings out in the fields of Mulbarton with a trio of dogs racing ahead of him as he walked. He could have been thinking of the fair-haired girl in the Boswells' shop in London Street, Norwich, 'who would often trill like a bird, playing her own accompaniments on a piano standing among chairs, china, tables and pictures', and whose name he did not mention when recalling her in print fifty years after. She was Miss Elsie Langham and her clear soprano echoed long and pleasurably in some Norwich memories. Of the seductive charm of those musical interludes in the top-lighted gallery of the shop there is no doubt. They could only happen, he said, when the Boswell brothers were away. 'I was attracted by her.' Perhaps the Boswell brothers were not away often enough.

There was for a certainty one obtrusive topic, money. It had been coming to him more easily than to most young men of his age and class. He spent it as if in no doubt of the continuance of that fortunate state. His first impulse on receiving it was usually self-indulgent. He sold the weighty gold medal of the Poster Academy to the Boswells for six sovereigns, 'and spent the money the same night on a dinner'. He wondered what was the fate of the gold medal and wished that he had not sold it. Not until sixty years after did he learn that the real buyer was his early Norwich admirer and patron, Thomas Henry Porter, a builder, who was told, after acquiring it, that Munnings regretted the transaction and who thereupon handed the medal back to the Boswells, expecting them to return it to Munnings. Apparently they never did so. It was worth more than £6 melted down.

For the time being, he was in a condition of financial restraint. He had been spending too freely on pleasure and work was in suspense. At Barclay's Bank, Harleston, where the manager, George Stebbings, looking at him through gold-rimmed glasses, was less respectful of his talents than of his kinship with one of the branch's oldest customers, Munnings senior, his account was well below the £70 which he regarded as his economic safety margin. Why £70? 'Seventy pounds, more or less,' he would say if pressed, while being unable to explain why he had fixed arbitrarily on that amount.

Or the problem of the Royal Academy may have been in the forefront of his reflections out there in the fields. He *dreaded* – his own emphasis – rejection by the Royal Academy, now that he had once been accepted there. He dreaded it so much as to be darkly reserved about his sending-in plans, telling no one what pictures he was submitting. He wrote of 'the discordance, the jolt, the shock', of being rejected, 'after weeks of waiting here in the country'. He found a phrase to define his feelings when that crisis occurred; it was 'a pause in life', as if his entire career hung in the balance, as if art existed only at Burlington House.

Those low-tone preoccupations were always at the mercy of his response to nature, to Hazlitt's 'wrinkle in a leaf, the tinge in a cloud', that filled every day with new excitements of the senses and quickened in him the pleasure and the pain of the artist's life. The cry was constantly on his lips: 'If only I could paint what I see!' He did not see heavenly hosts in the rising sun; he did see the miraculous in the stippling of a bird's egg, in the explicit unfolding of a bracken shoot. For him there was absolutely no tedium in nature. His eyes had a ready-for-any-thing look, his sight was the instrument of the liveliest curiosity and the channel of a delight in the natural scene that could bring him to reverential tears.

He was sensitive to the wonder of existence, yet seldom troubled by its mystery. The fates had granted him the boon of a happy childhood, its perennial symbol the Millais little-girl study famously known to the Victorians as 'Cherry Ripe'. A reproduction of it, one of the hundreds of thousands issued with the Christmas number of *The Graphic* in 1880, hung in his bedroom to the end of his days, placed so as to be the first object to meet his eyes on waking: 'facing me as I lie in bed, she always looks demurely down on me'. He was not cursed with the ingrowing temperament which, coiling upon itself, springs its hateful tensions on others. The tensions that chiefly beset him were those implicit in the artist's struggle to answer the question: 'How in God's name can one do it?' Almost in his last year he wrote: 'Meeting old difficulties again, I realised more than ever that the artist lives and works alone.'

The ease with which he detached himself from the gregarious-ness in which he revelled when the mood was on him was noted by more than one of his contemporaries of the Norwich days. It seemed at odds with the mercurial mental briskness, which in turn was hardly characteristic of his yeoman context. Land-scape, the matrix of his visual imagination, was a formative influence that always excluded the urban scene from the range of his sympathies. It was one of his most frequently repeated pleasures to walk alone by the Waveney river that was the source of his father's livelihood as a miller. Friendship for him was apt to be an affair of hearty acquaintance rather than the deeper state usually implied. Places meant more to him than people. No human relationship assisted the realisation of his gifts and powers so completely as the scenes of nature that were his birthright.

(2)

England is a land of noble views. They are not to be found in Norfolk. The county is more memorable historically than scenically. Its sea-level landscapes, its fine church towers disposed on gentle contours, its great elms embossed on modest skylines, charm the heart rather than seize the eye. It is our fifth largest county and its heritage of history is rich indeed. In some respects the most English part of our country, all its prospects pleased Alfred Munnings and that not only because they offered him escape from the quasi-commercial life in Norwich to which his indentures had committed him for six years.

Idling away his few days' holiday at Lodge Farm, Mulbarton, with an aunt and uncle named Hill, 'who bred hackneys and farmed in a considerable way', he thought about his future as an artist aspiring to be free of the mental limitations and physical disciplines of applied art, then his means of support. 'Working to order' was for the craftsman, the blacksmith, the thatcher, the harness-maker: the artist could be in chains to no taskmaster but his inspiration. Munnings found it in landscapes which, for all their lack of the larger splendours, produced in him the passion to do his best and probably his most lasting work.

'Fresh discoveries of all that paint could do led me on', he wrote. 'What joy there was in finding out and seeing colour – becoming aware of beauties in everything, beauties never seen before; and although I lazed away precious hours . . . I must have worked most of the time during that first free summer, for I lived in a painter's paradise.' He thought then, and long after, that East Anglia was the most paintable part of England.

(3)

That day, as he walked over his uncle's farmland, one of the dogs started a hare and coursed it, the others frantically follow-

B

ing. The chase took them through a quickthorn hedge into a field of swedes. The hound puppy, which was being walked on the farm, struggled to find a way through. Munnings lifted the puppy over a hurdle and set it down among the swedes. As he straightened up in readiness to swing himself over to the other side, a twig rebounded from his weight and he felt a sharp prick of pain in his right eye. When he shut the other eye, he saw red fog. He stood there by the hedge, experimenting with his sight, shutting first one eye, then the other. The red fog did not disperse. Calling in the dogs, he returned to the farmhouse, hoping for the best because it was not in his nature to fear the worst.

The doctor from Harleston prescribed fomentations and a lotion. In the evening Munnings called on the Drapers at Hall Farm, Mulbarton, a well-known local family, whose daughter Emily remembers him 'going out of the room several times to bathe his eye. He seemed to be in pain'. Possibly too late, he was sent to see the best-known Norwich eye-specialist, Johnson Taylor M.D. The diagnosis was alarming. The eye had been pierced by a thorn, which had set up complications.

Johnson Taylor, formerly resident medical officer to the Severn Tunnel scheme, was a Norwich personality long remembered by his patients, particularly the poorest, to whom he was as likely as not to say after an examination: 'Toss you half-a-crown or nothing.' He was known to take a catapult to meetings of the British Medical Association in London and shoot paper pellets at long-winded speakers. He had no hospital appointment in Norwich and, therefore, no beds for his patients, on some of whom he performed major operations in his consulting-room at 44 Prince of Wales Road. He was well thought of at Moorfields Eye Hospital, London, and it was there that he sent Munnings, who was one of the early subjects of X-ray examination. It showed that he had lost, beyond recall, the sight of his right eye.

CHAPTER 2

People of the Valley

(1)

As an eager young artist whose dreams of success had been amplified by his unusually early foretaste of it, Alfred Munnings showed a good spirit in his misfortune, which, by the compensatory processes of nature, proved to be less calamitous than he and those around him had at first feared. Uniocular vision has its temporary advantages, as every artist knows. All artists are used to occluding an eye in contemplating or judging certain technical effects. The problem for the artist who is permanently deprived of the use of one eye is how to conserve the power of the other, a consideration that caused George du Maurier to turn from drawing for *Punch* to writing *Trilby*. Eye defects have had more important consequences for the visual arts than for literature; for example, El Greco's astigmatism, Durer's squint, Turner's cataract, Constable's colour-blindness.[1] Recourse to the Royal Academy library yields remarkably little information about one-eyed artists. Alfred Munnings stands out among them as a shining example not only of success but of fortitude.

After the accident he was professionally nursed in one of the five-storey, white-stepped Georgian houses of Surrey Street, Norwich, where the Misses Bunting had their Boarding-house for Young Ladies, where Professor Leopold Sloenitz taught languages, and where other brass plates announced homoeopathic practice and that of orthodox medicine and the law. Lying there, the upper half of his face severely bandaged, he was often

1. P. D. Trevor-Roper M.D., F.R.C.S. (London) reported interesting observations on the subject in the *Proceedings of the Royal Society of Medicine*, September 1959.

heard to raise his voice in song: 'Sweet Rosie O'Grady' and
'The Blue Alsatian Mountains', his 'star turns', he called them.
'What a go!' he would call out as the door opened to admit his
latest visitor, inaugurating an exclamatory habit of a lifetime.
The nurses were impressed. They thought him a remarkable
patient, if careless of his language. Long before Shaw introduced
the word 'bloody' into *Pygmalion*, Alfred Munnings was doing
his best to immunise society against the shock of that innovation.
There were rare down-phase intervals in the graph of his
recovery. Disturbed by the depth of his depression during one
of them, his mother sent a young orphan cousin, John Read,
to sit with him. His services were not needed. By the time he
arrived Alfred was in full song again.

Unfettered by the darkness, his thoughts must have ranged
over many aspects of the familiar past. Its dominant figure was
his father, John Munnings, the Waveney Valley miller, who
combined strictness of character with a kind of rural Bohemianism
that made him a popular frequenter of the village Red Lion and,
at the same time, a church lesson reader of such dramatic force
that people came from other parishes to hear him. He liked to
declaim in the masterful way known as 'holding forth'. Alfred
said that he read the lessons 'in the grand manner'. He gave the
Prayer Book responses in a loud resonant tone, standing with
his right hand firmly cupped over the carved poppyhead that
adorned the chancel end of the family pew. A Mendham contemporary who made notes for private circulation recorded that
'there was a touch of the actor about John Munnings'. His
wife remarked over the Sunday joint: 'John, I wish you wouldn't
work yourself up so, as you did this morning over the Agony
in the Garden.' He answered: 'Ellen, *I* wish you'd mind your
own business.'

Alfred recalled, as a chief memory of his church-going at
Mendham, looking through his fingers during prayers at a
long-haired girl sitting with her sisters in a pew across the aisle.
Her name was Ethel Notley – 'an old sweetheart of yours', he
was reminded years after, by which time she had become the
wife of a famous circus proprietor, Bertram Mills.

He also recalled his father's sharp temper, usually a sequel to overnight indulgences at one or more of the Valley inns, where he was given to drinking gin in his beer. Blustering hotly to his mill engineman, named Sowter, he threatened: 'You deserve to have your backside kicked. And I've a good mind to kick it!' Sowter's knuckles whitened over his occupational oily rag as he answered with a gleaming eye: 'I shoon't do that, master. People's backsides get riled sometimes.' The retort gained the engineman legendary status in the village.

Stockily built and short-legged, with a good forehead and a laugh that seemed to come from his eyes rather than from behind the beard that did not so much grow on his face as hang histrionically from it, John Munnings liked to cut a dash in his light red-wheeled trap drawn by a grey mare with a silvery mane, especially when the object of the drive was a session at the Magpie at Harleston after a call on George Stebbings at Barclay's red-brick bank opposite. On summer days he would put on a light alpaca jacket and a grey topper, with a yellow rosebud in his button-hole. It pleased Alfred to recall 'the spruce appearance of the whole turnout'.

He remembered more vividly still the evening when there was a commotion among the millhands and, leaning from an upper window of the mill house, he saw his father limping down the lane with blood on his face. He was frightened when someone asked him: 'What would you have done if your poor father had been killed?' Recalling the episode, he said that he had 'trembled with fear'. His father had cut too much of a dash rounding the corner into the mill lane and was thrown out. 'Irish whiskey was the cause of that spill', Alfred remembered, and it was a potent factor, too, in diluting their relationship into a lukewarm affection that, later, Alfred regretted and wished had been otherwise. 'I never made a friend of him until later in life and then, alas, too late.' His mother's admonition to his father echoed down the years in Alfred's memory: 'John, you've been drinking again!'

His happiest recollection of his father was of him reading to the family in the winter evenings. 'Supporting his forehead with his left hand as he turned the pages with his right, he was a picture, sitting at the table, the shaded lamp throwing its light over him and upon the book and part of the green tablecloth. To increase the light on the page, a pair of upright candlesticks stood on either side of him', giving him the consecrated look of an Old Master subject, especially when he was reading from *The Pilgrim's Progress*. When he read from Dickens, the candle flames were apt to cower before the explosive family laughter. ' "Sam," said Mr Pickwick. "Sir," said Mr Weller', and John Munnings's smiling eyes would anticipate one more hilarious climax. To hear him read Dickens, Alfred said, was 'a thing to remember', an experience buttressing his contention that it was impossible to have a dull childhood 'with a good story going on each night interwoven with our work and play'. Home life at Mendham Mill had enough of enduring happiness in it to be always gratefully recollected by Alfred Munnings.

'I see it all so plainly', he wrote in mournful retrospect, when the mill had changed hands to become 'a luxuriant riverside dwelling' on which £20,000 had been spent. He saw himself back there on peaceful Sunday afternoons, 'the flat, calm islands of the water-lily leaves' patterning the mill pond, as he took tea with the family under a weeping ash tree. 'Brown wheat loaves, cakes – sometimes ham or sausage rolls, with cream in the tea, if all was well or guests were staying. What days! Great, healthy girls to work and do in the house. Always there were Pollys and Sarahs and Nellys or Marys. . . . Peaceful enough, with the heavenly light of a summer's day over all. Alas! "The past is over and fled." '

(2)

Both parents were of farming stock, their roots deep in the English soil. John Munnings was born at a farm at Little Horkesley, near Dedham, auspiciously for his artist son, who did not hide his satisfaction in being able to say that John Constable's father was a miller too. John Munnings appears to have learnt the miller's trade at Shonks Mill, Ongar, Essex. As a young man he gained local prestige by his spirited contributions to the Penny Readings that were a favourite form of instructional entertainment before the 1870 Education Act provoked large-scale newspaper and periodical production and distribution.

The family history interested Alfred only in his later years, when he regretted having so little information about it. He could write of his father: 'We knew nothing of him, his life, his brothers and sisters', of whom there were nine, 'his beginnings, his thoughts'. One of the brothers, James, having worked in a Colchester bookshop, became a professional reader for Bentley, the London publisher whose list had at one time been headed by Charles Dickens. The paternal grandfather farmed at Scotland Place Farm, Stoke-by-Nayland, where in the shadow of the high church tower painted by Constable there are Munnings graves with headstones dated 1817, 1830, 1842 and 1848.

Beyond that, Alfred's knowledge of the family line was sketchy to vanishing point. He went back to the Stour valley in later years on a pilgrimage of piety with his father. They saw Flatford Mill, 'beautiful, unspoilt, as in the days of Constable'. There were the locks, the barges, and horses on the towpath. 'Only the sound of the mill, ducks on the stream, and the breeze in the trees'. With the passing of time, pain and anger took the place of pleasure in his reminiscence of the scene. 'No bottles or food papers littered the meadows. No sound of car or charabanc. Constable's age has gone. Ours is here.'

Like many of his class, he played with the notion of superior antecedents and filled a page of one of his autobiographical volumes with not wholly beguiling extracts from *Suffolk Manorial Families*, which encouraged that fancy with a hint that the name of Munnings once had its prefix of nobility. 'It appears that my true name should be de Munnines or de Mooninges', a possibility that attracted him more than another arising out of a suggestion that he had inherited the genes of a Dutch flower-painter of the seventeenth century named Johan Moninckz. A coat-of-arms was attached to the Norman alternative, but he was never enticed into inquiring after it. The petty social embellishments were not essential to his pleasure in life, though he was susceptible to and jealous of the traditions ensuring their existence. Reaching in due time socially higher planes, he seemed to find satisfaction in referring to himself as 'a mere plebeian'. In any event, according to the historical source-book, the Munningses, variously spelled, were considered as far back as 1659 to be a family 'long since almost worne out'.

(3)

Less forcefully obtrusive into Alfred's nursing-home reveries was the image of his mother, born Ellen Ringer, one of the daughters of William Ringer, who was a farmer and also the agent for a local landed estate. When he died, his widow continued farming at Walsham Hall, Mendham, a farmhouse having no claim to the status implied by its name. The Ringers were a large farming clan. William Ringer boasted having sixty cousins.

Darkly attractive, in some eyes handsome, his daughter Ellen was classified as 'refined' by local standards because she did not pronounce 'have' as 'haive', or use the word 'say' when she meant 'says', and because she could play the piano and sing to her own accompaniments. That assessment of her quality was assisted by the strain of melancholy in her nature. Strongly evident in the entries made in her diary, kept on Sundays only, and reflecting the Victorian obsession with mortality, it offset her husband's assertive style and was capable of evoking from him what to some was a surprising tenderness of concern.

'I have been reading Longfellow's verses (she wrote) – *The Rainy Day* – it is typical of my feelings. At times . . . I think – What use is Life? But no doubt there is still something left for me to do. The daffodils are in full bloom; as I stand near dear little Joe's grave beneath the ash trees, I live over again the happy times we passed in their shade, the summer tea parties, when I lay there so many days on my sofa. In the years to come, when Mendham is only a memory, I know they will all look back to the happy summer afternoons and talk about them, perhaps when I am in my grave. Writing of graves reminds me, that before church this morning, I sat on the wall by the old floodgates, and made a wreath of daffodils which I placed on my mother's grave when I went to church. The service was not, to my mind, refreshing or peaceful.'

The particular grief was for the family dog. Alfred, too, could not put it from his mind. 'Butchers' carts were always driven at what we then thought was a terribly reckless speed; and thus ended poor Joe's life. The misery we suffered – that I suffered – on that afternoon was deep enough, and the memory of that scene at the end of the lawn brings tears again': this was written more than fifty years after. Joe, of mixed terrier breed, had been his inseparable companion. He delighted in the memory of Joe being out with him for an afternoon walk when they met staghounds returning from the hunt. Ignoring the hounds' deep disapproving growls, the little dog placed himself at the head of the pack and proudly led them home to the kennels.

Munnings said that his mother was 'full of organ-playing, music, poetry, of Scott, Thackeray and Dickens, and a hundred sunsets over the river', rhetorical implication of the basis of his own self-expressive impulses and of her superiority to his father as a source of creative encouragement. She played the organ in other churches besides Mendham's. After hearing Mozart's Requiem in Norwich, she wrote in her private pages: 'I would work a month to hear music like that, and what few chances I have had!' She confided there on another Sunday: 'Oh, the blessedness of being able to work! I have so many worries that I cannot rest long except I have a book to divert my thoughts.'

The occasion of that declamatory outcry was the Balance Sheet (capitals hers), which in April every year was a cause of household apprehension, not allayed until it was clear that the mill accounts had 'come out on the right side'. Dating from the fifteenth century, Mendham Mill was the largest on the Waveney, a river with other mills at Hoxne, Syleham, Needham and Weybread. Flour was sent from Mendham Mill as far away as Hull and Newcastle-on-Tyne. Apart from bad harvests, John Munnings was sometimes handicapped by bad debts.

Another recurring hazard was the price-cutting of the big millers at Ipswich and Norwich. He was sustained through difficult times by his friend Stebbings at the bank at Harleston, who held out the helping hand that was then a freer prerogative of bank managers than it is today.

Sometimes John Munnings drove to the bank with 'considerable sums' in wash-leather bags stowed under the driving-seat of his trap; once, Alfred remembered, £200 in gold. For protection, he carried a pistol. His boys could never hear often enough how one night, returning late from market, his horse's bridle was seized by two men demanding money. He fired the pistol over the horse's head. The frightened grey mare lunged forward, knocking one of the men down, the trap wheels bouncing over him as John Munnings whipped the horse on into the darkness.

The 'considerable sums' spoken of by Alfred in his references to his father did not mean affluence for the family. Ellen Munnings complained that she was never able to buy enough furniture for the mill house and some of the rooms remained forbiddingly bare. A cousin (Mrs Horner of Yoxford) remembered in after years: 'As a girl, I dreaded bedtime when I stayed at the mill. I was scared by the noise of rats running round the walls.' Life there was often harder than Alfred chose to reveal. In the good years a governess was attached to the household; once a Miss Tongate, another time a Miss Woodcock, not only instructing the four Munning boys but raising the family status in the village. More often, local girls were engaged to walk them out like foxhound puppies in the lanes and fields. Alfred, looking back over seven decades, preferred to remember them as governesses too.

CHAPTER 3

Boyhood at the Mill

(1)

H E was born at Mendham Mill on 8 October 1878, the second of John and Ellen Munnings's sons. On his fourth birthday his father had put into his hands a toy horse. It became so much a part of his childhood that he remembered it affectionately all his life. It was the inspiration as well as the subject of his first drawing, done when he was six. Thereafter to him the horse was a creature of destiny – 'my destiny' – and the noblest animal in creation. East Anglia was its kingdom. The Suffolk Punch and the Norfolk Bay were still supreme in their native scene, where the ringing of the blacksmith's anvil was as familiar a sound to local ears as that of the church bells.

There might not be profit in speculating on what meaning, if any, the toy horse had in Munnings's life. It can hardly be construed as a symptom of psychological morbidity that in his adult imagination he liked to play with the idea of Amazonian nudes on horseback. He had an inheritance of sound health, sustained by the enfolding peace of his earliest surroundings, Mendham's weather-boarded water mill, swan-white and serene amid the poplars and willows of the long green valley. He insisted, looking back: 'Environment is everything. Mine was all that I could wish for.'

His formal education began at the village school at Mendham, a fact not mentioned in the account of his early years given in his first reminiscent volume, *An Artist's Life*. All that he remembered learning there was to memorise the Marlborough battles by the code word BROM, for Blenheim, Ramillies, Oudenarde and Malplaquet, never dreaming that a day would come when he would paint a Duke of Marlborough at his palace of Blenheim. From the village school he and his brothers William and Frederick went on to the small grammar-school, at one time known as the Commercial School, at Redenhall, a daily walk of about three miles each way. He afterwards wrote: 'We liked that school, with its headmaster, Christopher Hall. He encouraged me to draw.'

Three weeks before his thirteenth birthday he was sent to Framlingham College, founded in 1864 as the Suffolk county memorial to the Prince Consort. He was there four terms only. The fees were paid by his mother. She had gone into stock-farming in a small way on her own account, hiring land for the purpose between the mill and Walsham Hall, where two of her sisters still lived.

He left Framlingham at the age of fourteen with 'bitter resentment', his own words. 'I hated the place. I was damned miserable there.' He could not forget a particular experience during a preparation period. 'I was drawing something or other. Suddenly the master spoke. "Will Munnings come here to me and bring with him what he is drawing?" ' Disapproving of what was shown to him, the master gave him a caning before chapel. 'There in his room did I bend over a chair, receiving in spite of my "Please, sirs", six vicious cuts, all on the same spot. How I sat in chapel I can't tell. This was villainous treatment for what I had done.' The villain of that account was the second master and senior modern languages master, Alfred Pretty. Young Gainsborough, over at Sudbury, a few miles away, had been more fortunate in his day. When he played truant from the grammar-school to fill his exercise-books with sketches from nature, his father proudly exonerated him with the boast: 'Tom will be a genius!' John Munnings watched his son's development as an artist with little curiosity and even less encouragement.

At Framlingham, *alma mater* of the sons of Newmarket trainers, well-off farmers and successful tradesmen, Pretty was the outstanding personality next to the headmaster, the Rev. Dr Oliver Digby Inskip (1852-1934). Pretty incurred Alfred Munnings's lasting dislike as 'a cross-grained fellow' who inflicted other chastisements upon him with a severity their victim for ever after thought unjust. 'One day we rushed up the corridor a minute late for breakfast in the large hall. For this slip he ordered us to get up each morning at seven, fill his cold bath, and then parade up and down the school drive from the statue [of the Prince Consort] to the gates and back before breakfast, and until further notice. . . . We cursed that fool of a master.' Not every Framlingham old boy of that period would have endorsed Munnings's unyielding verdict. Alfred Pretty, who died in 1940, was considered by many to be a successful deputy headmaster at a time when the College prospered in numbers and repute.

Art teaching at Framlingham consisted of the symmetrical free-hand drawing from copies that was the usual form of school art instruction. The art master was Edward Walter Lynch, who was genially proud of Munnings's early successes as a painter. Munnings never acknowledged any benefit from the art teaching at the College, an omission not entirely due to his brief tenure as a pupil there.

Visiting Framlingham years later with Mr and Mrs Marshall Sisson, he told them how he used to stand in front of the school gazing at Framlingham Castle in the sunset, imagining it as Torquilstone Castle in *Ivanhoe*. 'I really thought it *was*.' He recalled his father, on his regular Wednesday visits to Framlingham Corn Exchange, bringing with him 'a cardboard box full of cakes and pies from home, all tied up with odd bits of string'. He spoke of the College as 'a rotten place', and said that he had been 'clapped and cheered' for stating as much in a speech at the only Old Boys' dinner he ever attended.

(2)

The mill that was his home was still shaking to the motion of its water-wheel, with smoke going up from the tall chimney-stack of the engine-house that supplied auxiliary power. Lying in the nursing home, he could see himself as a schoolboy watching Sowter, the engineman, going about his business with oilcan and waste-rag, a being of secret knowledge whose nonchalant intimacy with the moving parts excited envy and admiration. To have the heavy hinged door of the wheel-house opened for you was always a favour and meant submitting yourself to another experience of the spellbinding sort, the wheel's revolution were so massively inevitable, the air dank and mossy in there, an underworld of ominous possibilities. There was the less intimidating pleasure of watching the sacks of corn being hoisted skyward on the brightly polished chain, clicking like castanets, that raised them from the farm-waggons below to the high jutting platform called the lukem, which received them into the bins. His father had a fright once when young Alf looked out of the door on one of the upper floors just as a sack of flour was being sent down on the chain. The sack hit him on the head. 'They thought I was killed.'

He remembered a morning when a waggon came early with its load. The family were at prayers before breakfast. John Munnings sprang up, leaving the rest on their knees. He went through to his office, took a sample of the wheat he had bought in the market at Norwich, and joined the waggoner outside. Putting a foot on a spoke of the front wheel of the waggon, he hauled himself up among the corn sacks to compare their contents with the sample in his hand. That done to his satisfaction, he let himself down, called out to the driver: 'All right, cocky, on you go', and returned to resume family prayers where he had left off.

(3)

Nursing-home visits from colleagues of his at Page Brothers, the Norwich lithographers, letterpress printers and wholesale stationers, were a congenial reminder of the long apprenticeship which gave Munnings his sound proficiency and a lasting prejudice against those aspirants to the successes and rewards of art who disdained 'serving their time'. He had gone to Page Brothers straight from Framlingham College, when he was fourteen. His father paid a premium of £40 to put him with the firm, who required him to work from 9 a.m. to 7 p.m., with a half-day on Saturday. He seemed to revel in the disciplines

rather than to resent them. 'My life was happy there, in spite
of the long hours . . . the work was thrilling and engrossing', a
declaration of the zest that was the hallmark of his personality
and the source of a kind of envy that is all too readily transmuted
into enmity.

'How we laughed at times!' Some of the relish was imparted
by the good-natured head of the art room at Page Bros, where
he worked with six men of various ages, 'a Mr Macready, a
well-read Scotsman, grey, sober and proper, with a clipped,
iron-grey beard and moustache and gold spectacles', who
recommended to him 'all the good books I got out of the Free
Library. He was my literary adviser, and soon I was full of
Tennyson, Scott and Dumas'.

The occupants of the art room at Page Bros wore 'long
painters' blouses' and sat at their work on high stools, each at
his own wide bench below a high north window and isolated
between frosted-glass partitions. The work most usually in
hand was commercial in origin and purpose: showcards,
chocolate and Christmas-cracker box-lids, wrapper designs,
display advertising for toothpastes and bicycles and beer, and
double-crown posters. A coloured design Munnings did of a
jovial innkeeper, pot in fist, is still displayed on the Bullard
public-houses in Norfolk, these seventy years after.

If high art could hardly flourish in those surroundings, the
impulses and emotions springing from it assuredly did. The
talk in the lunch breaks was of the great masters, the splendour
of their imaginations, the mighty techniques, the breathless
fulfilments. Commingling with the dreams and aspirations,
frustration would be expresssed in sad harmonious melodies
that filled the art room with spontaneous outpourings of feeling,
each man at his bench joining in with the best that his tenor or
baritone or bass could give. Munnings recalled that, while it
did not often happen, when it did there was a permanent enrichment of his memory. It amused him to touch the recollection
with bathos. 'We sang to perfection if I had brought in with
me two round, flask-shaped bottles of wine called Canary Sack
from a grocery stores near by.'

Not that theirs was a wholly unhallowed art. They needed

no reminding that in France especially it was given the im-
primatur of genius. The lithographs of Daumier and Géricault
were famous. Those of Toulouse-Lautrec were a new excitement
of the Paris Salon. In England, despite a refusal by the Royal
Academy to admit lithographs to its Black and White Room
on the ground that they were not original works of art, Charles
Shannon, William Rothenstein and the two fine painters who
styled themselves The Beggarstaffs, namely, James Pryde and
William Nicholson, were bringing fresh distinction to litho-
graphy, while Whistler, practising a less direct version, found
himself defending it, successfully, at the Royal Courts of Justice.

The lithographic training gave Munnings the linear firmness
that enabled him to handle his brush as a painter with an assurance that was the envy of his fellow-artists. For one of them,
Cecil Aldin, 'there was such a directness and certainty about it
that it was quite uncanny'. Like Renoir before him, who had
first painted on china, Munnings acquired the directness and the
certainty as part of the lithographer's irrevocable craft, in which
a faltering hand was not to be tolerated. 'Not a mistake could
be made – even a finger touch on the stone would print!' It
endowed him with the facility for painting first and drawing
afterwards which Sickert said was 'ideal for the formation of a
painter'. Even mixing the lithographic inks was a grave matter –
'it had to be done exactly right' – and he was kept at it every
morning for months, until his services were deemed worthy
of something better. He was receiving half-a-crown-a-week
pocket-money. His brother William said that their mother
paid for Alfred's board and lodging. He lodged with one of his
Ringer aunts, whose husband had recently failed at farming.
She was keeping a small boarding-house at Catton, Norwich.

The hours at Page Bros were long, yet he behaved as if they
were not long enough, ripping off his smock at seven o'clock
each evening, five days a week, and rushing off to the School of
Art for two even more congenial hours of work that had in it so
many elements of pure pleasure. The School occupied the upper
floors of the Free Library and its head was Walter Scott, whose
memory Munnings always revered: 'An honest soul if ever
there was one.' Something of Scott's quality was imparted to his

Alfred Munnings (right) with his father and brothers at Mendham.

The Mill, Mendham, in Munnings's boyhood.

favourite lecture theme, 'Sincerity in Art'. His students were told and told again: 'Whatever you do, do well. Don't play about.' Scott had been a contemporary of Clausen at South Kensington, an association that endowed him with something like sanctity in the eyes of the young men at the Norwich Art School, for Clausen was among the sponsors of the New English Art Club and a bold transmitter of the new ideas about colour originating in France.

Scott was probably the most influential personality in Munnings's early years. 'He was the first and foremost of my guides', and Munnings never forgot Scott's words to him on many occasions: 'Whatever you do, Munnings, don't forget the tone.' He passed out of Munnings's life at the beginning of the century, pictured in memory 'with his bowler hat worn slightly forward on one side, looking fresh, rosy and happy'. His wife, Munnings remembered, always called him 'Worlter' and saw him off faithfully every morning to the Art School from the front doorstep of their home in Queen's Road. When Scott's deputy, an art master named Cooper, saw some of Munnings's work in the School exhibition for 1899, he remarked to those around him: 'That boy can become President of the Royal Academy if he likes.'

(4)

Musing among the pillows, Munnings probably also pondered the local eminence of James Reeve, curator of the Norwich Castle museum and art gallery, who had given him an easel belonging to one of the painters of the Norwich School, on which Reeve was the greatest living authority. His home at Thorpe was a treasure-house of Cotmans principally, but of the other inspired Norwich artists also, including Crome, whose work he was said to know infallibly at sight. His judgment was behind the fine Russell Colman collection of the Norwich School, provincial England's most illustrious body of painters.

Reeve knew more than anyone else about the forgers of Constables and Cromes; in particular, about the activities in that line of a man named Paul, who was concerned in a Norwich

c

murder case. When the Director of the National Gallery in London, Sir Charles Holmes, went to Norwich to discuss a proposed exhibition, Reeve 'produced with pride' some studies in water-colour done by a young student at the Norwich School of Art. Holmes wrote: 'So completely accomplished were they that I made a note of the young man's name. It was Munnings.'

Munnings never doubted that Reeve was another of his 'guiding influences'. He sketched Reeve in words as 'this old bachelor with a large clean-shaven face, grey side-whiskers, searching grey eyes and short stiff figure, a massive gold watch chain across his stomach'. He could recall himself, at the age of eighteen, being shown Reeve's private art collection for the first time, a privilege entailing his first experience of smoking a cigar. Reeve clearly saw merit in Munnings's work and wished to encourage him. At the same time he uttered the warning: 'You want to run before you can walk.' Later he bought a picture painted by Munnings in the carpenter's shop at Mendham, one of four separate versions of a subject called 'The Horse Fair'. Reeve paid him £85. Munnings recalled it as 'a vast fortune to me then'.

That he should have had easy access to Reeve's great experience and sage advice, and to his collection of pictures, was a fortunate circumstance for Munnings. 'Consider the immense authority of the veteran curator and collector,' R. H. Mottram, the East Anglian novelist, wrote of Reeve in 1951, 'his weight with wealthy patrons, and add his seniority in age. Who could be kinder or more helpful, who could be more bluntly withering when extravagance or insincerity vexed him?'

Shortly before his death in 1920 at the age of eighty-eight, the greater part of Reeve's picture collection, formed over many years, was sold to the British Museum. It meant that for the first time metropolitan students of art were able to see a fully representative collection of works by the Norwich masters.

(5)

When Shaw Tomkins, manager of Caley's chocolate and mineral-water factory, was ushered into Munnings's room at the nursing-home the patient's face glowed a particular welcome. 'He brought a breeze with him.' Tomkins had the laugh of one who not only enjoyed life but thought it an altogether jocund affair. He was a natural hustler, walking with quick pattering steps, eagerness in every movement. He was full of ideas. He persuaded Caley's to make milk-chocolate blocks and bars well ahead of the larger firms of Fry, Cadbury and Rowntree. He introduced the first fancy chocolate-boxes to the British confectionery market. He took Munnings with him as a travelling companion on his business trips to Germany, Switzerland and France, giving Munnings the chance to visit the best of the Continental art galleries, while Tomkins went about his local business affairs. For the young artist it was a romantic and rewarding experience which impelled him to write years after: 'I can never pay sufficient homage to my old friend for those early travels.' He spoke of Tomkins, a staunch Congregationalist, as 'the jolliest teetotaller of my acquaintance, a Christian in the real sense'. That definition was tempered by his recollection of bargaining episodes in which he found himself 'cut down to a low figure' for his poster designs and advertising work: 'We haggled over shillings.' Tomkins's private patronage of Munnings was doubtless his way of showing where his real sympathies lay. 'I look back [Munnings wrote in *An Artist's Life*] and know that it was all hard work, which had to be done so that I could live and paint.'

He never forgot the Good Friday of that period when he took his painting things home to Mendham, where he was spending Easter, and loaded them, with food and drink, into the mill boat. It was his intention to find what in his artist's vernacular he called 'a spot' and to spend the day painting it. Rowing along between the Waveney's willow-shaded banks, its water-meadows shining with golden kingcups, the morning air filled with warbler song, he was completely happy. Finding at last 'a spot' to inspire him, he set up his easel. 'What joy! Like any other artist about to begin a picture, I was filled with ecstasy.' He stooped to open the japanned paint-box in the grass at his feet. A malicious hand had replaced its tubes of colour with pebbles. He always recalled the incident in the accents of despair: 'The blow hit me hard. I was utterly beaten,' dramatising his disappointment as further proof of the ardours and endurances of an artist's life.

CHAPTER 4

Making of an Artist

(1)

JOHNSON TAYLOR, the opthalmic surgeon, had urged him to
rest his good eye for six months, advice that may have saved his
career. Behind the bandages he had nothing to do but think in
pictures, invaluable mental exercise. His visualising power
gained as it were an extra magnification, so that eventually he
saw with one eye more than most of us do with two. Not long
before the accident, his artist's imagination, first kindled by
Caldecott's fairy-tale illustrations in *The Graphic* of the '80s
had received its most violent stimulus, a visit to Bungay races
in celebration of his first success at the Royal Academy.

'This was a plunge into the most vividly coloured phase of
life I had so far seen. I had known horse sales in Norwich,
local races and regattas; but what were they compared to
this vast fair and meeting combined on Bungay Common?
There were roundabouts, shooting-galleries, swinging-boats
and coconut shies; large eating-and-drinking tents, flags
flying, and thousands of oranges blazing on stalls in the sun. I
had never seen such droves of ponies and gipsy lads. But all
this, with music and noise, died away and dwindled to nothing
when I saw the thoroughbred horses and jockeys – professional and gentlemen riders . . . in bright silk colours,
going off down the course.'[1]

For him it had been a phantasmagoric stirring of the soul –
'the greatest day of my life' – uplifting him to the point of
1. *An Artist's Life*

inspiration. Bungay races was his most exciting experience so far. Apart from its panoramic splendours, had he not set eyes on Kiomi, the gipsy woman model who spoke of 'Mr Rossetti' and 'Mr Millais'? He had an old fear of the gipsy tribe, dating back to his village infancy and his first 'dreaded glimpse' of a tent in a lane and a dark man sitting by a fire. 'Our hearts stopped – we stood transfixed – then, turning, we dashed back in terror to those behind.' That haunting horror was at last dispelled. In his nursing-home solitude the Bungay race-meeting crystallised reminiscently as 'that stupendous day'. He did four brilliantly impressionistic pastel drawings of the scene and sold the set for £20. One of them later changed hands at auction for £275.

At last the bandages were removed. He was 'allowed to see the light of day again'. He then realised that he was sorry to leave the nursing-home. 'What a happy Christmas it was, what nice women the nurses were!' It was a strange experience, going back into the world with one eye. His perspectives were confused. He poured water on to the table-cloth instead of into the glass. Trying to paint, he made stroke after stroke in the air, missing the canvas.

He did not look like a one-eyed man. The accident left no obvious mark of abnormality. One of his friends thought it had improved his appearance. 'It gave him a touch of odd distinction.' A London editor, meeting him a long time after, said that he had 'the knowing jockey look', quoting Leigh Hunt's remark about Hogarth.

(2)

The Norwich that he knew differed not notably from that painted by Crome from Mousehold Heath. True, the smoke of industry flowed over the madder-pink pantile roofs and the towers and spires of its seemingly myriad churches which made such a clamour with their bells every Sunday – 'how I hated those bells!' It was still a city of restful interiors, glimpsed through Tudor and Georgian doorways approached over cobbles, and of latticed windows overlooking some of the busiest streets. That was, and to some extent continues to be, one of the charms of Norwich, an intimate conjunction of private and public living, as of a community in which everything happens just round the corner.

Munnings saw Norwich in retrospect as 'a beautiful place . . . an old city of gardens, with its cathedral, its fifty churches, its river with wherries, boats and barges, quays and bridges . . . and gabled houses in narrow streets'. If its famous school of painters was in debt to the Dutch and Flemish strains brought into Norfolk in the course of seventeenth-century Continental trade, it owed even more to an environment which he said was 'a playground for the artist. Such an unlimited wealth of motifs', he insisted, 'would tempt the dullest painter'.

Norwich gave him more than ideas about painting; it helped to improve him culturally in a number of ways, endowing him with the freedom of its library, museum, picture collections; giving him access to musical experiences that were a valuable part of the refining process. At the triennial Festival concerts in St Andrew's Hall, half church, half concert hall, he heard famous singers, noted instrumentalists, fine orchestras; and, if the Theatre Royal less often evoked the inspirational mood, it widened the range of his conversation, which increasingly tended to become a solo performance.

The city was also a base for ecclesiological excursions prompted by artistic impulses rather than religious feeling. With a friend from the life class at the School of Art, Walter Starmer, who was studying stained-glass design, he visited nearly all the churches in the southern half of Norfolk, experiencing refreshment of the soul in 'their impenetrable, brooding silence, broken only by the slow ticking of the clock in the tower above', as it beat out 'the little lives of men'. They explored most of the churches from nave to belfry, and Munnings, whose mother had taught him the rudiments of piano-playing, always looked out for unlocked organs, on which, with Starmer blowing, he would play the hymns of his childhood. Above all, as that companion's lasting impression of Munnings in those days, 'there was his contagious sense of joy in painting'. In his humility, as in his enthusiasms, he seemed to Starmer to be a dedicated man, his constant heartcry: 'Oh, God, if only I could put down what I see!'

He could readily credit others with Christian impulses and actions. For himself, religion was an emotion rather than a positive concept. An elderly lady in one of the villages where he frequently went to paint was troubled because he was never seen at a church service. When she finally beat down his evasiveness, he explained: 'I'm sorry, but I wouldn't know what to do with my hands.'

(3)

He became one of the most conspicuous of the younger members of the Norwich Art Circle, where, if there were no self-effacing painters like George Borrow's brother, who declined to paint the Mayor of Norwich because he knew someone who could do it better, the corporate experience was necessarily more mature than at the Art School. He specially valued the friendship of a senior member of the Circle, Savile Flint, a gifted painter whose hope of more than local recognition went unrealised. Munnings said that Flint might have walked out of a play 'in the part of a Victorian bachelor artist of quality and tone'. He had a 'frizzy' ginger moustache; a Wellsian character who wore white spats over brown shoes and a straw hat with a band of faded club colours. A great-grandson of Sir Charles Flint, private secretary to the Duke of Wellington, he went on water-colour sketching tours with Munnings, who said that Flint knew 'every trick of the trade', at the same time implying that Flint was inclined to dip his brushes in whisky as well as water.

There was also Bagge-Scott, President of the Art Circle, 'the best artist Norwich had seen since Cotman', in Munnings's later judgment. Munnings never doubted that Bagge-Scott, who had studied on the Continent, had painted at least one masterpiece, a work that nourished Munnings's own resolve to do better. At the same time it was a warning of the fate that could befall an artist, whatever his gifts. 'He spent much time on that picture and, I believe, sold it for fifty pounds. No wonder he was pale, bitter and needy. His end was sad. He died in poverty.'

Seeing that Munnings was selling more of his work than most of them, members of the Art Circle were sardonically amused by his grumbling about the price of paints. In a mood of economy he bought a keg of green paint from a house decorator, whose yard he had seen it in and whose hand-cart he borrowed to push it up over the cobbles of Elm Hill to the friend's studio he was using at the time. Shortly afterwards an extravagantly large acid-green landscape, signed by Munnings, appeared in the window of a dealer named Nightingale. It remained there so long unsold that it became almost a city landmark, known as 'Munnings's keg green picture'.

He did a fine water-colour of a frog which made such an impression on his old colleagues at Page Bros that they insisted on lithographing it. Munnings was begged for 'pulls' by friends and acquaintances of the Art School and the Art Circle. To each he said: 'You buy me a sixpenny glass of wine at Back's in the Walk,' a noted Norwich wine-shop, 'and you shall have a copy.' He told a young woman (afterwards Mrs Porter) who who called on him for a donation to charity: 'I want a new cushion for my studio chair. You make me one and I'll give you something for your fund.' Sixty years after she retains her conviction that he was 'a bit mean'.

At Bungay he hired a pony and trap from a coachbuilder of that place, who duly sent him a bill. Munnings drew a pen sketch on each side of the bill and returned it with the note: 'To one pen and ink drawing for Edgar Watts, coachbuilder, jobmaster, true-blue ham cutter, antique dealer and rink proprietor – take £1 1s. from £1 1s., that leaves nothing, so we're square.'

He assumed by general consent the place of leader in any group formed for the pursuit of the bucolic pleasures. One such group foregathered weekly at the Dove Inn, Homersfield. To celebrate his success at a Norwich exhibition Munnings was given a supper by the group at a public-house in Bungay. After the meal Munnings mixed what he called 'a flowing bowl'. Calling for bottle after bottle of spirits and other liquors, he

produced a punch of such potency that some of his friends
were afraid to go home for two days. There was trouble over the
bill, which by his impetuousness had mounted far beyond the
original reckoning. He left it to be settled by a Mendham friend
of his, Jack Cason, whose father, a saw-mill owner, cut his
wages as a punishment.

Meanwhile Munnings had made a private settlement of his
own with the Bungay landlord by crayoning some drawings on
the white roller blinds of the bar parlour. They were to be seen
there many years after.

(7)

According to a local newspaper writer Norwich 'treasures a
legend of the wildness of young Alfred Munnings'. The legend
is as hard to confirm as it is to refute. There is agreement
among the few surviving contemporaries of his Art School and
Art Circle years that he could fairly be charged with rakishness
in respect of two of its commonly accepted ingredients, wine
and song. As for the classical third, there is no general opinion
and all too little information. He was, it seems, no more active
in the sexual domain than the average young man who, at that
period and perhaps particularly in the East Anglian environment,
was still answerable to the codes of a puritan society.

Munnings's attitude to women generally seems to have been
subject to the inhibiting idealisation of 'Cherry Ripe', the
Millais picture of a little girl that had put such a spell on him in
his boyhood. In Norwich, when he was a student, the auburn
beauty and submissive charm of an amateur model gained her
the name of 'the Burne-Jones girl'. Munnings appeared to
enjoy being seen walking with her in the streets. Perhaps she
took their friendship too seriously. She invited him to her
lodgings. By the testimony of one who knew them both, he
thought it 'shocking' that she should do so. He was 'deeply
upset'. He ceased to go out with her.

CHAPTER 5

The Lights of Norwich

(1)

H is savings had gone. Financial recovery was possible only through the commercial art which he had hoped to put behind him. He resumed his bread-and-butter poster drawings of pretty girls in picture hats for Caley's chocolates and crackers. Soon he had the imperative £70 in the bank again.

To help with the nursing-home expenses he had sold his part of the carpenter's shop at Mendham. Three months after his release from medical supervision he set up as a free-lance artist in two unfurnished rooms at Shearing's Farm, Mendham, paying a rent of £10 a year and 15s a week for his keep. 'And what keep!' he would shout in recollection, reciting the good Norfolk fare of those days, the roast pork, 'with crackling, mind you, not a luxury then', the gooseberry pies, the home-made bread, 'so crusty and golden', the fresh farmhouse butter, and eggs laid by barndoor fowls, 'not by wretched victims in forcing houses or laying batteries'. The provender of his enthusiastic reminiscence was supplied by his farmhouse landlady, Mrs Corbyn. 'God bless her!' he wrote, always a fervent remembrancer of kindnesses and courtesies shown to him in his youth. 'A kindly ploughman' had given him his first horseback ride. A 'kindly and obliging' local station-master sent some of his canvases to Norwich. Nor did he fail to note that an income-tax official who queried his unkept accounts had 'a kind manner'.

One of his two rooms was the farmhouse parlour of earlier times. 'Its low ceiling, with an oak beam across the middle, gave it a snugness which could calm and pacify the tortured mind, however sorely distressed – as mine was when pictures were rejected, or the bank balance low, or a letter didn't come from my latest flame.'

He kept lovingly to his last days the furniture he bought for the two rooms, his first essay in domestic taste, a Jacobean oak chest, an old walnut veneered bureau, 'a gem when done up', a tall ormulu grandfather-clock with a lacquered gold cockerel on its door, a glass-fronted bookcase, and two Sheffield-plated candelabra, 'which gave tone to my parlour'. An eccentric decorative touch was his wall-hung collection of palettes, large and small and some of odd shapes. They were a reminder that the mixing of colours was a more serious affair than compounding the punch which he liked to give visitors on winter nights, 'and what a glorious, scented, steaming bowl of nectar for artists or anyone to sip! I can smell its spicy odorous steam yet, see its pale amber colour in the clinking glasses'. Alone, he spent long evenings in reading Thackeray and Surtees. He read Surtees so thoroughly and so often that he could repeat whole chapters from memory through the rest of his life.

Sometimes he went down to the village and climbed the rickety stairs leading to the loft-like dwelling of 'old Norman', a villager who remembered the 'Hungry Forties' and who had walked a hundred miles to London in 1851 to get work at the Great Exhibition. It was for 'Master Alfred' that the old man sent when in his late eighties he lay dying after a fall while apple-picking. Munnings read long passages from the Bible in the light of a guttering candle until the old man's eyes closed for ever. Munnings always remembered him as 'my staunchest friend of long ago, a nature's gentleman', and he perpetuated him in 'Whitsuntide', a much admired Munnings picture of those days.

(2)

Sitting at his easel in the village and in its byways and foot-paths, he was a familiar figure to the parishioners, who regarded him as being as much on his lawful occasions as they were on theirs. 'A passer-by greeted me, but no more thought of staying to take a look at what I was doing than he would at a man cutting a fence.' It was a party of trippers in a waggonette who goaded him by their inquisitiveness into throwing his canvas into the river.

There was a Sunday morning when his father, going to church, saw him painting a grey mare in a paddock. Showing no interest in the work itself, John Munnings called to him over a hedge: 'You'll never prosper, you know, if you paint on Sundays!' Alfred said he had 'queer feelings of doubt, a sort of chilly fear which went down my spine as I asked myself the question, shall I stop work and prosper, or get on with it and risk the consequences?' A scriptural antidote had at once suggested itself: *Whatsoever thy hand findeth to do, do it with thy might.* The painting of the grey mare was exhibited at the Royal Institute but rejected by the Royal Academy. 'I thought it was my number one picture of the year. A judgment!'

Some of the local gossips hinted that Alfred was 'drinking, like his old man'. His drinking was not a physical need. It was a social habit. He drank 'because others were thirsty', as Kipling is supposed to have said; and his natural animation was more than likely to suggest conviviality to the sternly sober-minded. A lady who knew him by sight in those days wrote to him in 1953: 'Often on Saturday nights, coming off the 10.20 train from Harleston, on the Bungay road, I met you on your horse – the latter finding its way home. I had to dodge it on dark winter nights when it took an erratic course!'

Shearing's Farm, known as Street Farm in older parish records, took its name from John Shearing, a mid-nineteenth-century farmer whose wife, Damaris, managed the farm after his death, a woman of presence and authority in the village. Munnings believed that the hands that clutched and pulled his bedclothes were those of Damaris Shearing's ghost, 'for there was a ghost in that old house'.

He was not intimidated by the notion. He liked to fancy that dead friends retained or recovered some measure of their awareness of this world. 'He may know I'm writing this,' he remarks in an autobiographical passage about Walter Scott, the Art School headmaster. 'I hope he does.' James Reeve, too, the Norwich connoisseur of Crome and Cotman: 'his eye followed

me afar then, as I humbly hope it does now.' Or the friend who
took him to the never-to-be-forgotten Bungay race-meeting:
'He may be at my elbow as I write.' He confessed to having
'tried hard to get in touch with Joe,' his dear, dead dog, 'who
was my most faithful queer little companion,' and he hoped to
paint again his mother's white pony, 'amongst poppies and
marguerite daisies', in some world elsewhere. He had another
poetic fancy, that of scanning the passing crowd in Norwich for
faces matching those of effigies seen in local church interiors.

If there was little that was morbid in his nature, he was no
stranger to melancholy, which he thought came from his mother,
with her private musings about life and death. Anatomical
studies at the Art School induced it and, still more strongly, a
Norwich Museum exhibit of 'the most perfectly set-up skeletons
of a man and horse', the man a murderer, hanged at the Castle.
They were 'a gruesome sight to encounter in the shadows or
with the white light of the moon streaming through the sky-
light'. He said the skeletons often caused him 'to conjecture on
Nature's extravagant wonders'.

He was 'overcome with horror' when he saw at the cavalry
barracks on Mousehold Heath the skin being taken off a dead
horse. He agreed that as a student his sense of wonder should
have insulated him from the shock he felt, but it did not do so.
'It failed then, as it does now,' writing in his seventies. As it
failed, for example, when he was painting at the Pytchley
kennels and saw 'a good-looking horse' being led to the slaughter-
house and the kennel-man, minutes later, starting to flay the
corpse. 'At the sight, I fled', more sensitive to what Arnold
Bennett called 'the sickening bases of existence' than many
realised, knowing only his combative temper, and themselves
insensitive to the latent poet in him.

Stubbs's *Anatomy of the Horse* had been a notable discovery
of his Norwich time, his original copy of it procured for fifty
shillings after a local dealer had advertised on his behalf. Stubbs,
'an indefatigable colossus', in Munnings's esteem, was 'a
landmark' in his art career, inciting him to intensive comparative studies leading to his mastery of horse structure, form
and stance. He not only learnt from Stubbs but set himself out

to discover 'all that there is to know about him'. He was more impressed by Stubbs's reaffirmation of the superiority of nature over all art than by his water drinking, while admiring his walking feats; for instance, missing the coach at Marble Arch, he cheerfully set out on foot for Lord Clarendon's place between Tring and Watford, sixteen miles. He was then seventy-nine. To Stubbs's achievements on canvas he bowed the head with the humility of a true disciple, while reserving the right to criticise many of his hero's backgrounds as 'afterthoughts'.

An acquaintance of Munnings in those years, Dr Alec Ross, who later practised at Hurlingham, remembered him 'wandering about Norwich in riding kit and a disturbingly dirty old hat, smelling of horses and dogs'. Another Norwich contemporary, Owen Bales, recollects Munnings 'making horses almost come to life on paper' in Low's Yard, St Giles's Street. Low was a veterinary surgeon and horses were brought to his yard for shoeing, harness measuring, and for sale as well as for treatment.

As an art student, Munnings was often seen there making notes of anatomical details and tracing them out on paper, studies that helped to give him his great understanding of horse symmetry and characterisation. Another of his haunts was the station yard, where there were always cab-horses to be studied and sketched.

Endorsing, without necessarily knowing it, the Shavian might-of-design theme, Munnings's anatomy studies made him write Nature always with the capital N. The whitened skull of a thoroughbred, which he brought to his rooms, evoked from visitors the comment, 'How horrid!' To him it was a thing of awe-inspiring wonder. 'Ivory traceries and shapes. A miracle of creation – of God; a mere trifle in a world of mysteries, of millions upon millions of God's masterpieces.' He placed it on the Jacobean oak chest. 'The grain of the wood is God's design, the grain of the bone is God's design. I know less than nothing. Looking at the perfect symmetry of the forehead, the curved occipital bones, I am astounded. What are mere paintings – politics – anything? Nature is lasting – supreme.'

(3)

His Royal Academy rejections were few; in 1903, 'five works hung out of six', 'The Last of the Fair', 'Sale by Auction, Michaelmas', 'A Country Horse Fair', 'A Gala Day' and 'The Wood Cutter', encouraging more ambitious projects during his six years at Shearing's Farm. He was selling everything he sent to the exhibitions of the Royal Institute of Painters in Water-colours. Chiefly, his subjects were horses and men of the East Anglian cattle markets and fairs, but landscape, where his heart lay, inspired 'Langham Mill Pool', an almost perfect rendering of the green and gold gaiety of a late spring day, its effects of light and air space seized with an intensity of vision that seemed to make the canvas quiver. He painted it 'for sheer love of painting', he said, and felt sorry 'for the townsmen who must toil laboriously through the schools'.

Through the first decade of the 1900s he lived a near-nomadic life within the Norfolk bounds, varied by intermittent visits to L'Atelier Julian in Paris, where, according to his ramshackle autobiography, he had some 'blissful experiences'. His appearances at that celebrated centre of Paris art teaching were in the nature of brief visits. He never enrolled for more than a few weeks at a time. Of what he learnt there that was important, he tells little in his sketchy autobiographical references to that period; chiefly, the monotonously reiterated advice of the principal, M. Bougereau: *'Continuez toujours.'* Possibly, like others before him, he gained more by inference than by example. The portrait-painter, Sir John Lavery, who was there earlier, wrote that 'the training came from what I saw rather than from what I heard'. On that hypothesis Munnings's competence was heightened by the model for the nude study, done at Julian's, which he reproduced in *An Artist's Life*.

The prospect of Paris was suggested to him in the bar of the Castle Hotel, Norwich, where 'a swell bachelor with side-whiskers painted glowing word pictures of the life'. There were hints of perils by night. The effect on Munnings was unnerving. Crossing a Seine bridge at midnight not long after arriving in Paris, he heard a splash in the river. 'There you are,' said his

Munnings, the art student, painting at a Norfolk fairground.

Munnings aged twenty-seven in 1905.

dour Scotch companion, 'they've thrown a dead body into the water!' Munnings said that he shivered down the spine. He liked to make others shiver with his highly dramatised rendering of *The Raven*. Now Poe and the murders in the Rue Morgue were making him shiver.

He returned home aglow with the inspiration of great pictures seen in the Paris galleries : 'I lost myself in profound contentment and admiration. What are pictures for ? To fill a man's soul with admiration and sheer joy, not to bewilder and daze him.' He took back with him to Norfolk an enormously enhanced regard for the gifts of Bastien Lepage, Fantin Latour, Degas and Tissot, who, he never doubted, were 'on the true path'. Compared with them, 'the old Norwich school and the Art Circle faded away into insignificance', the artist in him easily subjugating the sentiment of the local patriot.

(4)

A letter from one of the students he had known at Julian's bore the postmark 'Finchingfield'. Munnings had never heard of it. Invited to that Essex village, he found himself in a setting to be described in the manner of one reporting on a work by Watteau or Fragonard: 'An Arcadian scene it was . . . whilst all around at easels, standing or sitting, was a bevy of damsels and one or two men who didn't count. Many of these fair creatures belonged to what is known as The County. In studious, graceful attitudes, they looked most wonderful to me.'

The young women were pupils of the School of Animal Painting organised and conducted by Frank Calderon, a son of Philip Calderon R.A. and himself a regular Academy exhibitor for many years. Munnings felt his social inferiority and his situation was the more uncomfortable when he fell in love with one of the girls, Una Bell, who showed no interest in his feelings for her and may have been unaware of them. She was an accomplished horsewoman, compelling in him a lasting admiration for equestrienne *chic* as well as nerve.

There were compensatory happenings. His visits to Finchingfield gave him introductions which opened to him the door of the

D

Langham Sketch Club and the London Sketch Club, at which
centres of metropolitan art activity he was brought into touch
with men of a calibre that he had not met before, among them
Phil May, Dudley Hardy, Tom Browne and John Hassall,
familiar personalities of what he supposed was 'the true Bohemia'.
That some of them remembered works of his at the Royal
Academy naturally increased his pleasure in their society.

As yet he had no professional warranty for joining them and
their like in London and it may have been to appease resulting
discontents that he rented rooms in Norwich, over a solicitor's
office in Prince of Wales Road. The truth was that his expenses
were rising. The young women at Finchingfield had stirred in
him an urge to shine in the drawing-room and on the dance
floor, not to say in the hunting field. 'I was climbing into higher
circles', which meant, he soon found, higher tailors' bills and
other liabilities. Commercial art kept him solvent, but 'there
were some narrow shaves'; for example, 'a stinger' from a
tailor and an overdraft reminder from the bank, 'sending a
tremor down my spine'.

Pursuing overdue payments from private patrons, one of
them a local grower known as 'Tomato' Adcock, he gathered
in £35. There lay on his table an unanswered letter from
Bullard's Brewery, of Norwich, asking him to submit a new
design for a calendar. 'Never did I sit down to do a job with
such an intent to finish it and get the money', £10. His sense
of 'the uncertain future' remained.

He painted horse portraits at £10 apiece. One commission
took him to the village of Shotesham, ten miles south of Norwich,
where he put up at the Duke's Head. He is still remembered in
Shotesham from that visit of more than fifty years ago; by the
landlord's daughter, for instance, then seventeen. Her father
let him 'run up the bill' until he received the money for the
picture he was painting for the squire at Shotesham Hall. At
the old Bush Inn at Costessy he lodged for long periods at 14s 6d
a week for his bed and board. When he ran out of cash there was
always the landlord who would let him have food and drink in
return for a sketch. Subsisting largely and happily on bread-
and-cheese and beer, he was also based for varying periods at

the Hawk at St Peters, the Fox and Goose at Fressingfield, the
Wolf at Laxfield, and the White Hart at Scole, the last-named
venerated by him as one of the great inns of the coaching era.

(5)

The rooms in Prince of Wales Road, Norwich, were for work,
not residence. Mendham was too far out; it was *fast vanishing*,
underlined words expressing his restless state and leading to
what he described as his 'disloyal flight' from Shearing's Farm.
Like any other real countryman he grew into the places and
scenes that he knew best, and uprooting was always painful.
Nearer and more convenient was Church Farm, Swainsthorpe,
five miles south of Norwich and owned by the uncle on whose
farm at Mulbarton his eye accident had occurred. He arranged
to rent one end of Church Farm, with his board provided by the
wife of the bailiff, who lived in the other part. His uncle let
him put up a sectional studio, built for him by Boulton and
Paul of Norwich, in an adjoining field.

A wayside encounter of that time stayed long in his memory.
Just before leaving Mendham he was painting a familiar figure
of the village, a thatcher, in the church lane. The owner of
Shearing's Farm, a farmer named Wharton who also farmed
the land of Walsham Hall, driving in his low-slung gig, pulled
up to greet him as he worked at his easel. Munnings was
deeply absorbed in the technique of which Fragonard was the
master, involving a swifter, almost panic, pace of painting, to
seize the living minute. 'Don't leave this part of the country,'
the farmer counselled him. 'It's brought you luck. Mark well
what I say,' and, clicking his horse into movement, drove
slowly on. It was the voice of wisdom and Munnings heard it,
'but the die was cast'.

The farmer was unlikely to know that there had just been
published in a leading London literary journal, *The Athenaeum*,
an art notice in which Munnings was referred to as 'perhaps the
most vigorous of the younger nature painters. Although his
pictures show no refinement of handling or colour, they indicate
considerable natural talent'.

CHAPTER 6

A Vagabond in East Anglia

(1)

H E was in his middle twenties and on his own at last. He was riven by dual feelings. He wanted to grasp his freedom with both hands and yet was uneasy about his severance from old familiar things. 'Goodbye to the skewbalds, to Charlotte's pony, to Gray and his old gun . . . to the sound of Redenhall bells over the hill', sentimental attachments as real to him as 'the little green spot' that endeared a certain place to Rousseau or the courtyard post to Pope. But a noticeably different air gave charm to Swainsthorpe, or, as he put it, 'a more sophisticated atmosphere', and it increased the distance between Mendham and himself. Swainsthorpe being nearer to the county centre, the local farmers drove into Norwich on Saturday mornings (with high-stepping hackneys in rubber-tyred ralli carts with red or yellow wheels. His uncle Hill of Mulbarton owned a high-stepper named Hamlet – 'a liver chestnut, in the Stud Book'. He had a memory of 'being driven into Norwich with my Aunt Polly behind that mover, looking into the plate-glass windows as we went down St Stephen's to put up at the Boar's Head. These horses scarcely touched the road in their action. Fourteen miles an hour was an average for many'.

At Church Farm he kept a hunter and a groom and rode out with a regularity designed to aid his social preferment as well as improve his horsemanship, though he had to be content for the time being with the approbation of the bailiff's wife, Mrs Lodes, who, seeing him accoutred and spurred, called him 'an amazin' man'. He reckoned himself a 'hell of a fellow', dressed for the Norfolk Staghounds in a dark grey Melton jacket, white cord breeches, boots with dark-brown tops, and a black velvet cap, sartorial elegance that drew him, by his own admission, to the mirror. 'The white string gloves looked well and my boots shone', naïve rather than vain self-admiration.

His keenness on the pleasures of the chase was part of his hearty appetite for life, but it was subordinate to other responses. 'I saw many things on those days: bright winter sunlight on bare trees, on stacks, on farmhouse gables; the riding out after a slight frost; the riding home with a frost beginning and a young moon in the sky; puddles already crisping over as I said good-night to friends. Such were needed to freshen my mind and vision.' He was not making excuses for his indulgence in a controversial sport. The Norfolk Staghounds hunted the carted stag. He was not a blood-sport partisan. He was content to be named by the Master as 'artist to the Hunt'.

He rode forth into landscapes that impelled him to paint some of the finest of his early works and confirmed him in the opinion that the challenges of that branch of art were 'so difficult that if a young artist were too aware of what is ahead he might never dare to begin'. He could not look at a successful landscape by another hand without bringing his mind to bear on 'disheartening obstacles encountered and overcome', Hazlitt's 'friendly strife with nature', that is more often an exhausting wrestling with reality. It was not only the internal conflict. Munnings wrote in *An Artist's Life*:

'Working against the climate through the seasons wears an artist out. That is why artists should be forgiven for all the exaggerated stories told of them. No indulgence in pleasures of all kinds can be too well-deserved a reward, or can recoup the wearied soul of the painter, whether he loses or wins the struggle. He deserves a jolly good dinner if he wins and needs a jollier one if he loses.'

Generally, he approached landscape with the gravity of a trustee of the 'natural' tradition in English landscape art. The spirit in which he painted landscape was contemplative, a fervent concentration on what to him was 'beautiful, romantic and restful'. He had no mind for what we now call 'involvement'. He painted landscape for the pure pleasure of it, a comment that does not fit the commissions that were later to make him rich. He was happiest at opening magic casements, as in 'Gravel-pit in Suffolk' and 'Evening at the Ford', and his landscape painting of the years in East Anglia may be the largest part of his title to the esteem of that posterity which survives the poisoning of the wells. If he perishes, it will be in good company.

One of his most impressive Norfolk paintings, 'The Timber Gill', depicting a familiar scene in the autumn woodlands, prompted its purchaser, Thomas Porter, the Norwich builder, to suggest to Munnings that he was 'capable of handling more important things'. Munnings wrote to him from Church Farm in or about 1906:

> Dear Mr Porter, Your advice is perfectly right – I know it well enough, but to conceive a great work and carry it out is not as easy as one thinks.
>
> I myself know just what I ought to do and no one better, but it is the *Idea* that I want. It's no use painting just anything.
>
> Your picture I know is a good sound piece of work and painted with a spirit that I hardly seem to have now, but in the R.A. it would be *very* small, indeed it would.
>
> I am at present in a state of unhappiness and unsettlement. Simply because I cannot hit upon *just* the *good* thing.
>
> You never said a truer word in your life than what you said today when declaring that it is no use painting these unimportant things.
>
> Alas! every man knows himself only too well. But we are all victims of circumstance!!
>
> Ever yours,
> A. J. MUNNINGS

He wrote to the same patron about the same picture a few weeks later: 'There is nothing about anywhere of mine like it, or won't be either, as I shall never paint anything like it again.' Of a more precise cause and nature of his grievances there is no hint. There were ominous stirrings in the art world. Perhaps he was breasting the waves of unrest generated in Paris against all art based on 'horrible resemblance'. His mother made an entry in her Sunday diary: 'Alfred has been over. He seems to be happy, at least as happy as it is possible for him to be – he really very seldom seems quite satisfied or happy.'

(3)

During the years at Swainsthorpe Munnings was often seen on the roads at the head of a curious little procession that might have been mistaken for the tail-end of a bankrupt circus. It was headed by himself on horseback, leading a string of seven or eight nondescript horses and ponies. Behind them came a swaying blue-painted caravan with a chocolate-coloured roof, drawn by a horse in charge of a gipsy boy outrider nicknamed Shrimp, whose real name was the euphonious one of Fountain Page. Following the caravan was a long cart with a bright-faced older man named Bob walking beside it. The cart was loaded with canvases, an easel, palettes, cans of turpentine, oil and copal varnish, quantities of paint rags, jars of water, a large tattered umbrella and a sailcloth for windy days. Bringing up the rear was a donkey. 'Jasper Petulengro, Swainsthorpe' was scrawled in white chalk on caravan and cart, hurriedly applied when Munnings was reminded that a name on a vehicle was a requirement of the law. The horses, the caravan, the man, the boy, the donkey, were his models. He spent months painting them in his favourite region of the Ringland Hills, his holland smock smeared with cadmium yellow expended in trying to capture the glory of the gorse. Wearing a once-white linen haymaker's hat, a jacket that had a secondary use as a brush-wiper, and trousers of several colours acquired when he absent-mindedly sat on his palette, he led his vagabond cavalcade farther afield to Buckenham and Massingham and Burlingham, to Rockland St Mary, Surlingham and Limpenhoe, to Sisland and Saxlingham Green, names that jingled like the brasses on his horses' harness, every signpost luring him to new vistas and 'more exploits'.

The man Bob, and Shrimp, 'that tough and artful young

brigand', who, 'having no home, no family ties, no parents he
knew', slept under the caravan with the dogs, sometimes showed
unruly instincts that annoyed the master. Sent on ahead to a
rendezvous, Bob and Shrimp would dally at pubs, often emerging
from them in a fighting mood. Angrily Munnings would ride
well ahead of the procession, as it resumed the journey, 'pretending to have nothing to do with it.' The characters, the
situation, the comment, might have come from *Lavengro*.

Seated at his easel, painting Shrimp astride one of the mares,
Munnings was interrupted by the arrival of the Norfolk con-
stabulary, one an inspector. 'Have you a young fellow of the
name of Page here?' A summons was out against Shrimp for a
breach of the peace at Bungay. 'What's the fine?' Munnings
asked without parleying and, on being told, paid it, Shrimp
meantime not shifting his pose on the horse's back by as much
as the flicker of a muscle. Munnings never forgot riding back
to Church Farm late one night after a long day out with the
caravan: 'The rising moon, the scent of dog-roses, honeysuckle,
the smell of road dust, the sound of horses' feet and the Norfolk
voice of Shrimp telling me of his last appearance before the
magistrates, are still memories that remain as clear as day in
my mind.'

The reserve of canvases carried in the long cart partly explain
his prolific output at that time. 'I never started a large picture
until I had painted smaller canvases of thirty by twenty-five
inches, or twenty-four by twenty inches. Of these, one or two
might be worthy of a larger subject.' The subject decided, he
would begin work, 'with canvas set, a half-bucket of water hung
from the easel to steady it against a fitful breeze, palette and
brushes ready. For weeks I was free and happy on those hills.
After painting awhile, the beauty of the gorse and the sunlight
on the ponies became a problem and a joy. Days flew by. Two
or three good efforts pointed the way to a larger subject. A
fifty by forty canvas, with others, was now laid in the long
cart each morning, and pulled up to the hills, on the summit of
which I was working in a sort of gravelly hollow. The white
ponies stood up against the sky in sunlight, with the distant
blue Taverham country across the valley showing beneath their

bellies'. Some of his subjects were repeated in a dozen different versions. 'The Ford', one of the more notable of his early works, was painted over and over again; his 'White Canoe' twenty-five times. Always there was the gamble of the changing light, of cloud shape mutations, of unpredictable weather. 'Look, sir,' the man Bob would say, turning away from the horizon, 'look at them old clouds comin' up. They're goin' to stop us today, sir!' Too often Bob was right. 'No artist can tell a layman of the hopeless blight that falls upon him with such a change,' Munnings wrote. 'He is doomed, beaten; but only for the day. To the artist of experience there is a way out, his second canvas.'

So, if there were wasted hours, there was no wasted day; and the discarded canvas was returned to the long cart and a new picture started. For every large-scale work he attempted there was a whole series of variants, the product of the artist's discontents. 'I am at work in the fresh mood, recovering from the setback.' From just such a setback came one of the outstanding works of his nomadic period, 'The Coming Storm'. 'Shrimp said he knew we were going to get it. I had gone on painting, aware of a portent in the air – hearing the far-off boom of thunder; watching the ominous, dark storm clouds gather and slowly advance. What a background!' He said that he revelled in painting that picture. 'Shrimp riding the white mare and leading the white pony was the principal mass of light, showing against a dark, threatening sky.' He had seen drama in earth and sky and had set himself to seize its forms and atmosphere, in so doing proceeding beyond the impressionist mood with its absorption in the pursuit of light. Mere illusion, however lyrically conceived, could never content Munnings. He had to discover his own truth. 'The Coming Storm', exhibited at the Royal Academy in 1925, was bought for £850 by the National Gallery of New South Wales. The Duke of Gloucester told him that it was one of the pictures that he, as Governor-General, had chosen from the Gallery in Sydney to hang in his official residence. Passing on that information in a letter, Munnings commented: 'What a go!'

His furious energies at that time drew a warning from the

Norwich art patron, Russell Colman. Seeing some of his gorse pictures in the Boswells' shop, Colman remarked: 'That young fellow's painting too much. He ought to be knocked on the head.' Colman missed the point. Munnings was painting for the sheer joy of it.

(3)

When the days drew in and the sunlight in which he rejoiced became pale and fitful, he sold all but one or two of the horses, paid off the men and went back to work in his Norwich rooms and to experience afresh the amenities of the city. Prominent among them was that 'warm, cosy little bar at the Maid's Head', the oldest Norwich hostelry, 1287, 'a real and true haven of peace and comfort'. The little bar is still there as he knew it. 'To look at A.J. in those surroundings took you back a hundred and fifty years', wrote Dame Laura Knight R.A. She spent an evening there with him a little later in his life. 'He fitted into the antiquity; even his clothes had a cut that belonged to the past.' Not less distinctly she remembered that he was annoyed because, by having a bath, she put a shilling on his bill as the host, though afterwards he spent extravagantly on the dinner.

There was also the City Club, gathering place of the more prosperous professional and business men. At 2 a.m. on the night of 29 November 1907 one of several members with whom he had been having 'an evening' challenged him to do a drawing. The implication was that he had taken too much wine to comply. When someone offered to send for paper and pencils, he went to a window and ripped down a four-feet-square blue linen roller blind, which he spread on the billiard-table. Taking the marker's chalk, he did a superb drawing of a jockey on a horse. To match it, he took the blind from the only other window and did a second drawing, equally effective. Both drawings still hang in the City Club. He enjoyed the pleasures of wine but not at the expense of self-command.

Offended by the charge that he considered the proper study of mankind to be the horse, he did a drawing of a poacher character in one of Rider Haggard's novels. Dr C. F. Bunting of

Norwich has a dramatic Munnings sketch of a young woman, intended to illustrate lines from a Burns poem, one more impulsive proof of a versatility that may have ministered to Munnings's self-esteem but did little to advance his reputation. At twenty he had painted a portrait, 'Daniel Tomkins and his Dog' (1898), which sufficiently indicated a line of development that he could follow with a firm guarantee of success. Inevitably it would have led him to the studio and he was not a studio man. The call of the sun was one of the strongest forces in his career. No one remembers seeing him willingly at work indoors on a sunlit day. That was a French influence which he never disclaimed.

CHAPTER 7

Personalities of the Newlyn School

(1)

'D A T E S fail me,' he wrote; and only his biographer can appreciate the full significance of that admission. There is no one now to say precisely when he forsook Norfolk for Cornwall. The attractions of the Newlyn School were impressed on him by a young woman student at Finchingfield who had spoken of going there after finishing with Calderon and the animal-painting course. Munnings paid two or three short visits to Cornwall. He settled there on a more or less permanent basis from about 1911.

As a painter with more than the glimmerings of a reputation and whose left thumb was curved by a longer acquaintance with the palette than some members of the Newlyn circle, he was warmly received into a group in which John ('Lamorna') Birch, Harold and Laura Knight, Ernest and Dod Proctor, Charles Simpson and Harold Harvey were gathered round the central personality of Stanhope Forbes R.A., who, with Napier Hemy the marine painter, was a founding father. Others of the School at that time were Frynywyd Tennyson Jesse, Crosby Garstin and C. E. Vulliamy, each of whom ultimately made a name at writing.

All were living and working and studying in a community then still obstinately at odds with the artist's way of life. For example, there was almost mortal danger in Sunday painting. Easel, canvas and the offending artist were likely to be pitched into Newlyn harbour. Mrs Augustus John, arriving with her husband soon after Munnings had settled there, was criticised for being seen outdoors without a hat – 'and on a Sunday!'

To him, it was all excitingly new. The people, the scenery, the strong Atlantic air, put such a spell on him that he feared for his native loyalties. 'To lie on the sweet-smelling turf, watching sea pinks trembling in light winds, and listening to the unceasing sound of the surf and cry of gulls, gives peace and rest to body and soul. Nothing quite like this coast exists anywhere'; and his mother wrote mournfully in her Sunday diary: 'Now I feel I have lost Alfred.'

There were 'rough, primitive' race-meetings at St Buryan, where he experienced again some of the elemental excitement that had seized him on the ever-remembered day at Bungay. One of the pictures he painted at St Buryan, his first of a race start, was bought by the donor of the Walker Art Gallery at Liverpool. For some months he was in lodgings at Zennor, finding accommodation there also for his man Ned, 'a simple soul, who grew into a useful combination of groom-model and posed for many a picture'.

In winter he rode out with a local hunt, the Western Hounds Master, Colonel William Bolitho. There was a late December afternoon when the fox got away over the cliffs near Morvah. It was seen crouching on a rock far below. Munnings and the whip went down after it. As they approached, the fox leapt into the sea, swimming for its life. They watched it battling with the waves until one swept it ashore. Looking a sorry sight, it sought the haven of a fissure in the cliff. The hunt whip started to go and get the fox out. 'No, you don't!' protested Munnings. 'That fox has run for his life and saved himself. Leave him alone!' He made it clear to the huntsman that he 'didn't give a damn' what the Master said. What the Master said was: 'That's the last time we'll let *him* go down after a fox.'

Keen rider to hounds that he always was, Munnings never took pleasure in the kill. His experiences later with the Essex and Suffolk were not always congenial. 'I enjoyed many a day out. For all that, I could tell stories which do not go with good sporting traditions.' He was upset by the digging out of a fox with a wire snare embedded in a foreleg. When he expressed his feelings about it, the Master shouted at him: 'If you don't like it, you can go home,' and home, in anger, Munnings went.

He also 'never took to shooting'. The day in his boyhood
when he went along the Waveney with an airgun and killed
'a poor little water-rat quietly nibbling a succulent end', left
him with a permanently scarred conscience. He joined 'syndicates
of jolly men', among them the Boswells and other Norwich
friends, but he walked the stubble and mangolds without even
taking one shot, 'a mere looker-on'.

(2)

Between the early visits to Cornwall and on several occasions
later he spent weeks in painting the gipsies at Alton in Hampshire, introduced to them by Olive Branson, one of the older
women students at Finchingfield, 'the kindest and sweetest
person'. A competent painter, trained in the school run by John
and Orpen in Chelsea, she made annual trips in her own gipsy
caravan to that part of Hampshire, where in the last weeks
of summer the gipsies went for the hop-picking. It was Munnings's first encounter with the tribe *en masse* – 'at least two or
three hundred men, women and children' – and by the end of a
month he was not sorry to part from 'these folk with importunate
ways and wild habits', who were 'well enough for a time but no
longer'.

It was hardly generous acknowledgment of services rendered;
for among the gipsy Lees, Grays, Stevenses and Lovedays at
Alton he found not only some of his most memorable models
but painted, with their willing if too often fidgety co-operation,
some of the pictures that helped to make his name and fortune,
including such notable examples as 'Departure of the Hop-
pickers' (National Art Gallery, Melbourne) and 'Gipsy Life'
(Aberdeen Art Gallery). The gipsies of Alton always called
him 'Mr Money', he having quickly put himself on good terms
with them by his free and easy manner and racy vocabulary,
and as effectively, if less consciously, by his unstinted appreciation
of their primitive colour sense. In the opinion of the Australian
artist and art critic, Sir Lionel Lindsay, 'it was in itself a stroke
of genius to have found this wealth of painting material'.

Unlike that other rampantly zestful East Anglian, George

Borrow, Munnings never romanticised the gipsies. By painting them in the way he did, Lindsay suggested that he 'established an indisputable claim' to the letters-patent which Constable proposed should be awarded to the artist, as to the scientist, who discovers something new, 'adding the distinction of a personal point of view as well as new subject-matter to his art'.

It was to Cornwall that Munnings always returned after his Hampshire excursions. The commercial element was not so strong in Newlyn as it was in Norwich, where the dealers had been constantly plucking at his sleeve. In Cornwall he was free to exert his will or to follow his inclinations, never beyond range of a self-discipline that could detach him with little more than a token show of resistance from lighter preoccupations.

He went out sketching one day with Augustus John. Not long before, a Slade School functionary said that John had arrived at the School as 'quite an ordinary art student', that on his first summer holiday he went for a bathe, struck his head on a rock, 'and returned a genius'. Munnings was engrossed at that time by his discovery that a horse's coat, like other textures, reflects the lights of day. He made much of the problem, walking towards Land's End with John, who listened carefully and then, after silent reflection, gruffly asked him: 'If you see a brown horse, why not paint it brown?'

Munnings's new friendships were stimulating and, though he was not a pupil of Forbes's school, he attended what were jauntily known as 'the Saturday crits', at which Forbes examined and commented on work brought in by outsiders as well as by students. Munnings was prominently identified with the Newlyn artists' colony but he had no direct connexion with it. As a social being he was popular from the first in that circle, a born master of ceremonies who could inject liveliness into the dullest group and be counted on to make any party 'go'. It was a later boast of his (to Marshall Sisson) that he had 'organised more parties, picnics, outings and Christmas festivities than anyone in this country'. The first intimations of his virtuosity in that line were apparent in his activities at Newlyn, where no congenial gathering was regarded as complete without him.

As before, at Norwich, his hearty enjoyment of the social

pleasures left its trail of problems. Unlike some of the Newlyn artists and art students he was entirely self-dependent, having no private means or well-off relatives to support him. Back at Swainsthorpe for a brief visit, he wrote to Dod Procter (Mrs Procter R.A.): 'I wonder if there would be any horrors about a court of bankruptcy?' He told her that on his way through to Norfolk he had stayed in London longer than he had meant to:

'I tried to end my "blues" there, but couldn't, and they've followed me right through since leaving Cornwall and I have them now. Last Sunday in town was rotten. We loafed in my friend's studio in Hampstead and looked over some Cornwall sketches. I was simply withered up with the "blues" for the rest of the day, until at night my body – without the soul – went finding its way from Hampstead to Kensington, where a select Bohemian gathering was held at the house of a good fellow – a publisher or something. About 2 in the morning we were leap-frogging over a red letter-box, but as it was too high to clear we got stuck on top.'

He could agree, he wrote, that 'London is all right for a bit, but Lamorna is best. I wish I was there now, tying your shoes.' He posed the question: 'Why ever did I have a memory?' and quoted Tennyson: . . . a sorrow's crown of sorrow is remembering happier things."[1] 'Alas, that's true.' He continued in the mood of melancholy:

'There is a moon tonight. Outside now and again a distant dog barks or a horse stamps in the stable. The moon seems about the size she was when we went and sat in the wood and tried to conjure up the spirits.

Why haven't we £10,000 a year?

Have you read any of Matthew Arnold's verse? There is one piece, *The Buried Life*, that I like, and another, *Marguerite*. And *A Summer Night*.'

Soon back in Cornwall, he was the hero of an episode recalled

1. *Locksley Hall.*

'The Timber Gill',—"I shall never paint anything like it again".

Munnings sunbathing at Lamorna Cove, 1910.

by Mrs Procter. Wishing to help two artists who were short of money, Munnings persuaded her to go with him to the Queen's Hotel, Penzance, for the purpose of seeking the patronage of some wealthy people staying there. Hiring a dog-cart, they put a selection of the two artists' best pictures in it and drove to the hotel, Munnings wearing a red handkerchief instead of a collar. The hotel commissionaire was brusque. 'Nothing today, thank you,' he told them. When Munnings, with two pictures under his arm, marched forward into the hotel vestibule, there was a scuffle in which the commissionaire fell and sprained an ankle. While he was hopping around on one foot, Munnings slipped into the hotel and sold the pictures.

(3)

In Cornwall, painting among the brooding hills, the haunted woods, the sacrificial stones, he was at first happier than he had been since living in Norwich. The companionship was delightful and so was the seriousness of the devotees attending Stanhope Forbes's classes in the big converted sail-loft that was his teaching studio in Newlyn. Forbes's high standing as a Royal Academician was beginning to wane. He seemed as satisfied, and was almost as accomplished, with a cello between his legs as with a brush in his hand. The Newlyn School was passing the climax of its fame, though considerable reputations were still to come out of it. The School was no longer absorbed in the painting method of the 'square brush', initiated years before by Bastien-Lepage, who had abandoned his fine-pointed brushwork for the effects to be got by brushes two inches wide.

The Newlyn School had also survived the intolerance of the '90s, but its inspiration, like its leadership, had lost much of the old rapture. The impact of Roger Fry, a name that later had apoplectic implications for Munnings, inflamed the passions of a small inner group at Newlyn, whose methods Munnings described as 'painting figures as though cut out of pale yellow boxwood'. It was that group, 'this rather warm element', he called it, that set the pace at the Newlyn School in the last Edwardian year or two. He wrote:

E

'Imagine a long, low, top-lit sail-loft, converted into a studio, as so many were at Newlyn and St Ives, its real use and purpose in the world ended. No more brown sails and straight, long spars. Instead, a vast white damask tablecloth spread on the floorboards, it centrepiece a great pile of fruit – gilded melons, gilded pineapples, gilded grapes and vine leaves. There were dishes of food and troops of wine bottles, full and empty. In a blue haze of cigarette smoke, Roman revellers reclined on cushions around the feast on the floor. Japanese lanterns swung from the rafters and lit up the scene. Lovely, voluptuous, reclining women smoking cigarettes in long holders. Amateurs and students, they were rather more competent in the art of seductive make-up than in the art of painting. Their own attractive figures were totally unlike the strange shapes they put on canvas.[1]

Stanhope Forbes lived in a rambling house called Trevarveneth on the heights behind Newlyn. There Munnings organised a Christmas party that lasted several days and nights, an unforgettable festival for those who were invited, with every meal a banquet, and singing, music, dancing, games-playing, speechmaking and practical joking filling at least sixteen hours of every day. Dame Laura Knight remembers it, above all, as a display of Munnings's 'supreme vitality'. She says that he kept the affair going at top pitch from first to last, 'never faltering or showing the least trace of tiredness'. When others did, he rallied them like a ringmaster with doggerel lines for which he had discovered a tune: *For we are wonderful people, we are – we are – we are!* 'Come on, all of you!' he would cry. 'Sing up! *For we are wonderful people, we are – we are . . .!*

For a time he painted in the studio of a near-by house called Chyoone Grove, where he gave a punch party based on a formidable recipe obtained from the landlord of the Swan at Harleston, Norfolk: a pint of rum, a pint of brandy, a pint of sherry, lump sugar rubbed against the rind of lemons, a handful of simmered cloves, with boiling water added – 'and what a flowing bowl *that* was!' Four of his guests became 'stretcher

1. *An Artist's Life.*

cases' and were laid out on the verandah. One of them, coming to with the dawn, feared the worst when he heard Munnings intoning incessantly in his bedroom: 'Quoth the raven, "Nevermore," quoth the raven. . . .'

At a party given by Harold and Laura Knight at their house at Newlyn in or about 1910, Munnings and a young woman guest, Dorothea Allan (Mrs Coxhead), were told off to make punch. 'We brewed it in somebody's bedroom water-jug,' she reminded him in after years. Munnings was depressed about his work and future. He told her that he felt like 'chucking it all up', that he would 'never be any good', and so on. She gave him a lecture on perseverance. There was a portfolio full of his drawings which she had been looking at and admiring. He bade her: 'Take the lot – I don't want them', and a time came when she wished that she had accepted his reckless offer.

His much demanded recitation of *The Raven* by Edgar Allen Poe was invested with added awe during one of the nights of the long Christmas party when, as he spoke the line, 'Soon again I heard a tapping somewhat louder than before', the door shook to a knock that sent the colour from the faces in the lamplight. The landlord of the Lamorna Inn, Mr Jory, had called to take some of the guests home, producing a climax that Laura Knight said 'froze the hair on our heads', the garden reputedly being haunted.

Dame Laura remembers what she thought about Munnings after their first meeting at Lamorna Cove. 'He had the air of a poet and looked like a stable boy. He could have sat for a portrait of Robert Burns.' To her he was 'an arresting sight, standing straddled there; strong, upright, small head, wide shoulders, narrow hips. I could not take my eyes off him, he had such over-overwhelming vitality.' Mrs Dod Procter says that 'he held himself beautifully', and she also recalls his craze for 'doing his hair like Sir Walter Scott'.

One of Forbes's students, Clare Waters (Mrs Collas), says that he was 'surprisingly clothes-conscious', and that he told her that 'the cut of a jacket was important'. She has a memory of him sitting with Fryn Tennyson Jesse (later Mrs H. M. Harwood) on a cliff top near Lamorna, 'combing her beautiful auburn tresses'. There is another recollection of him painting at Boskenna Cove, where the daffodils covered the slopes down to the blue sea's edge, and the rust of a wreck, half-buried in the sand, shone like beaten gold in the sunlight.

Idyllic days that surviving members of the Newlyn art colony remember as if they were privileged to know a kind of happiness that has since gone from the world.

(4)

In 1911 the sister of 'Joey' Carter-Wood, one of Forbes's students, arrived in Newlyn to stay with her brother and to attend art classes. The Carter-Woods were understood to be members of a Lancaster family of substance, who owned, among other property, Artillery Mansions, Westminster. So it was said in Newlyn at the time. Florence Carter-Wood, a slenderly attractive girl of twenty-two, who had the rather less becoming nickname of 'Bloat', was tall, fair and blue-eyed. She has remained in one memory as 'a charming figure in a grey flannel costume with a bunch of sweet peas tucked in the waist belt', and in another as being 'very like the actress Shirley Ann Field'. She figured in a 'conversation piece' painted by Harold Knight, then of the Newlyn School and subsequently an R.A.

Munnings fell in love with her. After a brief engagement they were married early in 1912. They went to London for the honeymoon, staying at an hotel. While they were there Florence Munnings showed signs of mental disturbance. She attempted suicide by taking poison. Munnings hurried back with her to Cornwall. They went to live at Cliff House, Lamorna Cove, where he resumed his painting after what had been for him an upsetting experience.

Those who saw him at that difficult time remember his desperate ministrations to his young wife and his concern for her future. Almost from the day of their return from London it was clear that all was not well with the marriage. Florence Munnings's nature was in rebellion against the obligations of her sex. The wife of Charles Simpson, one of the Newlyn School's leading members, had recently become a mother. Florence

Munnings, calling to see her, asked questions about the birth.
'I couldn't stand it!' she cried and ran from the room. Her
mental health rapidly declined. Ten days before the world storm
broke in August 1914 she took cyanide and died. An inquest,
widely reported in the Press, was held at Lamorna on 26 July.
'The jury found that deceased's death was due to poisoning by
cyanide and that it was administered by herself during temporary
insanity.' The coroner voiced a general feeling of sympathy for
Munnings.

He went to stay with the Simpsons in the quiet of their home
at Carbis Bay. He told Charles Simpson: 'It was not a marriage.
It was never consummated.' He spoke hardly at all of the shock
he had suffered. He appeared to cultivate a jaunty indifference
to it. Simpson was playing chess with him, while at the far end
of the room Mrs Simpson talked with friends. They were
joined by a woman caller who, as she entered, asked loudly:
'What was it that Bloat took?' She then saw that Munnings was
there. Her dismay was obvious. Charles Simpson remembers:
'He looked up in silence from the chessboard. He then rose and
went over to the woman caller, who could not hide her distress.
He spoke soothing words to her, then returned to our game.
It was most gracefully done.'

There is no evidence that his work was seriously interrupted,
or affected, by his shattering experience. What is remembered by
his friends the Simpsons, and by others who can bear witness
from that time in his life, was the readiness and ease with which
he returned to it. For him, painting was the unfailing anodyne.
But for some time after he could not bear to read newspaper
reports of women's suicides. They caused him such deep pain
that his friends conspired to distract his attention from them.

CHAPTER 8

An Artist in the Horse Lines

(1)

W ITH the outbreak of war in August 1914 outdoor painting and sketching made every artist a subject of suspicion; in fact, a potential spy, involving the ludicrous possibility that artists might require police permits to pursue their vocation. D. H. Lawrence was a notable victim of the official and private harrying that went on in Cornwall, and elsewhere, in the first months of World War One.

Munnings hurried to London, where he found the members of the Chelsea Arts Club drilling with broomsticks and developing an untoward respect for the martial life. When he was rejected as a yeomanry recruit because of his lack of an eye, he went down to Hampshire with a friend who had been with him at Julian's to paint the gipsies again. 'Nothing seemed to have altered,' he wrote. 'The same families, the same horses, the same noise, as though no war at all were going on. Painting in that big pasture day after day we saw long trains with drawn blinds passing to Southampton. These trains, everybody said, were full of Russian soldiers, landed in Hull and going to France!'

In his enthusiasm to be accepted for the yeomanry, he had offered also the use of his two horses, kept at Lamorna, provided that they could continue in his charge. A telegram from Cornwall the next day, informing him that the horses had already been commandeered, came as 'a bad shock'. Hardly waiting to strip off his painting-smock, he caught the next train for London, stayed the night in Chelsea, and left the following morning for Penzance. There, that evening, he pleaded for the liberation of his horses. 'You have collected many,' he told the requisitioning officer. 'Surely you can spare my two?' He explained that they were his models and that, in that sense, they were part of his livelihood. The officer, 'that dear, kind man', was sympathetic and conspired with Munnings to get the horses away late in the evening, 'when there was no one about'.

With many thanks, 'many heartfelt thanks', Munnings rode one of the horses and led the other through the dim streets of Penzance, along the promenade to Newlyn, over the bridge, and up the long steep pull to Paul and on in the gathering darkness to Lamorna. Fumbling at the meadow gate, he let the horses loose and heard them go thundering off into the night, 'full split, in sheer joy'. He returned to London the following day and in another twenty-four hours was at his easel again at Alton, painting the gipsies. Later, he conceded that 'a too-passionate affection for horses may become a foolish obsession'.

His next attempt at enlisting was at Bodmin. 'This fellow's blind in his right eye,' said the examining doctor in the tone of a discoverer. Munnings went back to Newlyn, a C3 reject, resuming his painting at Lamorna Cove with the assurance that he was well enough known there not to incur patriotic doubts. He acquired the companionship of a white bull-terrier which he named Reggie. The dog developed a late-night habit, often not coming home until the sun was up. Munnings always patiently waited. Asked why he let himself be deprived of sleep by a dog, he answered that it gave him the quietness essential to a proper appreciation of Jane Austen's works. When one of his mares gave birth to a foal, he behaved as if it was an unusually blessed event. He went round the village, knocking on doors, announcing it. Loudly reciting obstetric details in the bar parlour at the Lamorna Inn, he had to be restrained, 'on account of the ladies'.

He was cheered by a letter from a Norwich dealer named Nourse who wanted to buy any pictures that he had to sell. He replied: 'Well, you are a sportsman to think of coming all this way and if I can sell you anything cheap I will. Of course, I am holding back my better work and can't part, but there will be something for you. You deserve to make £20 on every picture.'

(2)

A drawing he did in 1915 is captioned 'Evlyn' in his first reminiscent volume, confirming his habitual mispronunciation of Evelyn. The young woman of the drawing was Evelyn Castier (Mrs Noel). She was not an art student. She had come from Cheltenham to live with her parents at Penzance. The drawing was a sketch for a painting of her subsequently exhibited at the Royal Academy. It shows her to have been attractive. Munnings liked her. He taught her to ride and a letter from him, telling her that 'the horses will be ready', was found by her father, who at once assumed that an elopement was being planned. His telegram of urgent recall was delivered while she was at a studio party at Newlyn, where one of her songs at the piano, 'Roses are for loving, Loving dies so soon', touched Munnings deeply. She remembers that he told her he was twenty-eight, when his real age was thirty-seven. She also remembers that, responding one evening to an appeal to recite *The Raven*, he began in his customary dramatic style and then stopped, pointing with imperiously outstretched finger at a potted palm in a corner. 'I can't go on with that thing in the room,' he complained; nor would he until it had been taken out.

He kept some of his painting things at an old house far out on the moors behind Penzance. It was then occupied by a retired chemisty professor named Peartree and was approached over thirteen Cornish stiles. Going there one day with Munnings, 'Evlyn' was overwhelmed by what she says were 'horrible spooky feelings' which she could not throw off for days after, a shiver of the nerves experienced by other visitors to the place. 'There is something strange and weird lurking down there in the great peninsula which juts into the western sea,' wrote Conan Doyle in *Through the Magic Door*. The house is still there among its remote druidical rocks.

It was there that Munnings met Father Bernard Walke, incumbent of St Hilary, a noted High Anglican who wore bright-striped socks showing conspicuously below his high-hitched trousers and who described their first encounter in *Twenty Years at St Hilary*. 'Leaning against a bay horse was a man in a

flannel shirt without a collar, wiping paint brushes with a rag.
The poise of his body and the tilt of his head . . . suggested an
arrogant, almost insolent attitude. Here, I thought, was a man
whom I should certainly dislike.' The parson was immediately
converted by Munnings's smile, 'like that of an ascetic saint'.
It was the beginning of a friendship. When Walke became too ill
from T.B. to continue his wide parish rounds on foot, Munnings
gave him a chestnut cob, which Walke named 'A.J.'

He and Munnings joined an eccentric High Church parson
named Wason in an undertaking that caused Munnings some
inner disturbance. Wason's church was by the sea at Gunwalloe,
near Mullion. It had Victorian varnished pitch-pine pews and
'a hideous pulpit', which both Walke and Wason thought an
affront to the primitive character of the church. They resolved
to replace the pews with rush-seat chairs and to get rid of the
pulpit.

Munnings accompanying them, they went out to the church
in the early hours one morning and, borrowing the grave-
digger's tools, set about dismantling it. 'At the first sounds of
breaking,' Munnings confessed, 'I trembled with fear,' as if
dreading the arrival, at any moment, of the Diocesan Chancellor.
'Growing bolder, with Walke I heaved and sweated – clearing
one pew after another, while Wason walked up and down the
aisle chanting from some holy text.' The pews were sold to a
local tea-room proprietor, realising enough cash to provide the
few rush-chairs needed to accommodate Wason's small con-
gregation. Forbidden to use the church, he installed an altar in
his rectory. Munnings had no doubt that the church interior was
improved: 'Wason made it a picture'. There was a sequel of
ecclesiastical and police action. In due course Wason was ejected
from the living.

A letter from a member of the Welham-Clarke family of
Needham, near Harleston, Norfolk, touched a still responsive
chord in Munnings's memory. He replied from Lamorna on 25
September 1916 (one of his few dated letters): 'I often long for
the river and the river scenes. I know just how it is looking at
your place now. I can see the exact curves up at either end of
that reach – the water moss along by the edge of the bank and

the autumn colouring coming there . . . the willows, the distances, and all.'

Dame Laura Knight, who broke her leg at Lamorna in November of that year, still recalls the solicitude he showed her through the weeks of her convalescence. 'He came every night to read aloud', the first reading being from Compton Mackenzie's novel, *Carnival*. 'After that, Jorrocks. It was a treat I looked forward to all the day, for those who never heard 'A.J.' read Jorrocks missed something.' A rhythmic thumping sound late one night baffled her and her husband, who went outside to see what it was. He found Munnings out of breath at the door, an enormous log at his feet, part of a great tree-trunk; he had rolled it up the hill to put on their open hearth, where it burned for several days. The comfort it gave the Knights was dimmed by the fear that the neighbours who owned the log might discover that Munnings had stolen it.

At last, in 1917, he went off to the war. With the help of Cecil Aldin, accomplished artist in black and white who specialised lovingly in drawing horses, hounds and the old houses of England, he found a lowly place in the vast military apparatus that was being created for the defeat of Germany. Aldin, sometime master of the South Berkshire Hunt, was a temporary major in charge of the remount depot at Calcot Park, near Reading, where a thousand horses were arriving each week, mostly from Canada. Aldin got Munnings accepted as a 'strapper', a job that involved scratching horses' necks to see if they responded to mange (Aldin's definition). Munnings went to work with exemplary cheerfulness and was soon whistling and hissing with the practised earnestness of a Dickensian ostler.

There were heavy hearts in Newlyn and Lamorna when he said his farewells. Laura Knight never doubted that he had 'enlarged the lives' of others beside herself. 'His companionship, his extraordinary vitality, his joy in his work – none of us could forget him.' She had known him uplifted and cast down, in success and disaster. The strongest impression that he made on her was of his unflinching tenacity. 'He was a fighter. He fought the wind that shivered his easel and canvas. He fought the heat and the cold. He fought the shifting sun and the changing shadows.'

CHAPTER 9

Elected to the Royal Academy

(1)

HE scratched the necks of several thousand horses, and applied foul-smelling mange-dressing to most of them, making himself indispensable to Aldin, who, at the end of twelve months, deplored his departure to the front as an official war artist attached to the Canadian Cavalry Brigade. He had been invited by Paul Konody, a leading art critic, to join a group of painters who under the auspices of the newly established Ministry of Information were to record the war on canvas. Augustus John and William Orpen had already been posted to the British army with the rank of major. With no rank Munnings reported to General J. E. B. Seely (later Lord Mottistone), a dashingly brave soldier-politician who had succeeded Haldane as Secretary of State for War. His field headquarters were near the front line in the Arras sector, at a place called Small Foot Wood. 'But there was no sign of a wood,' Munnings wrote, 'only charred stumps of trees standing in desolate wastes of mud with duckboards about, leading to dugouts.'

With the easy courtesy that was one of his distinctions, 'Jack' Seely welcomed Munnings into his headquarters mess, jollying him about his civilian status and at the same time respecting it. A member of a Hampshire family with radical sympathies – they had entertained Garibaldi on his visit to England – Seely had a keen profile and a port-wine complexion; he looked the hereditary horseman. Munnings placed him as 'belonging to the Wellington period' of soldiering. Like Munnings, he could talk of things other than war and horses and there sprang up between them a fellow feeling that lasted into the years of peace, a latter-day conjunction of Xenophon and Hesiod.

The brigade-major was Geoffrey Brooke, one of the British army's great horsemen. He, too, thought well of Munnings because when Orpen, as a visitor to the brigade mess, severely criticised one of his drawings, Munnings 'took it in good heart'. Another of Munnings's mess companions was the brigade interpreter, Baron Roulleaux Degage, whose calm in a crisis Munnings found both admirable and comical. Seely's *aide-de-camp* was Prince Antoine d'Orléans, appointed to the Canadians because his position *vis-à-vis* the French throne might have been politically embarrassing otherwise. He made it one of his daily tasks to take Munnings's finished canvases off their stretchers and pin them on the mess walls, where they could dry and at the same time be critically inspected by the staff.

Munnings's discovery that there could be a picnic element in war was the more enjoyable because he had not imagined it. Seely gave him Irroy to drink, prescribing it as 'the champagne that makes you laugh'. Munnings responded with 'Julia', a ballad of romantic dalliance of which he had written both words and music for a Christmas party before the war. The old boy of Mendham village school was a great social success. 'All my command loved him,' Seely wrote. The cavalry corps commander, Eldred Kavanagh, coming upon him sketching near the line, asked him with a hint of asperity in his voice who he was. Munnings answered: 'I don't really know. When they sent me out here they said I was a genius.'

Though he fitted comfortably into that unfamiliar *milieu*, he looked at odds with it as he strode about in his check suit, cloth cap and box-cloth leggings, a dented paint-box under one arm, a bunch of brushes and pencils in one hand. He undoubtedly had a more realistic understanding of war than, for instance, the noted portrait-painter, John Sargent, who, on hearing a military band playing at Haig's headquarters at Hesdin before church parade, remarked to General Fielding: 'I suppose there is no fighting on Sundays.'

Munnings's first war subject was Seely, mounted on his splendid horse Warrior, which went through several battles with him, was wounded and returned home on Christmas Day,

1918, afterwards winning an Isle of Wight point-to-point. 'Sitting there on his charger,' Munnings wrote, 'in general's uniform, on a cold, still day, with a long brown woollen muffler thrown round his neck, Jack Seely was a picture.' Seely himself wrote afterwards: 'Warrior was painted by Munnings in full view of the enemy – I should think an almost unique occurrence on the Western Front! The Germans were husbanding their ammunition for their great attack of 21 March; although they would endeavour to demolish a battery that annoyed them and, of course, fire at any considerable bunch of men, one could play all sorts of tricks with them if there were only one or two together. So Munnings and Warrior survived several sittings, although a German artillery officer with a telescope must have been watching the whole proceedings, no doubt amused. . . .'[1]

Munnings's portrait of Seely on Warrior went to the National Gallery at Ottawa. For Munnings there was a more important sequel. The portrait helped to fix him in the public mind as an exceptionally skilful painter of formal equestrian subjects. From it flowed the long series of commissions which he never regarded as his life's work but which brought him money and fame in the years to come.

At the front he worked long hours to keep up with the variety of subjects presenting themselves to his eye at every turn. 'What a chance for an artist!' he wrote. He filled scores of sketch-books and accumulated a large collection of paintings in oils and water-colours that travelled about with the brigade baggage.

(2)

The German bombardment that heralded the Fifth Army rout of March 1918 was his worst war experience. 'I lay in bed trembling with fear,' he wrote. 'It became the background of all our doings; it went on, and on, and on.' The brigade had moved by stages to the Somme. He was painting in the horse lines when 'suddenly something was happening'. Men were running. There were shouted orders to saddle up.

1. Lord Mottistone: *Fear and Be Slain* (London: Hodder & Stoughton 1931).

'Can't you do something about a uniform?' he was asked by an anxious staff officer, who may not have relished Munnings's nondescript propinquity at a time of crisis when the local populations were beset again by spy fears. Munnings borrowed a tunic, a serge Sam Browne belt and a tin hat, and went off on a black Australian-bred horse. 'I was now an imitation captain.' He overtook some cavalry units, including the Scots Greys, whose horses were camouflaged with Condy's Fluid (permanganate of potash). 'Many of these men had fowls and dead pigs hanging from their saddles. We were in one vast retreat!'

He contrived to keep in touch with Seely, who joked: 'Munnings, in his false uniform, would most certainly be put up against a wall and shot,' if the brigade was overtaken by the enemy. '*Qui est-il?*' a French gendarme asked the General, as Munnings stood on a bridge watching a crowd of horses being watered below. '*Il est un Boche*,' replied Seely, whose smile sent the gendarme away satisfied. At Compiègne, Munnings thought he was riding through a street strewn with salt. It was glass from the railway-station windows, powdered by gunfire.

One evening Seely handed him dispatches to take to a Canadian military representative at general headquarters. In effect, it was his *congé*, as in the changed circumstances of the retreat he could no longer function as a war artist. He wrote that he 'felt the separation' from his friends of the brigade. He was left with a recurring dream of 'those uncertain, chaotic days'.

He had found the Canadians 'the finest and best fellows I ever met', men after his own heart, and there was his later tribute: 'I learned to respect and admire Canadians.' Orders were coming through, after many delays, that he was to return to London. The Canadians thereupon virtually kidnapped him and sent him off to the forests where their lumbermen were at work – 'grand fellows, who belonged to the illimitable spaces of Canada'. He visited the forest of Conche, the forest of Dreux, the forest of Bellême. Everywhere, the Canadians received him as one of themselves in their log cabins, 'with a stove at one end and an iron pipe going out at the top. In spite of the fug, I spent pleasant hours with them'.

He visited what he called Stendhal's country, and Besançon,

the birthplace of Courbet, seeing one of that painter's largest
canvases – 'quite one of the most superb paintings of a horse
that I know'. Those excursions were the more gratifying in that
'things were looking up and people cheerful. The German attack
had failed and their armies were finally on the run'.

'Munnings is to return home.' War Office orders at last caught
up with him. Other artists were waiting to be sent out, one of
them Will Rothenstein (later Sir William), who was to make
drawings of the sites of battles in which the Canadians had taken
part. Munnings offered to give him a chit of introduction to a
Canadian staff officer. Sucking a pencil and looking hard at
Rothenstein, diminutive and dark, he asked him: 'Would it be
correct to describe you as a good fellow?'

Returning to England via Paris, he found the French capital
under fire from the German long-range gun called Big Bertha,
one of the two 'secret weapons' of the First World War (the
other being our tanks). He saw 'the Folies Bergère quickly
cleared, though packed only minutes before'. His canvases and
drawings had been sent to Paris-Plage, where, he sorrowfully
recorded, one of the young Canadian officers with whom he had
often made merry was drowned while bathing. Munnings
never afterwards heard 'Roses of Picardy' without being
reminded of 'that young, well-bred lieutenant, who had a
charming tenor voice and who sang that song so well'.

Collecting his canvases, he took them back with him to
London, some rolled in a golf-bag. Forty-five of them were
prominent at the Canadian War Records Exhibition at the
Royal Academy. They provided formal evidence of his com-
petency to be elected an A.R.A. in 1919. He had modestly
believed that he would never be a member of the Academy,
though he had agreed to his name being put forward by Richard
Jack R.A. His election quite genuinely surprised him. He still
considered himself a provincial artist. He had no London studio.
His smile was appreciative rather than rueful when Derwent
Wood R.A., the hatchet-faced, argumentative sculptor, told him
in the Chelsea Arts Club: 'Mind you, I didn't vote for you – I
voted for a gentleman.' The roar of laughter rang long in
Munnings's memory. Perhaps in that moment there occurred the

transformation of the Bohemian A. J. Munnings of Norwich and Newlyn into the prospective P.R.A. and K.C.V.O. 'It was a stirring event for me at the time', receiving the distinction of associateship of the Royal Academy. 'My ambition after the election was to work and win the next honour – that of being full R.A.' He did not dream then of reaching the highest place.

The last of his war commissions was to paint the Earl of Athlone, brother of the Queen, on a charger at Windsor Castle. Princess Alice, Countess of Athlone, had seen and liked the Seely portrait with Warrior. On the day that he was to go to Windsor he was a guest at luncheon at the Hampstead home of the Sunlight soap plutocrat, Lord Leverhulme – 'a terrific affair, with much toasting and many speeches'. He left for Windsor in the late afternoon. The next morning he rose early to keep his appointment with Lord Athlone, who with the Princess, a groom and the charger, was ready for him to begin work. He then found that he had left his paint-box in London. 'What a go!'

Hurried telephoning and quick action by the steward of the Chelsea Arts Club produced the missing paint-box by the first available train. Lord Athlone filled in an awkward wait by showing Munnings the bays and greys used in the royal procession at Ascot. The sitting was deferred to the afternoon, when Lord Athlone mounted 'the quietest horse ever foaled' and passed the time by humming snatches from Gilbert and Sullivan. Opening his paint-box to begin, Munnings found in it an envelope containing a Chelsea Arts Club bill for £85. 'It showed the reckless manner in which some of us were living after the First World War.'

(3)

He was forty and by then he can have had no doubt where his future lay. Apart from its working amenities, London opened before him a far wider vista of social enjoyments than he had previously known; its clubs, for example, where a man could be comfortably sure of finding more of his equals than of his betters. He always preferred the company of his own sex. With

Dear old
munnings
I did not mean
any harm. —
over looke it!
orps

Munnings caricatured by Sir William Orpen R.A. in the 1920s.

Castle House, Dedham

the help of H. M. Bateman, of *Punch* fame, he found a well-lighted studio in Glebe Place, Chelsea. It had a bedroom and a kitchen attached and the rent was £65 a year.

'And what a studio was mine!' he wrote. 'Being a countryman, I had never spent so long a period in town before. In 1919, free in Chelsea, I was becoming all but a roysterer – in fact, I may have been one.' Any doubt he may have had on that point would have been removed by his Chelsea Arts Club contemporaries, including the steward. It may or may not be in the club records that he was asked to leave it. That situation certainly arose. He was accused of using bad language in the hearing of an Irish waitress, who lodged a complaint. The honorary secretary was asked to see her and to try to settle the matter without resort to the committee. The waitress was told: 'We are all sorry that this happened, but with Mr Munnings allowances have to be made – he's a genius.' Confusing the term with a proprietary brand of stout emanating from her native land, the waitress remained unmoved. 'The bar wasn't open at the time,' she insisted. Supported by influential members, an accusing faction succeeded in having Munnings suspended from the club.

The committee man charged with conveying to him the order of banishment was Captain Adrian Jones, sculptor of the great bronze figures of the Quadriga on Constitution Hill. Munnings thought it proper to disclose Jones's emotion while keeping silent about his own. 'I looked at Jones; he looked at me. There was a tear on his cheek.' Jones, formerly of the Regular Army, told him: 'It's a terrible thing to be asked to resign a club,' as if it was the final shame.

Munnings sought sanctuary at the Café Royal, which had been shorn of some of its gilded glory but which was still a meeting place of kindred spirits as numerous and varied as those at the Chelsea Arts Club, including Augustus John, William Orpen, William Nicholson, James Pryde, C. R. W. Nevinson and Wyndham Lewis, with the added attraction of prominent actors, writers and musicians and their ladies. Napoleon brandy could still be had there and the wine list was as good as any in London. Munnings made himself at home to the extent of expecting the company to listen when he rose in his place among the red plush *banquettes* to declaim whatever ballad of his own composing he thought suited to the occasion. Usually the audience was tolerant, if not necessarily enamoured. Occasionally he was clapped and cheered.

He had been encouraged in his balladry by a future Poet Laureate, John Masefield, who in 1913 had been so gratified by meeting him that he wrote to tell him so: 'A real pleasure, because I found in you and your work a sense of English country life which is very rare in English art, and a quality I always look for eagerly.' After the war Masefield read *Anthony Bell*, a fox-hunting ballad of sixty verses written by Munnings in his Norfolk days and thereafter occasionally revised. Masefield told him that he read it through 'with huge delight', and suggested that not a word should be altered. He believed that it would be 'a joy to people in this land for generations to come', a kindly compliment not endorsed by all those who had to submit to listening to its unseasonable sentiments on sweltering summer evenings at the Café Royal.

Chastened or not by his departure from the Chelsea Arts Club, he was elected to the Arts Club in Dover Street, Piccadilly, where a table in the dining-room was reserved for members of the Royal Academy. 'For years I dined in happy company round that table.' He celebrated his contentment there by lending the club his treasured Tissot, '*La Danseuse le Cord*'; 'A lovely girl in pink tights! With pale blue corsage and pink rosebuds. Only Tissot could have painted her – poised, balancing on a tightrope, above the crowded tables in the Jardin de Paris.'

There was also the Royal Academy dining club, dating back to the days of Sir Joshua Reynolds, the first President, and providing pleasurably anticipated dinners four times a year, beginning with a whitebait feast in May. At first they were held at a restaurant, until pressure of sentiment caused them to be given in the Reynolds Room at the Royal Academy, as they still are. Munnings was delighted by those surroundings, 'one of the many rooms in Lord Burlington's house which have remained untouched as they were in his day. A great home for a dining club of such traditions!'

Not long after he had left the Chelsea Arts Club, he was

invited by Sir Edwin Lutyens R.A. to dine with him at the
Garrick Club. Another guest was Asquith, the former Prime
Minister, who wrote in his diary that 'conversationally, the
situation was saved by Munnings, the artist', who recited
some hunting ballads which Asquith presumed were written by
Masefield. Noting that, in fact, Munnings was the author of
them, Asquith added to his diary the comment: 'He delivered
them with marvellous *brio.*'

Dining again at the Garrick with Lutyens and E. V. Lucas,
the London essayist and bookman, Munnings was asked to
recite *Anthony Bell.* Among listeners at other tables was a
member who belonged to a well-known hunting family and
who, at the end of the recital, urged Lutyens and Lucas to put
Munnings up as a candidate for the club. 'To my astonishment,'
Munnings was writing some weeks later, 'I was made a member.'
He called the Garrick 'the club of all clubs'. It gave him, among
other satisfactions, access to some of the best works of Zoffany,
the great colourist and master of the secrets of tone. In due
time, too, he was reinstated at the Chelsea Arts Club, though
his newer club loyalties precluded him from taking full advantage
of that act of grace.

(4)

He had not found it necessary to invent another personality
for his own. The social pressures in the village of his birth and
upbringing had never been such as to force him to resort to
protective colouring. There was no great resident landowner
to touch the cap to, no overpowering ladyship to whom he was
required to bend the knee. Thus it was easy for him, on becoming
a Londoner, to behave as if he had no intention of being mistaken
for one. He spurned the affectations of the town. His East
Anglian accent rang out as defiantly in the smoke-rooms of
Pall Mall as in the Norwich bar-parlours. He could be flam-
boyant, but it was rarely a conscious pose. With his whipcord
strength and his well-weathered look he was like a force of
nature, impulsive, perverse, aggressive – and impressive. His
way of putting his whole personality into an utterance and into

most of what he did was memorable. His copious use of exclamation marks in his letters manifested the same intensity of
feeling.

He still wore his tweeds and checks and his lemon-yellow
muffler, still laid down the law with a switch of his riding-whip.
His free and natural and totally unaffected manner could be both
embarrassing and enviable. Standing up to declaim in the
Café Royal meant nothing to him. Calling at the Magpie at
Harleston and hearing sounds of Rotarian revelry in another
room, he demanded of the landlord: 'Why shouldn't I join in the
fun?' and strode in on the assembly, to be at once accepted
and welcomed as a guest. Lunching at Claridge's, he did not
flinch from telling the head waiter in a voice to startle the
dowagers: 'The crust of this apple pie is nothing like as good as
my mother's.'

The Suffolk author-farmer, Adrian Bell, wrote in a local
newspaper of a car-ride with Munnings through some of the
more remote East Anglian villages. 'If a house took his fancy,
he would stop and lead me up the drive as if it were his own
home, pointing out admirable features.' When they were
accosted by an owner, resenting their trespass, Munnings looked
at him, 'head cocked back, screwing up one eye, as though
judging the irate squire's paintability'.

As for the too-free speech, at least it demonstrated vitality
in the English tongue, a quality that may have been lacking in
some of those whom it offended. It was more usually amusing
than objectionable, especially when it included the extravagant
analogies of his invention. His adjectives likewise could be
picturesque. 'Yellow-booted' was one of them, producing a
comical effect in conjunction with the indelicate noun to which
it was generally attached. Constable's caustic speech was said
by one of his biographers to have been 'the sole crookedness
of his nature'. Something of the kind could be said of Munnings's
expletives, which were probably a behaviour reflex of his village
youth; like smoking, a sign of manhood. To those who knew
him best it was an unconscious habit. That it derived from dark
psychological impulses, as possibly in the case of Cézanne,
whose profanity was notorious, may be doubted.

Munnings's worst outbursts were later associated with the gout which plagued him from the age of thirty. 'No victim of gout,' he wrote, 'could ever describe to anyone the utter misery and suffering, the obstinate pain of it,' and the irritability arising from it has long been a literary *cliché*, with or without benefit of medical endorsement. Munnings's 'bad' language was not the expression of an uncouth mind and it far from disfigured all his conversation. We can see it as a manifestation of his resolve to be irredeemably himself, a man from East Anglia with not only the will to preserve his identity in the mass anonymity of the urban scene, but the talent to stamp it on his time.

Like many other men of zestful appetite, the scabrous elements in life amused rather than repelled him. And, like Mark Twain and Max Beerbohm in their degrees, he wrote a number of unprintably witty things that entertained more of his friends than might have admitted it. Often those bawdy exercises relieved the indignation he felt at various aspects of modern progress. Walking along the littered shore between Snettisham and Heacham, he composed some verses which he called 'The Tortured Coast of Norfolk'. Not all the lines could be comfortably printed even under the latest legal dispensation. He changed the tone of several of them for publication in his volume of ballads. They were intended to point a moral about which he felt strongly, the mob's desecration of the English natural scene:

> With squads of children squalling.
> The summer day begins;
> Tradesmen's vans are calling
> With apricots in tins,
> Adulterated peaches
> And lovely crimson jams,
> Potted shrimps and lobster
> And constipating hams. . . .

CHAPTER 10

Painting the Prince of Wales

(1)

OFTEN, opening letters commissioning him to 'paint somebody on a horse', he was spurred to anger. 'Oh, damn it – *no!*' he would shout, throwing the letter impatiently aside. He would then adjust his feelings with the reflection: 'Better men than I spent their lives painting commissioned pictures', the great Sir Joshua among them. Admitting that many of his commissioned equestrian portraits were 'failures and disappointments', he put forward the excuse: 'I am one of those artists who want to paint pictures. Worse than that, I long always to sit by a river and paint.' He mused in *An Artist's Life*:

> 'A pleasant way of life, painting to the sweet music of water running over stones and pebbles; the high sunlight piercing the foliage, flashing on leaf and stalk – throwing pools of light on transparent, rippling sandy shallows. What colour in the running water, the reflections, the sunlit ripples; what subtle blue passages in the shadowed currents!'

He was claiming kinship with Crome and Constable rather than with, say, the turbulent, soaring spirit of Turner, who raised the art of landscape painting to a plane on which the familiar was lost in the cosmic. Munnings's letters contain many vivid word-sketches of the natural scene, as if there was solace in describing what he had too few opportunities to paint. He sees an autumn sunset as 'the flare of funeral pyres in the west'. At a Norfolk crossways he sits astride his horse and surveys 'the desolate beauty of a wintry day', the December light reflected in a watery lane, and listens to 'a rising wind making its solemn chords of eternity through the bare branches of the spreading oaks under which I rode'.

His first painting of a racehorse known to the sporting millions was of Poethlyn, winner of the Grand National in 1919. He painted the horse at the Flintshire home of the Peels. A registered parcel, arriving there for him, contained the 'formidable manuscript' of John Masefield's new poetic work, *Reynard the Fox*. The poet wished to be assured by Munnings that all was well with the hunting passages. Munnings felt deeply favoured. He read the poem aloud to the house party one night over the port. 'All were enthralled. It held them from start to finish', and the poet might have been the first to say that his work was embellished by Munnings's power as reciter.

What brought Munnings financial success and new reputation that year was not racehorses or equestrian portraits but gipsies. He went to the Epsom Spring Meeting, where he was soon surrounded by members of the gipsy families he had known at Alton before the war, the Lees, the Lovedays, the Grays and the Stevenses. 'The costumes of the women surpassed all dreams. Large black ostrich-plumed hats, black ringlets, big ear-rings.' Seeing them in their unrivalled finery, he nodded ready assent when they asked him: 'Are you a-comin' down this 'op-pickin', Mr Money?' He made some sketches at Epsom which he worked up later that year at Alton into two of his best-known gipsy studies, 'Gipsy Life' and 'Arrival on Epsom Downs', for which he received £850 and £800 respectively. 'What a blessing the gipsies did not know these figures. I should have been skinned alive!'

His companion on one of those days at Epsom, A. Egerton Cooper, remembers Munnings's concern that his real name should not be made known to the gipsies and, more important for him, that they should not know the prices fetched by pictures for which he paid them half-a-crown-a-sitting. He carried a hip flask of whisky and that, too, had to be kept a secret from them. He crept behind bushes to drink from it.

The Epsom pictures were seen by two Scottish brothers named Connell, who had a gallery at 47 Old Bond Street, London. They proposed an exhibition of the gipsy paintings. When he showed them a number of unsold pictures done at Alton before the war, they changed their minds and asked him to name a price 'for the lot'. He adopted a firm stance. 'I was not going to let them get the better of me', and held out for his price, 'running thrice into a few thousands.' He afterwards agreed that the Scotsmen had treated him well; at last he had 'a solid nest egg in the bank'. From that time forward he had no real cares about money.

(2)

It was the fulfilment of a dream when he became a man of property as the new owner of Castle House, Dedham, near Colchester. He had an eye for small country houses of character, noting quaintly that 'they are usually occupied by parsons'.

The furniture, 'the few good pieces', of his farmhouse lodgings at Swainsthorpe was still stored in the studio in his uncle's field. There was another studio full of unsold pictures at Lamorna Cove, Cornwall. At St Erth, not far away, his five horses were 'eating their heads off' and running up bills that at last he could pay with an easy mind. He now owned a fine Georgian house for his furniture, a garden for the studio, and thirty acres of pasture for the horses.

The dream had not been of a house but of a river, that paramount memory of his childhood. The Regency bow windows of Castle House opened on to a valley with glimpses of the Stour. Although he was committed from his heart, he had feelings of mental panic before and after putting his signature to the documents. Before: 'I should never be able to keep up such a place! Who was I? A mere painter.' After: 'I tramped up and down the rooms, cursing my folly for having saddled myself with such a responsibility. I believed that I should never paint again under the weight of my possession.' For the moment, the satisfaction of owning a house in the heart of Constable's countryside could not prevail against those doubts. Riding out for the first time from Castle House stables, he was troubled by the thought that 'pride goeth before a fall'.

The first work that he did in the sectional studio brought from Swainsthorpe and set up in one of the paddocks at Castle

House was the modelling of a bronze figure of a mounted cavalry officer to be placed in a side-chapel at Mells church in Somerset which Sir Edwin Lutyens had designed as a memorial to young Edward Horner, killed in action. Munnings put everything else aside to carry out that commission; and perhaps he owed more than he knew, in making a success of it, to the tactile awareness developed by his fondling of the toy horse of his childhood. More than any other painter of horses in our time, he achieved effects which, according to one sound judge, 'reached the farthest limits to which a painter can go in approaching the art of the sculptor'.[1] If he could not hope to emulate the equestrian glories of Velasquez, he could help to displace a convention of the nineteenth century which ignored the convincing genius of Stubbs and Marshall and reduced the horse on canvas to little more than an idealised silhouette or studies for a classical frieze.

As for the equestrian bronze which he did for the Mells memorial, it showed that he had as great a mastery of form in that unaccustomed medium as in his painting. Many people, seeing it, were surprised to find that it was the work of his hands.

(3)

In the same year, 1919, the gods who inflicted that grievous hurt on him in Cornwall five years before, made compassionate amends. They decreed that he should marry again and know long contentment in that state. At Richmond Horse Show he was struck by the immaculate appearance of a rider in the Ladies Hunters' Class. Riding a dark chestnut named Dandy II, she showed firm command of her mount and of herself. Her white gardenia button-hole fixed itself in Munnings's mind as a badge of perfection.

Looking at the show-card, he remembered painting a picture to the order of the owner of the chestnut. Seeking him out, Munnings secured an introduction to the rider, Mrs Violet McBride, a young widow. She had ridden horses since childhood

1. Charles Simpson R.I.: *Animal and Bird Painting* (London: B. T. Batsford, 1939).

for her father, Goldby Haines, an Edgware riding-master. She had won the Gold Cup at Olympia and many other prizes. When Munnings asked her to sit for him, she declined. She had already sat for an artist in Chelsea and found it tedious. She turned aside, leaving an impeccable image in Munnings's memory. A day or two later, riding in the Row with Sir George Holford, she asked him whether the name of Munnings was known to him. He replied that it was 'of some account in the art world'. Munnings said that 'if he had not spoken thus, I doubt if she would have thought any more about me.'

They were married in March 1920. Violet Munnings soon saw that 'A.J.' needed not only a wife but a comptroller of his household, that he required to be relieved of the petty cares, the business correspondence, the bills, and other wearisome matters that can come between an artist and his work. Recognising her level-headedness and resource, he gave her his power of attorney, with the result that he went to his bank only twice in forty years, saw his investments flourish, rarely signed a cheque and, save for intermittent explosions about income tax, gave comparatively little thought to a subject that obsesses nine-tenths of mankind.

His wife's early acceptance of the fact that to 'A.J.' his clubs meant as much to him as his home was a further guarantee of the success of their marriage. She was often lonely, but considered her situation to be inevitable and necessary. Nor did her exemplary tact and understanding go unregarded by Munnings. His letters to her over the years tell of an appreciation that was more than dutiful. He wrote to her from Woolsthorpe, Grantham, that autumn: 'I wouldn't want to be anywhere long without *you*. When I slip off on these excursions of work I know that soon I'll see you again and that all I do is partly for you; not all – a lot for my own sense of doing my best.' His postscript to another letter was: 'Good-night, my dear – you certainly are a good wife to me and well I know it.'

Retrospectively Violet Munnings saw their marriage as a dividing line in 'A.J.'s' career. 'He was never such a good artist after he married me. He had establishments to keep up, more expenses to meet. It meant painting for money.' All through his life he was capable of working productively at two levels.

Reviewing an exhibition of his work at the Alpine Gallery in 1921, Paul Konody, art critic of the *Daily Mail* and *The Observer*, wrote that he had expected to find 'a brilliantly-gifted artist being led astray by his own cleverness and facility'. He recorded, 'with relief', that he saw 'no evidence of hasty production, no slackening of energy, and, above all, none of the monotony that so often attends the effort of a single artist to fill so large a gallery.' Mr Munnings, he wrote, 'has taken a big stride forward in the direction of coherent design, colour emphasis, and constructive or form-giving brushwork'.

The Alpine Gallery exhibition advanced Munnings's reputation. People crowded in to see what was for them an authoritative protest against the confusing clamour of Vorticists, Cubists, neo-Impressionists, portrayers of the diseased and the malformed, who seemed intent on perpetuating aspects of reality which the recent great war had sufficiently emphasised. Munnings's paintings were a splendid reminder of the beauty that is as great a truth as ugliness.

(4)

Damning the fate that harnessed him to the equine theme, between the wars he was a familiar figure at Blenheim Palace, Eaton, Belvoir, Berkeley Castle and other great houses. That he was always and entirely at his ease amid the often sumptuous hospitality is made a matter of doubt when we read his comment: 'Unlike Mr Sponge, I never stayed long, and was ready – perhaps anxious – to finish work and get away.'

The Duchess of Rutland wrote to him on 15 May 1921: 'Do come to Belvoir to stay for two nights. Why not come next week-end? It would give us so much pleasure. Diana [Lady Diana Cooper] would come, if she knew you were coming,' but she does not recall meeting him. The Duchess was herself an accomplished artist. 'Stay with us for a year,' was the handsome welcome given him by the Baron Robert de Rothschild at the Chateau de Laversine, near Chantilly, where he sat down to dinner with the Duke and Duchess of Alva, Prince Murat, Field Marshal Earl Haig 'and all the nobility for miles round', among them, he wrote to his wife, 'beautiful women glittering with diamonds'. He told her what she hardly needed telling, that 'this was an entirely new experience'. More than the glittering diamonds, he was impressed by the butler and footmen moving slowly round the vast dining-table, whispering the year of the wine they were serving.

Often at those dinner-tables he was assailed by conflicting interests, listening to good conversation and making mental notes of a sitter's face. It meant taking his wine carefully, otherwise 'tomorrow I should not be any good at work. What a life!' He said that many times at table he sat 'with dull care perched at my back all through the dessert and port'.

His letters to his wife, written nearly every day while he was away on those occasions, show that he had an eye for much else beside the subject of his painting. His host at Woolsthorpe, Grantham, was Major 'Tommy' Bouch, Master of the Belvoir Hunt. 'Whatever he wants he can have – but he can't get sport; that elusive thing is not his,' and, after discoursing in the same letter on the secrets of the successful M.F.H., he wrote: 'He is not very happy.' That was the condition of another member of the same house party. 'Ralph Peto very dismal. He has lost a lot of money and is down on his luck.'

His comments on the genial and generous Master of the Belvoir seem a little too coldly objective in that it was his host who had given him his first impetus, and exceptional facilities, to specialise in a type of painting that helped to bring him money and fame. More than that, Bouch was discerning enough to buy Munnings's work long before he was well known. He had first seen it in the antique shops of Norwich. He had bought one of the four studies Munnings made of the Bungay race-meeting and fair on 'that memorable day'. They first met across a St James's dinner-table not long after the war. Bouch invited Munnings to be his guest at Woolsthorpe and to paint 'what he liked'. He was given the freedom of the Belvoir Hunt.

Arriving at Woolsthorpe for that first visit, he was quick to observe a picture of a white pony that he had painted in the

Norfolk years. He was critical of it, insisting that it was not 'up to standard'. A few mornings later, Bouch noticed that it had disappeared. Without a by-your-leave, Munnings had taken it down and painted over it a study of hound couples being walked in the heavy snow that had fallen overnight. He made the excuse that he had run out of canvases. Visiting London a little later, Bouch saw in a gallery what looked like the same picture. It had been sold to the Hon. Evan Charteris, who was annoyed to find that it was virtually a copy of the picture at Woolsthorpe.

Twenty-five years later, writing to Bouch, Munnings recalled that it was 'you who put all those splendid ideas into my head'. He hoped, he wrote, that he had 'made a full response to and recognition of your generous help, and all you did for me at Woolsthorpe'.

Staying at Blenheim, he wrote in a letter to his wife that 'the Duke wept at breakfast. Yes, the tears ran down his cheeks because the little Peke was dead – one of 30!!' From Eaton, where he was painting the Duchess of Westminster, he wrote: 'I can't tell you what a business this is – all the time wishing one was home and out of it and not having to paint anyone who doesn't want a real portrait. But I forgive. She is such a woman and can't help it.' At Cirencester Park, 'to see Lord Bathurst surrounded by the pack gazing up at him, dispelled all else from one's mind. He is the most modest person I have ever met. "I think you deserve a good bottle of claret," he would say at dinner – and there was the Lafitte.' Dining with Lord Berkeley in the great hall of his castle, Munnings's gaze went again and again to a pink cyclamen in full bloom in the centre of the ebony table. 'There we sat, dining in candle-light, among the shadows,' the pink cyclamen to be recalled as an abiding emblem of a gracious occasion. He watched his host next morning preparing to mount the horse on which he was to sit for a portrait – 'a tall figure in a yellow plush coat, a sufferer's smile on his red countenance. Slowly and painfully he put his leg over the saddle, a man helping him. Each effort was agony; gout in the knee.'

As he sketched those vignettes of a vanishing age in his letters, Munnings's eternal melancholy rose to the surface in a phrase that recurred in them: 'Life is sad.' It was not only for love of great poetry that he knew Gray's *Elegy* by heart. Its mood was his strongest emotional undercurrent.

'I felt I was up against it,' he wrote in reference to his misgivings about the portrait he painted in 1921 of the Prince of Wales (the present Duke of Windsor) on his hunter, Forest Witch. The portrait was commissioned by the proprietors of *The Field* for presentation to the Prince as a souvenir of his season with the Pytchley. 'Yielding to an ambitious impulse', Munnings went to work on a canvas larger than was expected by those who were paying for it. Velasquez painted a monarch's son on horseback. Munnings may have had a dream of sending a mounted Prince of Wales down to as remote a posterity. Each morning the Prince arrived at the Glebe Place studio, changing there into hunting pink. Munnings observed that, seated astride the wooden horse, 'he now and then looked at himself in the mirror, giving his hat a further slight cock'. Acting as a sort of extra equerry, the editor of *The Field*, Sir Theodore Cook, followed as the bearer of a basket cradle containing a bottle of vintage port, with glasses, and two handsomely bound volumes of Surtees, from which he read to the sitter. Munnings's task may not have been made easier by a procedure which obliged him to shut his ears to accomplished renderings from his favourite author. There was the further complication that the Prince was 'always in a hurry'.

Munnings was not pleased with the result of his labours and neither, it appeared, was the Prince, who thought the portrait more like his brother, the Duke of York. A less critical viewing public saw it in their thousands at the exhibition of 'A.J.'s' Belvoir Hunt pictures at the Alpine Gallery. The exhibition manager, Knewstub, had a flair for publicity and was accused of exploiting the picture to the benefit of the Gallery. When representations to that effect were made to the King, it was removed to the Royal Academy, where it was shown on an easel placed at the top of the stairs. The editor of *The Field* considered that 'the treatment of the mare is masterly', thus confirming his amateur status as a courtier. He remained one of Munnings's greatest admirers. 'He has recaptured the very spirit of the brave old school and has added to it a knowledge, a dexterity, and a lucid treatment of reflected colour, which are his own.'

There was another invitation from the Duchess of Rutland. '*16 Arlington Street, S.W.1* – Do look in here on Thursday afternoon – 3.15. Queen Alexandra is coming at 3.30 to listen to wonderful Russian singing by the *ruined* Prince Alexis Obelensky. She is stone deaf but knows how to manage it. One must talk to her, heard or unheard. The Prince has an enormous voice, so I *hope* she will just hear that.'

Munnings's path and the Prince of Wales's crossed again when he went to Kirby Hall, Melton Mowbray, to paint Robert Strawbridge, an American sportsman who had been Master of the Cottesmore Hunt (not the Quorn, as Munnings wrote). For once he was persuaded to lay aside his brushes and go hunting. In a tweed jacket and trousers, he rode out with the smart hunting throng – 'a formidable line in black and scarlet that extended more than half a mile'. His mount took him over 'the most wonderful gated country in England – never on a road'. During the going, he called to mind 'that lovely creature, Harriet Wilson, who stayed at Melton with some hunting swell of the period'. He wrote to his wife:

'More work to do than possible. Rich Americans all at me. Young Whitney is here with Sandford and his mother instructed him not to go back without Mr Munnings painting him. Never had such a week in my life. Got here Teusday [*sic*].

Wednesday, concert for charity. All the *élite* there. All in scarlet evening coats. I had to do *Anthony Bell* in first half, *Gloucester Spot* in second. Brought the house down.

Afterwards, forty of us went on to a big house, the Higginsons, to a huge champagne supper party. Everyone there, all in scarlet. What a go!

Next day, Strawbridge insisted on me riding to the first draw on a hack. Saw all the fun and rode like the devil, trousers and all. Both the Princes out. Then, that night, I'm blessed if they didn't dine here!! Prince of Wales, Prince Henry and only Mr and Mrs Strawbridge and myself to meet them. And then I'm blessed if I didn't have to do *Anthony Bell* after dinner for them.'

CHAPTER 11

Death of a Derby-Winner

(1)

THE lease of the Glebe Place studio ended. Munnings was content to leave it to his wife to find a site in Chelsea on which he could build a studio to suit his needs. He afterwards wrote: 'There was not the great thrill as when, at twenty-one, I took possession of the carpenter's shop at Mendham.' The new studio, in Chelsea Park Gardens, provided him with a working spaciousness that he had not known before. 'It became part of my life', a fact that he came to regret. 'Castle House, too often and against my desire, was forsaken for Chelsea to paint portraits of people.' He called his new London address Beldon House, taken from Surtees.

The times reflected the economic impoverishment caused by the war. 'Medici can't sell the Derby picture at all,' he wrote. 'Only sold about twenty proofs!!!' Telling his wife in another letter that 'Agnew says things are very bad', he seemed to be more troubled by her inattention when he saw her off by train from Colchester to London. 'You see, I haven't forgotten you not for a *moment*. You didn't even give *me* a parting glance.'

Privately he helped more than one of his Chelsea fellow-artists at that difficult period, his own circumstances being little affected by the worsening crisis of the post-war years. His water-colours sold exceptionally well at the Royal Society exhibitions, one for 450 guineas. He was never without a number of commissions of varying importance. In 1921 he was a guest for several months at Ascott Wing, Hertfordshire, painting the Southcourt Stud for Anthony de Rothschild. 'Paint whatever you like, just whatever you feel inclined to do,' that admirer of his work told him. He was looked after by the stud groom, named Kent. 'You'd be just too amused with the way he fathers me. He says I must dream about horses all night. I shall miss him frightfully when I go; a kinder man than Kent never lived.' He was given 'whole cases of ginger-beer to drink', and every morning there was 'a surprise packet of wonderful sandwiches – never the same from day to day'. At 4.30 each afternoon Kent would appear with 'a silver teapot, sugar bowl and cream jug on a silver tray'. Setting it down on the grass beside Munnings's easel, the stud groom would invariably say: 'There, sir, that should help to keep you going.'

Those were hot days in May: 'The heat and glare have tried my eyes frightfully. The sun is pitiless and the b — y trees are too green', for once censoring himself. At the end of another day's work: 'I'm dog-tired and weary; can't help it. I work all day.' He wrote again:

'Feeling very well and these days of work among the *dear, dear* horses and country soak into me. Each mare is an un-conscious friend. Each goes on eating grass and cares nothing for me, but I love them, and as for their children, they are too wonderful for words. So long as I'm with horses and people I'm at peace.

These days of work outdoors take me back to years ago, reminding me of Ringland, gravel pits, all sorts of things. I could do some great things here. I rang up Anthony de Rothschild today. He hopes I'll work on.'

A *contretemps* that befell him in his bedroom at the Rothschild house was a source of later reminiscent laughter. Attracted by the light on a writing-table, a May beetle flew in through the open window. When in its clumsy flight it came near 'A.J.'s' face, he struck out at it with the book he was reading and in doing so, knocked over the ink-stand. 'The ink flew all over Mrs Leopold Rothschild's pink rosebud wallpaper.' Describing himself as 'horror-stricken', he wrote:

'What a go! You never saw such a pattern as it made in all your life. The ink had run down in six long black marks to the skirting board. I seized a sponge and rubbed it off and the pattern too – Lord, *how* funny. I laughed till I cried. I think tomorrow I'll paint some more rosebuds on the wall.

Bless me, I forgot about everything else for the moment. Very good for one, these things: take one out of oneself for awhile. My word they do.'

Then the weather broke. 'Another b — y rough and stormy day.' He returned to Chelsea, to do finishing work in the studio. A glimpse of morning sun would see him dashing off to Euston to catch a train for Leighton Buzzard, where a car would be waiting to take him out to the Stud. 'After an hour's work, clouds would roll up, and then – rain. A repetition of past sufferings and frustrations of outdoor work.' Again and again it happened. 'What is one to do? Alas, all is vanity and vexation of the spirit.'

At last the pictures were done, 'quite a collection', delivered to Palace House, Newmarket, among them the portraits of two notable racehorses, Galloper Light and Radium. His studies of mares and foals at the Stud were particularly successful. 'Never have I enjoyed painting pictures more than those . . . how and when I liked, no time limit and plenty of canvases', with every inducement to make the most of the green and gold background of the English scene in summer. 'Never did an artist have a finer chance than this to paint what he would wish,' and there was the added satisfaction of 'being paid at my own figure'. He went to the Rothschild bank in the City, 'to be given the largest and most generous cheque' he had so far received.

Not that fortune was unfailingly kind. Humorist, the Derby winner of 1921, brought many people good luck but Munnings was not one of them. Through the *Daily Telegraph* racing writer, 'Hotspur', he was invited to paint a portrait of Humorist for presentation to the owner, J. B. Joel, on behalf of a number of his friends in the sporting world. Munnings heard about the horse from Steve Donoghue, the celebrated jockey who rode him in the Derby. He called for Donoghue one morning at his flat

in St James's Street, Pall Mall. They were to drive together to a
Newbury meeting. Munnings arrived to find the jockey's flat
being ransacked for a missing cheque for £2,000, the fee for
the Derby win on Humorist – 'not that he thought it at all a
large reward', Munnings noted.

On the way to Newbury Donoghue described his previous
rides on Humorist. They had given him the feeling that the
horse had a hidden constitutional fault. He approved a per-
ceptive report in the *Manchester Guardian* describing Humorist's
condition after winning at Epsom: 'Humourist, sweating and
trembling, played out with the fearful effort, standing there
with drooping head, surrounded by a mob of cheering men in
silk hats. They patted his shining hide, but he was too far gone
to respond. His owner and the great jockey, Donoghue, were
beaming with delight; but Humorist, the hero of the Derby,
tired of everything, walked away heavily through the shouting
throng, the glare and blare of the most tumultuous scene in
the world, to some place where he could rest.'

After Ascot that year 'A.J.' went to stay with Charles Morton,
one of the great trainers, at Letcomb Basset, near Wantage,
where Humorist was being rested. He wrote on the notepaper
of the Bear Hotel: 'What a place! Seven old barrows – downs –
downs – elms – fat old elms – farms – harvest everywhere. How
lovely!' Every morning Humorist was brought out of his box
so that Munnings could make sketches. On the Sunday morning
Morton invited Munnings to share a bottle of champagne from
one of several cases given him by an appreciative owner.
'After sitting on a garden seat in the shade and drinking a bottle,
Morton talked of horses and horse-racing and then went and
opened another.' Lunch followed and, for Munnings, deep sleep
under an old yew-tree on the lawn. He was awakened by a
woman's voice crying out: 'Mr Munnings – wake up – wake up –
Humorist is *dead*!' Sitting up, startled, he saw the trainer's
wife standing over him, 'wringing her hands like Ophelia in
Hamlet'.

Morton came out to him with a bunch of keys in his hand.
'You come along with me,' he said quietly, 'and I'll show you
a sight you won't see again as long as you live.' He opened

a loose-box door. 'There, did you ever see such a thing in your life?' Humorist, the Derby winner, lay dead on the straw, one ear pricked, one eye open. 'There lies fifty thousand pounds' worth,' said Morton. He motioned Munnings to leave and locked the door. Munnings said that Morton 'hadn't turned a hair; neither the horse's death nor the champagne had affected him'. Morton's version slightly moderates that impression. 'Mr Munnings could not believe his eyes. He felt almost as upset as I did', Munnings perhaps reminded of horrid moments in his anatomy studies of long ago. What distressed him most was the likelihood, from the signs in the loose-box, that Humorist had sensed his impending fate.

Munnings finished the picture, with sittings from Donoghue in the Chelsea studio. Morton had to tell him that Joel, the owner, was 'so cut up at the loss of his horse that he could not take the picture'. As for the friends and admirers on whose behalf it was commissioned, of them no more was heard.

(2)

'A.J.'s' numerous letters to his wife show how fully she played her part in ensuring him the completest possible freedom from domestic and business bothers. Few contain more than passing references to such matters; and fewer still, it may be added, to the state of the world or of society, to politics or current affairs. Nearly all reflect or imply the artist's single-minded resolve to do his best. Only occasionally did he reveal awareness of extraneous pressures, as, for instance, when a letter about income tax was inadvertently included in some correspondence sent on to him at Kilkenny, where he was painting a noted personality of the Irish hunting scene, Isaac Bell. Munnings to his wife:

'Dearest Lady, I came into lunch from working all the morning . . . dull, sad, dark weather and mild. No sun.

Each stroke I did was mixed up with income tax. A stroke, then the voice of the Commissioners: 'Where did you get' – another stroke – 'the money to buy' – another stroke – 'Castle

House?' My heart was in my mouth, my hand trembling. Another teaser of a stroke; dear, dear me – no answer. I couldn't think what to say, so did another stroke. So I went on, until the gates of the gaol closed upon me.

Your letter dispersed the nightmare . . . Lord, I can't tell you how glad I was to get it.

I sat alone last night and cursed and swore. I didn't take to drink, though, I am all but t.t. these days. Then I walked for miles in the mud and finally home. Woke up this morning thinking of it – damnation.

It is all so unfair, I think.

Oh, for *one* day of sun.'

Bloodstains on the green grass of Ireland told their tale of bitterness in 1922. Munnings went with Bell to Waterford races, where Sinn Fein took charge of the course. At Kilkenny Fair 'real rain; it poured all day, a scene of hundreds of umbrellas'. A Sinn Fein strike in the town left a great number of herded cattle 'standing up to their knees in water', and the silent misery of the animals was distress for Munnings too.

There were other distracting matters. Bell's domestic affairs had resulted in his sudden resignation of the mastership of the Hunt. 'I didn't think such a fine fellow existed. The whole country adores him. I'm so sorry this is happening. He only wants peace. He is giving up *everything*. His hounds he bred for fourteen years, such a pack. He built the kennels. He bought this land and this lovely house and is giving it all up. I'll try to finish the picture, but there seems an impossibility about it. I could paint here if it were not for this affair.'

Difficulties of another kind awaited him at Eaton, the Duke of Westminster's great house near Chester. He went on there from Kilkenny to finish the picture of the Duchess on her chestnut mare, Angela. The Duke, who called Munnings 'Mr Stubbs', had wanted her to be painted by Orpen. 'She said *no*, she wanted to be done by me.'

Describing the first sittings: 'She never kept still a moment and each time she got down they all came and said her eyes were too small, then too large, then the mouth, then the bowler

hat and, my God, the habit was *never* right. Then someone
wanted her done with a fox creeping under her horse's nose.
Someone else wanted a flock of startled sheep in the picture and
hounds and the Lord knows what.'

After another day's work he wrote out in dialogue form the
exchanges between his sitter and himself. For example:

'May I get off now, Mr Munnings?'

'Well, please give me a little longer.'

'Now may I come and look?'

'That's much more like me. Oh, please don't alter it, Mr
Munnings!'

He ruminated one night in his bedroom, in which there was a
blazing fire, 'which makes quiet *crumpling* noises, and a high
piping note sounds through the chink in the window. Most
melancholy. It is about 11.30 and we've gone to bed. The
Duchess has all but spoilt her picture and reduced me to a
miserable state of nerves. I like her. She is perfectly serious and
sweet and charming, but she can*not* sit still. I can't paint under
such conditions. Another job of this sort would send me mad.
Never again.' And apparently deepening his depression was the
thought that 'it takes a day to get out of this place'. He may
not have known that an earlier visitor, staying at Eaton, lost
his way going down in the morning until a footman came to
the rescue and showed him into the breakfast room. 'Good
God!' the guest exclaimed, surveying the vast apartment. 'Bacon
and eggs in a cathedral!'

A letter from his wife, reproaching him for not answering
one from her, produced the reply on Eaton notepaper: 'What
it is – you don't understand me entirely. Being *so* business-like
yourself, you don't overlook my failings. My failings aren't
criminal. All I know is that my life is all work and that it is done
against difficulties all the time. . . . Well, it's a sad world, my
masters.'

He pointed out that although his work took him into the
stately homes, he was often left to himself. 'I work all day.
After tea, it's always washing brushes and then walking alone
till dinner'; a glimpse of the journeyman artist for whom the
glittering diamonds and the prodigious hospitality were but

episodes in an essentially lonely life. 'I've done it for years,'
he wrote and repeated: 'Sad world.' A letter sent on from Margot
Asquith (Lady Oxford) may have brightened the gloom. He
had recently given her a picture. 'Dearest of friends,' she
wrote, thanking him. She was about to leave with her husband,
the ex-Prime Minister, for the election campaign at Paisley.
'The Coalition is damned,' she recorded in her letter to Munnings, 'Europe is in pieces, Northcliffe is in hell, Cadbury
in Heaven, and my husband in high spirits.'

Out of the travail at Eaton came a picture, 'The Duchess of
Westminster and her Harriers', that was a great success at
least with his patron. 'The Duchess is so delighted that she sat
on till dark; a large electric lamp rigged up, 600 candle power.
I really told her that I would paint her portrait if she would *sit*
and leave it to me. Today she is like a child over it, simply
delighted – says it's the best thing she has ever seen. I knew I
could do it. This picture will add to my commissions enormously.' It glowed with the charm of a Watteau and the Duchess
rounded off Munnings's satisfaction, and her own, by having a
room in her London house redecorated so that the picture might
be displayed to the best advantage.

There was a disconcerting sequel. Without consulting the
Duchess, Munnings painted a second version of the picture,
slightly altering her pose and changing the colour of her riding
habit from black, as in the original, to red. The second picture
was sold by a dealer to an American buyer and it was in America
that the Duchess first heard of it. She was 'deeply upset',
according to a well-known painter who afterwards had a part in
obviating the legal action which she considered taking. She
had commissioned the first picture. She sat for it. A duplicate
might lead to future doubt about which was the commissioned
picture. As for a lawsuit, Munnings might have been a
dangerously entertaining witness for his own defence. He could
certainly have named half a dozen artists more celebrated than
himself who painted and sold several versions of the same
subject.

He was expressing renewed uneasiness at the prospect.
Letters requesting sittings were 'a disturbing omen of the day',

and he wrestled again with the problem of 'whether to let the portraits go'. Invariably there came the corrective thought: 'You may live to want the money.'

So off he went to paint the Duke of Marlborough and his son, Lord Ivor Spencer-Churchill. 'A memorable visit. A palace beyond all dreams. Faded flags, trophies of victories and pictures by Reynolds and Sargent. . . . What noble courtyards, where I stood in cool shadow, wearing my soiled old painting-coat with easel, canvas and paint-box, ready for the fray.'

The fray was not so wearing to the nerves as at the ducal establishment he had recently left; but the ninth Duke of Marlborough had ideas of his own. 'We must have a signpost in the picture! Changing horses, four greys, with a second horse-man in full rig; what a subject! Mind you put me on the best horse, and why not have a stonebreaker in the picture?' Mun-ings wondered whether the Duke, whom he thought 'somewhat of an actor', imagined himself giving instructions to John Ferneley, the Leicestershire wheelwright's son who was a master of elaborate compositions for horse portraits.

He intended that the finished work should 'reach the heights', and had to admit that it 'fell far below'. The Duchess, he told his wife, 'is a *most* interesting woman', and 'the Duke very nice', but he reserved his highest admiration for the ducal trees – '*such* oaks and elms – my Lord, such elms!!!' There was so much to distract the curious eye. 'But there is only one thing for me to do and that is my work – no time for anything else. No one knows how hard it is.' He took the opportunity of assuring his wife: 'You are without exception a wonder,' and of subscribing himself, 'Your admiring and awestruck husband, A.J.'

'I'm sure you will like me better if I get to work and write less,' he told her in a letter from Hartforth Grange, Richmond, Yorkshire, whither he had gone to paint 'the popular and well-beloved' Master of the Zetland, Herbert Straker, 'a Yorkshire-man to the bone'. Unheeding his own warning, 'A.J.' wrote long descriptive letters almost every day of his three weeks' stay in a hospitable household, 'where the speciality is the big home-cured hams buried beneath tons of oatmeal to give them a mellow flavour. One is always on the sideboard at breakfast'; and, thinking of it, he said, he was 'always out of bed immediately in the morning'.

An evening walk along a woodland path suffused his thoughts with melancholy when he heard rooks crying in agitation among the tree-tops. 'Shooting the young rooks had been in progress for some evenings before, and here and there still lay little bedraggled black patches amongst the bluebells, their black feathers misplaced and beaks open. If they didn't shoot them each year a plague of rooks would result from sentiment being the order of the day, and so they must be killed. But certainly those dead rooks looked dismal and made me pessimistic – well – about things everywhere.'

His portrait of the Master of the Zetland was put on view at Wood and Sons' gallery in Darlington. Calling to see it, the Master asked the proprietor's younger son: 'Well, what do *you* think of it?' The young man expressed his admiration nervously, ending with the remark: 'Some of the dogs are exceptionally well done.' Glaring at him with autocratic contempt, the Master snapped: '*Dogs* did you say? *Hounds*, man – *hounds*! And they've all got a damned sight longer pedigree than you!'

Violet Munnings, who went to Exmoor every year for the hunting, wrote to tell 'A.J. that an abandoned hind calf had turned up in her garden at Withypool. She asked him what should be done with it. He wrote to her from Yorkshire: 'Poor thing, if it is put out it won't know what to do and in the end it will be chased and killed. If it stays with us it won't see its own kind again. All I think is, these animals are far better than ourselves. We're all damned awful.'

CHAPTER 12

Strenuous American Days

(1)

'DON'T tell folk I'm making a fortune,' he bade his wife, writing from the Château de Laversine, near Chantilly, in 1922. He was there to paint the young daughters of the Baron and Baroness Robert de Rothschild, and his warning and perhaps sardonic aside was made after meeting the artist Philip de Laszlo, who had arrived at the château at the same time. Laszlo was of Hungarian-Jewish origin and his loyalties were a subject of newspaper comment in the First World War, from which he emerged as one of the fashionable portrait-painters of the era. Munnings wrote: 'Although I do not greatly admire his work, I find him a very nice man and very kind. He is painting the Baroness – and he won't do a good one. Probably I'll do it when he's gone, on a horse – she's tall and slim and has the sweetest face in the world and will sit for me if I wish. We shall see. Damn the gout.' In another letter:

'I told you of Laszlo. That man makes thousands. In a week or so he has done two portraits, *very* alike but awful things. Sloppy – like all he does; worse than bad Birleys. He gets huge sums for these – £500 each probably. He built his new house and studio in Hampstead, he tells me, which for freehold land, etc., etc., cost him £28,000. Talking of taxes, he told me that he paid last year £7,000! He has an album of signatures of all those he paints – everyone in England from princesses to commoners; President of America [*sic*] and everyone there, and Spain and God knows where. Painted the Kaiser years ago. He gets a likeness and does it quickly.

My blessed horseback portraits are no go for money-making. You see, his sitters come to his London studio and he does them right away in two or three sittings. No journey to paint the horse in. No hounds. He coins money. No wonder they do portraits – no waiting for the sun.

I like Laszlo very much. He has good qualities.'

He found that 'as one gets to know them, the people here are more amusing and less stiff and snobbish than our folk'. The food was 'beyond anything in England – even the Irish stew'. His host, Baron Robert, 'is absolutely the kindest fellow I've *ever* met'. He wrote down what the Baron told him about the German occupation of the château in the war. 'It was the headquarters of von Kluck and his staff, and all was left as they had found it when they finally retreated.'

There was a great Hunt dinner-party, 'when the liveried Hunt servants with large, brass, circular hunting-horns played refrains from the chase in the outer hall. Never had I imagined such a night.' There was another great Hunt occasion:

'St Hubert's Day was celebrated and I was taken to the crowded church at Chantilly, and saw some hounds led up the aisle by two liveried Hunt servants. The priest blessed them and the Hunt. After the service, the hounds, Prince Murat, the Master, the Princess, huntsman and Hunt servants, all rode in a cavalcade from the great stables – the Grand Écurier of the Prince Condé of the past – along the ride into the forest of Chantilly. The Baron lent me a horse, and soon, with members of the Hunt, I was riding through the forest, hearing the melancholy, strange notes of the great brass horns sounding through the trees.

The Hunt wore a handsome livery: pale blue with claret-coloured facings – a colourful scene. Somewhere in the depths of the forest more hounds with the Hunt servants were waiting in a circular space from which many rides struck out into the forest. Blue liveries, the sun lighting on the circular brass horns and yellow foliage, the tufters giving tongue . . .

hollow notes of horns in far-away drives . . . sights and sounds entirely new to me.'

Before leaving for Paris each morning, the Baron visited all of his guests in turn in their bedrooms to inquire their wishes for the day. 'Well, Monnings, what is it you want this morning – the horses, the children, the dogs or myself – or what?', Munnings answered one morning: 'Well, let me think. It's a dull day. I'm working at the farm on grey days, doing the white horses.' 'White hor-ses?' asked the Baron. 'White hor-ses? I didn't know I had any white hor-ses!'

Munnings's letter to his wife continued: 'I tell you I find painting *very* difficult – don't like portraits. . . . Always thinking of you and how extraordinary it is that nobody else matters except you.' He begged her to read Surtees. 'So clever and witty. How Sponge goes out and looks at the stabling and then the children – oh, *do* read it.'

He made a discovery about French beds, that they enabled him to lie flat. He ascribed to it the cure of the backache that had been troubling his sleep. 'It never aches now – or my neck; all gone. I'm sure the cause of it was our dipped beds.' And: 'Do you know, the longer I'm away from London, the less I want to go back there. Beastly hole.'

On his way home he stayed briefly at the Rothschild town mansion, 23 Avenue Marigny, Paris. 'Your letter followed me here,' he replied to his wife, who hinted at ghostly visitations at Castle House. '*Damned* rot – you *know* there isn't any such thing at all. It's only the wind against the window. ROT. You annoy me when you get like that. You risk breaking your neck each day when you ride out and then are afraid of a noise in the night.'

He was not worried about ghosts at Castle House. What did worry him was its growing unsuitability as a painting 'spot'. He complained that his studio was in the *wrong* place. 'I've known it for ages. I *was* a fool. I could never have done these pictures there,' meaning those he had painted for Baron Robert de Rothschild. 'I'm glad of parks and large houses as much as I *hate* leaving home, simply because I've not got a good painting spot of my own.' Naming some particular drawbacks of Castle

House, he thought it necessary to declare in writing: 'Before I die I will leave an explanation to the world that if I had bought the *right* place, I should have done *great* work.'

He went on to say that he had reached a point when he wished to do the *best* work of his life. 'I have slaved and slaved to get money to do it with, but each time I attempt to paint there I despair.' In fact, Castle House was a shattered dream, 'but getting married to you makes up for *all* other mistakes. You're my one and only stand-by'; and, changing the subject: 'Such a nice Duke to dinner who knows my work well and is delighted with what I have done at Laversine. Tons of money, too – big house in in Paris and a château somewhere. Paints himself. Simple and kind and unassuming.'

(2)

Few men of Munnings's vital and forceful nature have been less critical of their fellows. In his many letters there is far more self-criticism. It was with studied moderation that he wrote of Fred Darling, the Beckhampton trainer, who, he said, 'dashed my zeal and hopes', when he went to paint the Derby winner, Cameronian. On the other hand, a Brighton racegoer, delighted at the chance of meeting him for the first time, was perfunctorily greeted and ordered to turn his attention to 'that dreadful creature over there – and that still more horrible b— beside him', a bookmaker in close conference with his clerk. 'Now do you wonder,' Munnings demanded of his somewhat crest-fallen new acquaintance, 'why I paint horses?'

Far more usually, he judged others with kindly tolerance, not from mere respect for the civilities but from a natural warmth of heart. He told his wife: 'I like to be kind to people and to enjoy myself at all times with them.' It was reported from Boodle's Club that Lynwood Palmer, a painter of horses for whose work he could find no admiration, had said on hearing that the commission to paint the Master of the Zetland had gone to Munnings: 'He will make a better job of it than I could have done.' Munnings was disconcerted. He reflected in writing: 'I do praise where it is due,' and attempted a somewhat oblique rectification of his opinion of Palmer by adding: 'He does the necessary portraits of horses as owners like them to be.'

Mostly he was direct and sincere in his appreciation, which often matched in zest the experience that evoked it. 'I'm afraid I use the word "excellent" a lot, don't I?' he asked in one of his letters, recounting the pleasures of a visit to the West Riding and the quality of the port given him after dinner. 'This is a generous part of the world. I can feel it in the air.' He found far more in life to like than to dislike. His smile was seen more often than his frown.

(3)

'I have the most feet in line space,' he noted with satisfaction on Private View day at the Royal Academy of 1923. 'Clausen gave me the measurements.' His six exhibits included 'Humorist with Donoghue Up', the thoroughbred stallion 'Radium', 'Mares and Foals at Southcourt', 'A May Morning at South-court' and 'Kilkenny Horse Fair'. He was up for election as a full Academician. 'I got some votes but Philpot [Glyn Philpot] got in easily – 30. He was next on the list. No good worrying. Sat next to Sargent at lunch and he was *very kind*.'

Writing the following day from the Arts Club, he told his wife: 'Not resting content with the fact that I shall see you again on Monday and that you are well and alive and so am I – I still write you a line because I must. A line or more to tell you that I spent a pleasant evening and drank only *just* enough and not too much. To tell you that I like your butter better than the Club's butter and my bed better than the Club's beds – and *our* house better than the Club.' After lunching at the Garrick: 'O'Casey, the writer of *Juno and the Paycock* sat next to me. Such a nice fellow. I like him. Mrs C— [a member of the domestic staff at Beldon House, Chelsea] is the nicest person going. *Perfect*. She is so quiet and kind – saw her ironing my linen before I went out this morning.'

He made another painting raid on the gipsy encampment at Alton; then went on to Marlborough to paint a future Oaks winner, Saucy Sue, under the watchful eye of 'the most famous of trainers', Alec Taylor. 'How lovely the country was. The loveliest little streams, crystal clear, and canals all bedecked with flowers and water moss lying in patterns on the surface.' As usual, he walked alone in the evening.

'A sunset which moved me to fountains of tears. Dusk followed and the moon showed through the clouds. All alone – not a soul anywhere. Sheep bells in the valley and the long ridges of the downs reaching away into vapours and hollows and more ridges. So still, and the light dying fast.'

The loneliness of his evenings away from home recurs as a topic in many of his letters between the wars. 'Awful!' he wrote from the Bridge House Hotel, Catterick Bridge, Yorkshire. 'Sitting over the fire in the hall here, feeling doleful', though he gave the highest praise to the hotel, parts of which reminded him of Castle House. 'It is dismal alone after 5 o'clock', usually the end of his working day. 'I just walk out and keep walking and then the sky loses all its dramatic portent and your artist fool of a husband has to walk without a sunset. He subscribed himself that time: 'Your most loving husband whose one certain comfort is that he has you somewhere in the background of his miserable existence.'

4

A letter from the Director of the Carnegie Institute at Pittsburgh invited him to go over as one of the judges at an international exhibition of pictures, 'fare paid, with a generous expense allowance'. He sailed in the *Berengaria* in March 1924, his only visit to the United States, 'a gloriously mad time'. The outward voyage had its enjoyments but also 'hours of suspense for a landsman from East Anglia'. He 'quaked with fear' at the sight of 'the mountainous deluge of water' breaking over the ship's bows.

Soon he was caught in a maelstrom of work and pleasure, with champagne corks popping louder and higher because the law prohibited them from popping at all, and handsome men and lovely women lining up to sit for him on their horses. One of the women said that if he would not paint her in America she would make the journey to England with her mount and sit for him there. Another was 'one of the best-looking women I ever painted', Mrs Bayard Tuckerman. She had 'the best-cut nose in the world and a lovely chin'. When her husband saw the portrait Munnings had done of her, he at once commissioned a portrait of himself. 'I was nearly dead with work.'

Some of the richest of his American patrons were the hardest bargainers over prices. 'Mr Phipps became very mournful when I told him my figure. He sat down at my side on a large, soft sofa, gently arguing that it was more than he could afford.' As they talked, the millionaire pulled a case from under the sofa. It contained two violins, one a Stradivarius, the other a Gounaris. 'Pointing to the Strad, he said: "I gave eleven thousand for that and ten thousand for the other." ' Another sitter, who was 'as rich as Croesus, haggled for hours over what he was to pay'. Munnings was touched when, having painted the hostess of the international polo-players then at Long Island, he went to his bedroom to change for dinner and found a letter and cheque from her husband in appreciation of the portrait. He met the great polo-players, Milburn, Whitney, Stoddard and Sandford.

In Boston a hostess asked if he would care to see her new Picassos, lately brought from Paris. 'There on the floor, resting against Queen Anne chairs, shouting their loudest amongst Georgian furniture and precious china, were the queer dis-tortions. Nobody liked them – not even our host and hostess; but they could not return from Paris without a Picasso or two. Never mind the cost! At least they were making some fun, helped by the cocktails. The noise increased a hundredfold at the sight of the "masterpieces" ', a foretaste of the equally noisy controversies in which he would be involved at a later time.

He ate and drank too much, had gout and lost sleep. For recuperation he went alone to the far-stretching sands of the New England shore – 'not a soul in sight, except the seals basking in the sun'. There was also the restorative charm of Old Salem, where magnolia trees 'as big as elms' budded sumptuously in the high-walled gardens of white wooden Georgian houses, and the sunshine was softly kind. 'It was all reminiscent of Hawthorne and Longfellow', and he left it with 'many regrets'.

His most outstanding personal encounter, he wrote, was with the America's Cup yacht designer, Starling Burgess – 'one saw at first sight that the man was a genius'. Burgess read 'page after page of Swinburne in great style', and had in his studio 'the largest bottle of gin I have ever seen', which may have been a *non sequitur*. Munnings delighted in almost every minute of his stay among the Americans of New England and Long Island, who called him 'Al' and initiated him into the agreeable if exhausting experience of being lionised.

One of his American patrons, Harry La Montagne, a well-known sportsman, was asked: 'How long does Munnings take to do a portrait?' La Montagne, a hospitable man, answered slyly: 'I guess it depends on how good the boarding-house is!'

He turned homeward from Montreal, after visiting Ottawa, where he was surprised to find a picture that he had painted at Lamorna Cove. Among other returning voyagers was 'a dark young man ' who joined him in the fun and games of shipboard life. More than twenty years passed before they met again. By then Munnings was President of the Royal Academy and his companion of the nine-day voyage in 1924 was the President of the Royal Society, Sir Henry Dale.

(5)

Munnings's picture, 'The Ascot Procession Crossing Windsor Park', was a central attraction of the Royal Academy of 1926. Painting it, he talked with Queen Mary, who had wanted him to do the picture and 'who was simply kindness itself'. The subject of their conversation was the exact shade of the pink parasol carried by Her Majesty. 'She wasn't sure. I told her that it must be just as *she* wished and she agreed': Munnings in the unaccustomed role of courtier. He was excited by the prospect of making a great picture success, seeing it as 'the chance of a lifetime'.

A little of the excitement, no doubt, was supplied by the daily

H

arrival at the Chelsea studio of a large maroon Daimler with
the royal cipher in front. In it, he was driven to Windsor Castle
to make his preliminary studies. Watching the procession of
ten carriages against a background of ancestral oaks and elms,
he thought it 'too magnificent to describe'. The scarlet jackets
of the outriders, the splendid livery of the postilions, the flash
of carriage wheels in the sunshine; 'above all, the red rosettes on
the horses' heads' stirred him profoundly. 'I found it difficult to
remember to lift my hat when Queen Mary gave me a kindly
bow.' He said that, tormented by flies, he worked as he had
seldom worked before. He seized the opportunity to paint a
large companion picture which he called 'Their Majesties'
Return from Ascot', 'not a royal commission but an ambitious
effort on my part'. It was inspected by King George V and
Queen Mary on the day before the Private View at Burlington
House. The King sent for him and spoke enthusiastically of his
work. 'The horses are moving,' he said, and the postilions, each
of whom His Majesty mentioned by name, were 'the very image'.

After being shown at the Royal Academy and at the City Art
Gallery, Birmingham, 'Their Majesties' Return from Ascot'
was sent back to the Chelsea studio. It was seen by the Chairman
and the then Director of the Tate Gallery, who persuaded the
Chantrey Bequest committee to buy it in 1938 for £850 – 'not
too large a sum for such an effort', Munnings remarked; but
he was glad to know that it would go to the Tate Gallery. He
had something to say about its reception there when a new
Director, John Rothenstein, took charge.

> 'For some reason, he has never given the picture a place on
> the walls. He has his Braques, his Picassos, his Matisses,
> Klees, Chagalls; but my picture of the King and Queen and
> the two Princes returning from Ascot has been kept out
> of sight, year in, year out.'

Munnings's dismay was shared by Professor Thomas Bodkin,
Director of the Barber Institute of Fine Arts, Birmingham
University, who wrote: 'It is shocking to think that this splendid
and most English picture has not been put on view in the

Tate Gallery for many years past.'[1] There was consolation for Munnings later when the Duke of Norfolk asked to be allowed to hang it in the royal pavilion during Ascot week. Subsequently the Tate Gallery was requested to lend it for a term of years to Windsor Castle, where it still hangs.

The figures in the picture, including the reigning monarch and two later kings of England, were painted in the studio. Munnings's wife held the pink parasol. Stanley Wade, a young director of Frost and Reed, print publishers and art dealers, then of King Street, St James's, was persuaded to 'stand in' for the Prince of Wales, wearing a grey top hat which Munnings sent him to borrow from Scott's. He was placed in a sideways pose on a settee, doing duty as a State landau. The sitting was a long one, the pose tiring. Munnings had to fight a battle with the light falling on Wade's face and ignored his discomfort. When pins and needles set in, Wade begged for a rest. Painting with fierce concentration, Munnings took no notice. Not then so experienced in the ways of artists as he has since become, Wade thought Munnings 'distinctly selfish'. Later, he came to know Munnings well.

He remembers 'A.J.' fussing about pens and pencils when signing contracts and autographing prints. 'He was quite likely to throw them out of the window if they didn't suit.' Wade went down to Chelsea to see him with a business proposal. He was received on the door-step with the demand: 'What the bloody hell can *you* do for me?' Wade pacified him by reciting some Longfellow verses. Another day Munnings was holding forth about Meissonier, naming him as great as Rembrandt. Wade ventured to demur. Munnings turned on him in a vengeful mood. 'What the devil do you know? You're only a picture *dealer!*'

A member of Frost and Reed's staff, handling a Munnings work for reproduction, accidentally damaged it. There was an insurance claim, arising out of which Munnings was escorted by Wade to an assessor's office in Lincoln's Inn Fields. They passed through a room in which a number of girl typists were busy at their machines. Pausing in the doorway to survey the

1. The *Birmingham Post*, 13 November 1951.

scene, Munnings shouted: 'Poor things - what a bloody life!'
After listening to a picture-restoring expert, he suddenly blazed
with temper, at which point the insurance assessor announced:
'Claim allowed.'

He became an R.A. on Derby Day 1926. The election produced
a dead-heat between him and Sir Walter Russell. Munnings
received the President's casting vote.

CHAPTER 13

A Welcome from Churchill

(1)

A VISIT to Spain in 1927, to see the Velasquez pictures in Madrid and the Grecos in Toledo as a first charge on his time, was overshadowed by his experiences of the bull-ring. It left a dark indelible stain on his memory. He could not forget 'a humble little white horse' awaiting its death in the sunshine. 'O little white horse! Little white horse!' he wrote, a monodic refrain in his letters home.

He went to Spain in the company of Lionel (later Sir Lionel) Lindsay, the Australian artist, and Bertrand Waterhouse, architect, a trustee of the New South Wales Art Gallery at Sydney. Waterhouse remembers Munnings as 'a mercurial and unpredictable travelling companion'. It was he who persuaded Munnings to make the journey. 'Oh – oh! how glad I am I didn't bring my painting things' (to his wife). 'This going about and loafing is a rest – and to try and paint in such a country under three months would be foolish; besides, I don't want to.'

At Ronda, he went off and climbed a mountain alone. 'I should think I lost a stone – never was in such a state. I rested and climbed and rested and climbed, until, trembling, wet and exhausted, I lay on top – on sharp grey stones – vultures wheeling round waiting for me to die.' Hearing a great bell tolling in Seville, he shivered 'at the thought of the Inquisition. I thought of the crowds of centuries ago, the *auto-da-fé*; burnings at the stake'.

It was to the bullfight that he returned again and again, writing his later account of the trip, compiled mainly from the letters his wife kept. Not the bulls but the horses were his chief concern, though he could not easily forget 'the scene of the bull, with its withers thickly impaled with gaudily festooned darts, their barbed ends deep in the muscles, and deep cuts from *picadors'* lance-ends, which cutting ends are never described'. Above all, there was the little white horse:

'His turn came. He, too, was lifted and hurled on his back, to the cheers of the crowd, and when beaten to his feet, was stamping on his own entrails, which stretched and split like pink tissue-paper. . . . Poor little once-useful horse, glad to work for only what it was given to eat – which had helped a human to earn his food too; and this was its end – a victim to a roaring holiday crowd.'

He saw a bay horse, 'its teeth chattering with fear, having been in the ring before', standing at the barrier below, 'the motley red-and-white striped bandage over its offside eye, its ears stuffed with tow, and tied with what seemed to be old electric wire'. After being attacked by the bull, 'the horse was beaten to its feet by red-shirted attendants. There, from the under-part of its belly, hung a large protuberance of bowels. . . . Not a soul cared, excepting ourselves. That I'll swear'.

He spoke his feelings to an American sculptor named Haseltine who had been in the ring at Seville modelling a bull with a horse caught high on its horns. 'He had to see it and say nothing, hoping that he could move people with the work he was doing.' The sculptor told him: 'The Spaniards don't see cruelty, where we do.' Munnings wrote: 'In England we hunt the stag (I do not excuse it) and the fox. To compare this with bull-fighting is senseless. Thousands go to watch bull-fighting where horses meet an ignominious end.' He sat down to write to *The Times* about it, then asked himself: 'What's the use?' Instead, he wrote to his wife. 'Last night it rained, and today is most beautiful, with transparent shadows on the grey mountains. Not a breath of wind. . . . Have been seeing some *Times* and read the news of Solario's defeat [the year's Ascot Gold Cup winner]. What a go!'

He went homeward by the Mediterranean way, his mind full

of Velasquez, El Greco and Goya; of Madrid, Toledo, Seville, Granada; of 'Roman aqueducts and clanging cathedral bells,' of immense sunburnt vistas taking the eye to far-off ethereal mountains; all shadowed by his memory of 'starved, weakened, half-dead horses. Their weakness and pitiable state enraged me', as if the only human spectacle to be seen in Spain was that embroiled in the tragic ritual of the bull-ring.

Munnings to his wife:

Hotel Victoria,
Ronda, Spain

Dear Violet, You will get this just after I have lived 48 years – awful. [His forty-ninth birthday, 8 October 1927.]

This is Africa, not Europe. Arab blood here – you see 100 mares with mule foals in a herd on an absolutely *parched-up* plain. They are everywhere, these mules. I've seen some really topping horses being ridden about; and now, my dear you can imagine me resting awhile among palms and olives and mountains – oh, Cordova was good – *the mosque*!!! Otherwise dirty.

I shall feel like work after all this. It only needs a change like this to make me realise that I shall always paint. But I want now to do *the* work – out of doors.

Toledo was wonderful. So is Wharfedale in Yorkshire, or anywhere – if it comes to that.

On the roads in the country you meet a donkey trudging with two men, 14 stones each, on it.

Love, much of it.

A.J.

(2)

'About my best portrait of a man on horseback': his private opinion of the picture he had done of the Earl of Birkenhead (F. E. Smith), some time Lord Chancellor of England, at his country home, Charlton Manor, Oxfordshire. His interest in the subject was deepened by the pleasure of being with the Smith family – 'and what a family they were!' To him, Birkenhead was a genius, 'head and shoulders above other men', and he had almost as great an admiration for Lady Birkenhead and their daughter, Lady Eleanor Smith, with whom, like Jasper Petulengro, he discussed 'the affairs of Egypt'. There was also the heir, Lord Furneaux, home from Oxford and 'full of the English poets', a sure passport to Munnings's regard. He was delighted when the young man 'gave us Keats's "Ode to a Nightingale" in true classical style'. He asked himself: 'Who would not want to paint in such an atmosphere?'

Birkenhead paid a compliment to his personality and attainments by making him a member of the small exclusive dining society known as The Other Club, founded in 1911 by Winston Churchill and himself. Its membership was and still is kept to fifty, not more than half being Members of Parliament. At the dinners, held in a private room at the Savoy Hotel, Munnings sat in the company of men as various as Sir Edwin Lutyens, H. G. Wells, Josiah Wedgwood, William Orpen, Arnold Bennett, Duff Cooper, A. E. W. Mason, Lord Burnham, Gordon Selfridge, Sir Roger Keyes, and his 'old friend and protector', as he called him, 'Jack' Seely, later Lord Mottistone. Churchill welcomed him to his first dinner and it was not long before they were on Christian-name terms.

Presumably that most distinguished of his fellow members would have endorsed the epithet bestowed on Munnings by E. V. Lucas in a letter of 3 May 1927: 'You are a vivid devil.' Arnold Bennett, writing one of the most readable diaries of the era, noted on 12 December 1929: 'Dined at The Other Club. Found that A. J. Munnings is a very considerable reader, including verse.' The following year, sitting next to him in the same place, Bennett noted again: 'Munnings talks well.'

He had his moments of success on the public platform but they were not many and, as often as not, arose from his disregard of the rules by abandoning the advertised subject and going off in full cry after another more congenial to him. An Essex audience that had gathered to hear him lecture on Constable had to be content, from the half-way mark, with a rambling discourse on river boards and their 'iniquitious neglect' of the amenities. In the realm of ideas he was not at home and rarely articulate. He was one of the top-table speakers at a banquet organised in 1930 by Sir William Crawford, the advertising agent and national publicity expert, who desired to promote closer relations between commerce and the graphic arts. Supporting that object, Munnings stamped his right heel loudly on the floor when he wished to make a point, a habit of his when speech-making. 'Like an old buck rabbit in a hutch,' someone murmured audibly enough to raise a sudden gust of laughter in the middle of the room. Munnings was put out. He lost the thread of his speech, muttered 'Damned scoundrels!' and sat down.

In private, as host or guest, he could be the best of good company, a talker who talked picturesquely if not always logically and who was more often persuasive than aggressive. He used emphasis freely, and no doubt it implies a lack of logic or the fear of it. He would resort to fist-shaking, but the thumb would be tucked into the palm, depriving the gesture of its force. There was the ready resort to adjectival violence; it depended on the company he was in. If it was not of his personal circle, he was ordinarily as reliable an observer of the proprieties as most people. It was exceptional when, speaking at a dinner of the Royal College of Surgeons, with ladies present, he turned and swore at a waiter who interrupted him by dropping some dishes. He had an enviable mastery of the art of social relaxation. With him at table, all affectations fled.

He dined one night in the early '30s in a private room at the Savage Club, then in Adelphi Terrace, as one of fifteen guests who included Sir Edwin Lutyens, Mr Justice McCardie, General Swinton (Chichele Professor of Military History at Oxford), R. C. Sherriff, author of *Journey's End*, Reginald Berkeley, dramatist and politician, Edward Hudson, the founder of *Country Life*, 'Billy' Bishop v.c., the Canadian air 'ace', R. D. Blumenfeld, Editor-in-chief of the *Daily Express*, and Tom Shaw, a Labour leader and some time Secretary of State for War. One of those present recorded: 'Munnings made a thoroughly entertaining attack on the drink laws, apparently in the hope of impressing the judge rather than the rest of us. Several times he held the table, our attention always given ungrudgingly to his demand. He recited with tremendous *verve* a foxhunting poem of many verses which he said he had written himself. At the end, he sat down in a little triumph – we all cheered.' The same observer noted that 'his is a bearable kind of egotism'.

In Laura Knight's opinion 'he might have made a success on platform or stage'. She was elected A.R.A. in 1927, he loyally active in her support, as he was in the case of another old friend of the Newlyn years, Charles Simpson R.I. Dame Laura said that Munnings arrived to congratulate her with William (later Sir William) Reid-Dick, the sculptor. Her studio in Langford Place, St John's Wood, was already full of people on the same errand, among them a number of artists' models, who had called to collect a tribute of guineas from the new member of the Royal Academy, by old custom. She wrote: 'From the moment he entered, the party became his. Such times as those made us love A.J. There was never anyone like him to make a party go.' As was said of Crome of Norwich, 'he was a boon companion, jolly in company; at the same time, firm and stern about work'.

(3)

In August and September 1928, long queues of sightseers were daily seen trailing from the entrance to the Norwich Museum and Art Gallery. The civic authorities had honoured Munnings with a retrospective exhibition by collecting three hundred of his pictures from other galleries and from private owners at home and overseas. Not all were willing lenders. The City of Birmingham Art Gallery was reluctant to deprive summer visitors of the pleasure of gazing on his 'Arrival on Epsom Downs for the Derby', one of his finest gipsy studies. The Duke of Westminster lent his portrait, on condition that Munnings replaced it with another of his pictures for the duration of the exhibition.

The exhibition, dominated by 'The Drum Horse', from the officers' mess of the First Life Guards, was a shining personal success for Munnings. An inaugural luncheon was attended by the Lord Mayor and the City Fathers, the High Sheriff of Norfolk, distinguished citizens of Norwich, with Lutyens,

Arnesby Brown and Henry Rushbury representing the Royal Academy. Lutyens, an irrepressible practical joker, seized the City swordbearer's cocked hat to wear in the Lord Mayor's procession. At the luncheon last-minute rearrangements of the seating at the top table were made necessary by the arrival of Roger Fry with an uninvited Indian guest. Munnings, the countryman, scorned Fry's Bloomsbury preciosity and could not accept as admissible logic the fact that Fry had become an art critic after failing to earn a living as a painter. Fry made a speech attacking civic art galleries. He sat down without mentioning Munnings or the exhibition.

That evening Munnings drove out with Henry Rushbury to dine at a country house. Rushbury was impressed by 'A.J.'s' intimate knowledge of the countryside. 'He seemed to know every gap in every hedge for miles round.' Seeing 'a poor-looking horse' in a field, he stopped the car, inspected the horse over a gate and then ordered the chauffeur to drive to the nearest farm, where Munnings asked for an armful of hay. He took it back to the field and fed it to the horse. Calling down curses on the neglectful owner, he rejoined the car, to find, arriving at the house a few minutes later, that the horse belonged to the host of the evening. Munnings would not leave the subject alone. Rushbury heard him muttering his disgust all through the dinner. 'Oughtn't to be allowed to own a horse – *or* a Crome!'

The exhibition at Norwich proved to be an event of more than local appeal. Not since Rembrandt's 'Mill' had been brought to London in 1911 had there been an art occasion in England more popular with the public. Nearly 100,000 people saw Munnings's pictures, a record at that time.

Among the breakfast-table reminders of his fiftieth birthday, on 8 October 1928, was a document composed by his wife for that occasion. He considered it 'an inspired warning'. It read as follows:

'. . . . Thou art fifty years of age. *Half a century* hath thy flesh and bones lived and partaken of the joys and ills of this life. BE THOU CAREFUL that thou abuseth not the good health the Blessed Lord hath given thee!

Go thou unto thy Club seven times seven, but be not carried away by thy *generous* heart. Thou orderest wine in abundance to pour down the gullets of thy guests, but, oh, Alfred, I pray thee pour it not down thine own gullet.

. . . Were I to pass to another world, where the cares of an artist are unknown, who would then take care of thee – thy finance, thy household, thy health and thy belongings? Go thee more to the country to inhale God's pure air. . . .

Yet your wife, who married thee for companionship, raileth not at thee; for life is full of compensations. Therefore, O husband, I am content to come second to thy Art, but I implore thee to regard thy fifty years spent in Art and work and revelry upon this earth, and while there is time *Take Heed*!'

(4)

'ONE more commission, only one,' he said to himself again and again. He agreed with his wife that 'to turn away good money was foolish: we might need it later'. Even so, he declined requests for portraits, usually telegraphing 'Sorry too busy' to save himself the trouble of writing explanatory letters. His sincerity also compelled him to paint pictures with no sale in view. Their subjects were never people on horses. There was 'The Friesian Bull', which did not find a purchaser until twenty-five years after he had painted it, a marble-solid study of bovine majesty which Masefield regarded with admiration and spoke of as a work of philosophic as well as artistic importance. It was finally bought for the Leverhulme Art Gallery at Port Sunlight and Munnings thought it a compliment well worth waiting for, recalling that 'old Crome painted "Mousehold Heath" for his own pleasure and it sold for a guinea after his death'.

The commissioned pictures brought in the cash but not the highest satisfactions of his painting life, though he far from spurned the praise with which his patrons often received his work. 'You've given me and my wife more pleasure than you know,' one of them told him after seeing the portrait he had done of a little boy on a pony called Canary. 'I'm more than satisfied and cannot thank you enough.' Munnings wrote to his wife: 'For twopence I would have given him the picture. Such kind appreciation is worth a cartload of cheques.'

The success of that picture, 'A Boy and his Pony' (Royal Academy 1929), he said, was due to his having put down what he saw, 'a summer Leicestershire landscape' prominent in his vision. He copied out on a half-sheet of notepaper a memorable letter of Constable's, dated 23 May 1802, as if it was refreshment for the spirit: '*There is room enough for a natural painter*. The great vice of today is *Bravura*, an attempt to do something beyond the truth. Fashion always had and will have its day; but *truth in all things only will last*, and can have only just claims to posterity'; and, if Constable had not provided the italics, Munnings would have. He wrote at the top of the copy: '26 years old', Constable's age when he wrote the letter. Munnings made another note, taken from the Twelfth Discourse of Sir Joshua Reynolds: 'I again repeat, you are never to lose sight of nature,' and that Gainsborough had declared himself 'sick of portraits' and yearned to 'walk off to some sweet village' to paint his heart's desire, which was landscape. Had not Romney found portrait-painting tedious and boring, merely a way of earning a living?

Munnings could not say, like Claude, that he sold his landscapes and gave away his figures. Significantly, he put as much of himself into his landscape backgrounds as into painting the horses and riders posed against them; for him, background was an organic part of the picture. Stubbs used background often incidentally, his 'afterthoughts', as Munnings chose to call them; in fact, they were sometimes painted by another hand. Munnings liked to manœuvre his subjects against backgrounds congenial to him; and it was the source of occasional clashes between him and trainers who would not allow a valuable horse to be exposed. Fred Darling, at Beckhampton, had told him that he would have to paint the Derby winner Cameronian in a loose-box. 'He's not going to be held out of doors.' That verdict confronted Munnings with an almost impossible problem. He wrote of 'irritations and vexations and difficult conditions'.

Rarely, but it did happen, the fame of a horse would hold his attention to the exclusion of all else. When he painted Coronach for Lord Woolavington he said 'scenery and oak trees were forgotten'. On the other hand, painting at Newmarket, he was 'lifted up with sheer joy' at having the chance to paint a Grand National winner, Sergeant Murphy, against a background 'such as no artist's imagination could ever invent', including old elms, a brown-tiled dovecote, and the round Saxon tower of Snailwell Church. He described the result as 'a happy picture, painted in happy moments, working in the English tradition'.

Sir Joshua Reynolds boasted that he had painted two generations of beautiful English women. Between the two world wars Munnings painted many beautiful racehorses whose names were household words. Writing from the stables and studs of their sometimes equally famous owners and trainers, he noted the horses' characteristics in hastily scribbled words. Foxlaw was 'so dark a brown that he could almost be described as black'. Tiberius was 'not a picture horse', Son-in-Law, 'a rich dark brown, with a short back and crested neck – all nerves, a lovely horse, "clothed in thunder"'. Mahmoud had 'a lot of Arab about him, darkish mane and tail, a white blaze and pink nose'. Bahram was '*the* horse; a beautiful rich, rather dark dappled bay, as near perfection as could be'. Dastur was 'a rich mahogany brown', Hyperion 'a beautiful little horse, far beyond the average in intelligence'.

Solario, 'a beautiful dark bay with a calm temperament and quite the thickest tail of any horse I ever remember seeing' (Munnings wrote), was sold to the Argentine for 50,000 guineas. Pleased with his painting of the horse, the owner, Sir John Rutherford, had a limited edition of prints made from it as gifts for his friends. A number of the prints left over were sent to Bond Street to be put on sale to the public. Munnings promptly bought them up and, by putting a *remarque* (marginal sketch) on each and signing them, he made a handsome profit. Rutherford was a wrathful man when he heard about it. As owner of the copyright he proposed to take legal action against Munnings. With difficulty, and after protracted negotiation, he was dissuaded from doing so.

That horse of legendary fame in our time, Brown Jack, incited Munnings to the extravagant flight of insisting that 'a more unassuming, kind or modest horse-character never lived'. He had been commissioned on behalf of the Jockey Club to make a model of Brown Jack for a bronze statuette. As with the cavalry horse that he had modelled for the memorial chapel at Mells, it was a task into which he put devotion as well as experience; an opportunity, perhaps, to reincarnate the beloved toy of long ago.

Brown Jack's owner, Sir Harold Wernher, sent the horse to Munnings's stables at Castle House, so that he could make direct studies. The horse remained there for six weeks, an object of pious pilgrimage by admirers from all over East Anglia and some from farther afield, who spent hours peering through the hedges and over gates in the hope of catching a glimpse of their equine idol. Brown Jack, Munnings discovered, had a comic-cartoon habit of 'almost seating himself on his manger in the corner of his box. I have seen him in this position and would never have believed it if I had not seen it'. When the time came to part with the marvellous little horse, he was downcast. 'We all missed him. What a horse was this!'

The Jockey Club continues to commemorate Brown Jack, and honours Munnings, by putting the statuette on view in the Royal Enclosure at Ascot when the Brown Jack Stakes race is run.

CHAPTER 14

Reflections at Cliveden

(1)

PAST middle age, he wonders whether his eye can go on supporting the strain he puts upon it. It waters more often, which makes it difficult for him to stand back and judge the effects he is trying to achieve on canvas. He questions the wisdom of his reading in bed, a perennial pleasure which has broadened his knowledge of our English literary heritage. No one understands (he complains to himself) the true nature of the artist's work, how much sheer craftsmanship underlies it: painting a small head in a hunting picture, for example, the head of a woman rider, say, at the back of a group.

He mixes flesh colour on his palette, giving it, precisely, a touch of copal varnish. He draws out the head with a fine pointed sable, using turps and red. He takes a small flat square sable, an eighth of an inch wide, to paint the eyes, the eyebrows, ears, facial arch, nose, mouth. The mouth will make or mar what he is trying to do. His brush hovers, awaiting the flash of certitude, for the face has to be a likeness: 'a hair's breadth and you lose it'. It is not only the unending battle to paint what he sees as he sees it. He is for ever repainting his work mentally, telling himself in the night watches: 'Not so good as I thought', and echoing Millais, who said: 'With every fresh subject I have to learn my art all over again.' Yet still he shows no sign of fatigue. His colour is still clean, if never subtle. The sweep of his brush, his breadth of handling, is still unfaltering. He can still impart to a picture an easy lyrical grace that is the envy of lesser men. He writes of painting being 'tantalising and exasperating', and tells his wife: 'What a life! I shall never paint seriously again.

It's all no good – dreadful', and in a tone of magisterial resolve: 'Small landscapes only.' Beset by self-criticism, he asserts: 'What a bad artist I've been. Miles out. What great fellows they were long ago', and it is true (as he may or may not remind himself) that he does not unfailingly paint with the glowing inner vision that lights the work of the great masters. Nor is there apparently consolation for him in knowing that he has brought sporting painting into the modern idiom, that he has in effect created a new form, the horsescape. For the moment he is under the dwarfing influence of Tolstoy.

At supper at the Café Royal with A. P. Herbert and the then literary editor of the *Daily Express*, he quotes extensively from his current Tolstoy reading, *What Then Must We Do?* The literary editor wrote in his diary that night: 'A.J. Munnings referred to Tolstoy with a proprietary air. When I mentioned that I too had lately read *What Then Must We Do?* he looked exactly as if he didn't believe me, which was annoying.'

He goes to stay at Cliveden, heading his first letter from there: 'Week After Silly Ascot', as if still in the grip of an indefinite disgust. It diminishes to a mild attack of his old melancholy as he makes notes for a diary with which he never persevered, 'Lying on a long sort of garden settee on the terrace at Cliveden, listening to the silvery sounds of fountains on the lawns below, I look into the western sky and at the elm trees silhouetted against its light. Cutting through the sound of playing fountains, the shrill whistling of happy families of swifts, birds whose ancestors wheeled and whistled over the same site centuries ago and whose descendants will wheel and whistle above the shell of Cliveden in years to come.'

From his high-up bedroom at Cliveden he looks out on 'that view of all views. Such a view as nobody could imagine, and what a room. Full of books'. The view is intermittently blotted out by driving rain, which upsets his programme for painting Lord Astor and contributes to his dejection. 'It POURED. . . . It is a b— and makes me sure I'll never do it again.' He proposes to pay more attention to the B.B.C. over-night weather forecasts and, providing he has no engagement to paint outdoors, he rubs his hands with glee when they prove to be wrong.

I

(2)

He pronounced 'naïve' as 'nave', always wrote 'never mind' as one word, and at no time bothered to correct his wrong spelling of Tuesday. 'Teusday, 17th December, 1929', he wrote on a sheet of Central Hotel, Glasgow, notepaper as a prelude to making more notes for the diary that was never kept. 'Just finished dinner. Hors d'œuvre, mixed grill, Camembert, coffee with milk, 1878 brandy. Brandy very dear. Never drink it. But the atmosphere of this place *very* depressing tonight.'

He had gone up to Glasgow to discuss an exhibition of his pictures with the fine-art dealer, Ian MacNicol, of West George Street, who admired his work and paid him good prices for it. MacNicol remembers his habit of nudging you with his fist in confidential moods. Perhaps it should be called the Norfolk nudge; it is a local characteristic in moments of conversational intimacy. He remembers Munnings's bold arm-sweep as another of his gestures when talking. MacNicol found him 'often testy to deal with' but always fair. 'You can't *order* art,' he told MacNicol, who had driven all the way down to Dedham as a result of hearing from Munnings that he was ready to sell the latest picture from his easel. He persisted in that difficult temper until after lunch, when he drove MacNicol through the Constable country and was 'the perfect host and guide'. As a Raeburn enthusiast Munnings took the chance of paying his respects to Scotland's great master at the Glasgow Art Gallery with passing genuflections to Courbet, Bastien-Lepage and Degas. His visit had an unexpected contextual surprise which he afterwards recalled with pleasure. 'All the while, the organ in the central hall was being played by a good organist, accompanying a woman singer whose voice sounded beautifully in this huge place. Wherever one went, the voice was heard. The hall was filled with every sort of working person seated amongst the sculpture, others leaning over the stone balustrades – all working folk, listening to this fine music and applauding it. I thought what a great thing and I also thought it helped the pictures;

some needed help and others were beyond it, hopelessly so. Terrible. Then I left and walked the whole length of Sauchiehall Street. What a long street and how dull'; and apparently it did not occur to him that in 1929 the presence of the artisan audience in the art gallery may have indicated something socially more profound than a free recital. Filling in another of the lonely evenings of his working life, he went into 'a huge elaborate cinema and there saw the damnedest rubbish – called *The Informer*. Sad to relate, it was British!! Dreadful.'

In the following spring he painted Princess Mary, Countess of Harewood, at Egerton House, Newmarket. 'No horse could have stood better – no sitter was more patient. I simply painted what was there: figure – horse – trees – shadows – sky'; and he decided that the resulting picture put that of Lord Birkenhead into second place as 'my best equestrian open-air portrait'. The Princess's mother-in-law, the Dowager Countess of Harewood, went to see it in his studio. 'Don't touch it again,' she told him. 'You have got Mary exactly.' He painted Lord Harewood at Goldsborough Hall, Yorkshire, where he was 'much taken with the two little [Lascelles] boys. 'Never have I stayed in a jollier or more homely household.'

Sargent said that every time he painted a portrait he made an enemy. Munnings had no such qualms, though always he painted to please himself as well as his sitters, however exalted. There was no interest for him in taking money to flatter a fancy. Not for him, either, the conventional side-elevation pose with the horse's points and colouring scrupulously recorded to satisfy uncritical sporting persons of no taste, the walls of whose dining-rooms and 'dens' were hung with lifeless portraits of their favourite steeds. The line of least resistance was never drawn by his hand.

(3)

He paid a return visit to Spain, to paint the American Ambassador, the Hon. Irwin Laughlin, at San Sebastian, 'a grand fellow with no nonsense about him and a face almost as red as a lobster, from the Spanish sun'. Dinners beginning with 'wonderful dry sherry' and ending with old brandy after champagne, activated Munnings's familiar enemy gout and he was laid low again. The only relief, 'an old one from Roman times', was colchicum. It had after-effects that sent him groping about the house long after everyone was in bed. 'Suddenly an oak door on the opposite side of the hall opened, and out came a black-haired, black-eyed Spaniard with a large revolver', who thought he was stealing the silver. Munnings had no Spanish. 'There he stood, whilst I patted my belly, making signs where I was going.' He was obliged to resort to the same part of the house several times. 'Each time the servant came out brandishing his large revolver.'

The gout, a chill on top of it, the heat and glare of Spain, culminated in work-weariness. He wrote to his wife: 'The pictures have proceeded under difficulties. Wet through with perspiration. This seems a sad story. Never was I so tired of work. Those pictures' – one of the Ambassador, another of the Ambassador and his family – 'got on my nerves. I *hate* doing pictures away.' He was not enheartened, either, by the conversation at the Ambassador's dinner-table one evening, when he had 'a titled Spaniard' as his neighbour. 'I heard things about bull-fighting not written of in books.' He saw 'miserable worn-out horses in every stage of neglect', tethered behind the bull-ring. 'It gave me a shock and filled me with a hatred for those who had allowed them to get into such a state.'

When the Ambassador took him to the house of Zuloaga, the renowned Spanish painter, he found a kindred spirit who was already fighting a losing battle against the new wave in art which had Picasso for its fountain-head. Zuloaga looked stern when Munnings said, with a sweep of his arm towards one of the largest canvases in the studio: 'I thought this and others we have seen belonged to the public galleries of Europe.' He told Munnings that 'the fine arts are being killed', and went on to argue that 'dealers need high prices to make big profits, and high prices can be made with clever handling of certain moderns. . . . Dealers must live. A faked sale or two in a saleroom, an expensive book or two, by a clever writer or two. The crazier the artist, the more foolish his buffoonery, the easier it is to expound his greatness.'

It rang true in Munnings's keenly receptive ear. He made a note of the Spanish painter's words 'on the back of some post-cards'. Zuloaga stood before him, 'a great and disappointed man, a tall, powerfully built figure with a touch of melancholy in his brown eyes'. When Zuloaga saw Munnings's portraits of the Ambassador and his family, 'he said it was a new style of work to him'. At dinner the Spanish artist delighted him by telling 'the oft-told true story' of Lola, the donkey of Mont-marte, which 'with a paint-brush tied to its tail painted a picture that was sent to the Salon and deceived the critics'.

(4)

Invited to Biarritz after leaving San Sebastian, he had the felicitous surprise of 'running into' his most ardent American admirer, Frederick Prince, of Princemere, Boston, Massa-chusetts, an extremely rich man who, as master of the Pau foxhounds, kept a stable of sixty horses in France. The American economic crisis had reached disaster pitch. Prince was one of the millionaires who were impervious to it, doubtless because his family fortune was in land close to Chicago. He lavished his hospitality on Munnings.

Munnings had never had a patron in the old sense of the term; like, for example, his friend Sir David Murray R.A., many of whose works were bought straight from the easel by the dis-coverer of the Broken Hill mines, or James Pryde, of the Glasgow School, who over a long period could count on the goodwill of Lord Cowdray, the oil magnate. Frederick Prince would probably have stood in that relationship with Munnings had circumstances required it. 'He says there is nothing I can't do – that I'm *the* man.'

Having had Munnings's account of his latest doings, Prince asked him: 'Why don't you for a change, before you die, try to paint people *off* horses? Come and start with us. I'll give you a good time if you'll come.' Munnings had grateful recollections of Prince's generosity to him in New England. 'How could I refuse such a prospect?'

Before moving to be Prince's guest, he went with Dudley

Tooth, the Mayfair art-dealer, to the Musée Bonat at Bayonne, looking at masterpieces that induced the reflection: 'These are but a mere fraction of the works of immortals,' a thought that he found almost overwhelming – 'one became more stunned'. Seeing 'The Jay's Wing', he recalled Durer's affirmation: 'I know now what beauty is; in truth, art resides in Nature; whoever can draw it therefrom possesses it. The more the aspect of his work conforms to life the better it will be. Therefore do not imagine that you can make something that will improve upon what God has created. . . .' For Munnings, the classic voices spoke with more authority than all others.

'It is like an Arabian Nights' tale,' he wrote from the Hôtel du Palais, Biarritz. 'Whatever I ask for I can have.' With his host and the *maître d'hôtel* he walked the softly carpeted corridors, visiting room after room in search of one that would serve as a studio. His host had bought him a new easel, canvases, brushes – 'sables and hogs in scores, and varnish and oil and God knows what!' The room, when it was decided on, was 'all that an artist could desire'. From its enormous, window he could see 'a succession of white rollers breaking in masses of surf that dazzled the sight'. He conceived 'a Zoffany-style' portrait of Mrs Prince, who ordered for the sittings a dress from Worth that was 'quite thirty yards round the hem'. He began the portrait, harassed by the sitter's unpunctuality, which sometimes shortened the day's work by an hour or more. Then his host suddenly announced: 'We're all going to the Ritz in Paris. You can finish the portrait there.'

Travelling in luxury – Mrs Prince had her compartment on the train covered with white sheets so that her clothes should not be in contact with upholstery exposed to the common use – he wrote to his wife: 'What wealth can do is surprising to me.' He toured the corridors of the Ritz Hotel, Paris, again escorted by the *maître d'hôtel*, seeking a room with a north light to work in. He could not find one that was suitable. His host told him: 'Munnings, go anywhere – go to the Meurice – to the Chatham – anywhere, so long as you get your good north light.' He found it at the Hôtel d'Orsay, across the river. 'Magnificent! Two windows looking out across the Seine to the Tuileries.' He

finished the portrait of his hostess and did another of her and
her husband which drew a letter of hearty approbation from
Sir John Lavery – 'your masterpiece, my dear Munnings'.

After the concentrated effort, the interruptions, delays, and
splendid hospitality, which was followed by more gout symp-
toms, 'there came the grand settlement'. Mrs Prince thought
his price too high. Her husband, leading him gently away from
the argument, murmured that he well understood the situation
and problems of an artist, and that he was well satisfied to
write his cheque, which he thereupon did.

Being in Paris was an opportunity for Munnings to go to
Versailles to see the Manet centenary exhibition in the Orangery.
He repeated the visit with Lloyd Osbourne, stepson of
R. L. Stevenson, who explained that he was in Paris because
the only place he could get a good haircut was at the Ritz barber's
shop. After his reverent viewing of the works of the painters'
painter, Munnings was forced to exclaim: 'What great artists
there have been in the world and to what miserable fooleries has
the world of art descended!' He always spoke the word art as
if it had a capital A.

(5)

He composed – and posted – a letter to a sick dog, Bingy, at
Castle House; autumn, 1933:

> 96 Chelsea Park Gardens,
> S.W. 3

My dear Bingy, I am sending you on some odds and ends of
pheasant and other bits which I'm sure you will love, but you
must give the bones to the cats, as they aren't good for you.
I really don't think you need be sentimental and give any to
the other two dogs because they are well looked after by your
mistress.

I had to send them because all the time I was eating I saw
that face of yours lowered on one side, staring and staring at
me as I ate the toothsome stuff. So, my dear Bingy, I hope
you'll like the snack.

Then there was a whole onion sitting up amongst some toasted cheese in a casserole all hot. I thought at first it was a baked apple. This was a surprise and very good too. So I send you a piece of cheese to try and a small piece of crust off the apple tart.

When I'm back on Saturday, we'll go for another walk and in the meantime I need not tell you to be good because you couldn't be anything else.

Your devoted friend,

A.J.

(6)

The gout attacks became severe again. In 1934 he suffered recurring crescendos of pain. Dining at The Other Club, he talked gout with Lord Moyne, 'a fellow-sufferer in a mild way'. Opposite was his old friend of the war, Major-General Seely, lately ennobled as Lord Mottistone, the name taken from his family home in the Isle of Wight. 'Why don't you come with me and my daughter to Bad Ems on the Rhine?' he suggested to Munnings. 'You can take the waters and get rid of your gout.' Mottistone himself was a bronchitis victim.

Munnings wrote to his wife:

London & North Eastern Railway
Continental Services via Harwich,
R.M.S. *Prague*
(Undated)

Dearest Violet, I feel leaving you as much as I did years ago and more. Bingy gives a sad touch. We are off now, going out to sea, and the old harbour was still reflecting afterglow. I saw Flatford in the distance and thought of Kaffir and Chips and Anarchist [his horses] and the rest up the valley! Through Stour Wood and Copperas and Wrabness Station!!!! Time flew.

Do get today's *Daily Mail*, splendid portrait of Mottistone, and all that he said in the Lords yesterday. It is all a royal progress, he with his pass. A coupé to ourselves, the attendants all attentive and running round. The same on the boat. Three lovely deck cabins.

I wouldn't mind leaving so much if the old dog were well. It's hard on you. Poor Bingy. I won't say more or else I'll cry.

Tell your Mother I'm very sorry I got annoyed. I shall never get any better. She will think me a bad, bad man.

Best love,
Yours, A.J.

'This is the place, my dear,' he wrote to tell her on the day of his arrival at Bad Ems. 'It's a beautiful little town, much better than I expected. Opposite this window are trimmed limes, then the river, the built-up wall and walk, and then a bright white hotel with balconies and red flags and limes, and white launches on the river. All very fine and just the thing. You see nothing of Nazis. We were received like royalty. I wish you were here. Love to Bingy and all.'

In another letter: 'The gout still hangs about. Can't walk far. What a go! All water – no meat; only eggs – fruit – fresh raspberries which grow wild. Lord M. is a wonder. He makes something happen every day. His daughter is devoted to him. She said to me at the end of the concert last night, after we had listened to a woman singer: "Did you see him? He was weeping – not just sniffling – *floods*!!!" He's a lad, certainly. He might be anywhere and would always find *something* to interest him. Love to Bingy and to you.' Mottistone was 'far nicer and kinder than I dreamt any man could ever be', the doctor in charge of his cure was 'the nicest and kindest of men', Mottistone's daughter Louise 'the nicest, sweetest child'. His good nature was extended to the local scene. 'Our Press writes rubbish about Germany. I'm glad I came and shall try to learn all I can.' Lunching with some of the spa officials: 'Mottistone made them all roar with laughter and it was like going about with royalty. He has a lot packed in that head of his and we laugh sometimes a great deal.' To Mottistone's young daughter Louise Munnings was 'inspiring company' throughout their stay.

Writing to his wife after 'the night of the long knives', when some of Adolf Hitler's oldest associates in the Nazi movement were shot without trial, Munnings said that there had been a telephone call for Mottistone from Whitehall. 'They wanted to know what it was like over here after the news in the papers. He just told them it was all as usual. And so it is. Everybody glad. To read that silly article by *Scrutator* in the *Sunday Times* was utterly and absurdly *misleading*. We are here at an interesting moment but nothing has altered. Nobody cares so long as the country is under Hitler and peaceful. Nobody wants anything more.' Dismissing the over-riding topic, he inquires about Bingy, the beloved dog. 'Your news about him is not too good. I can see him now, dashing and barking at the sparrows and chasing after the pigeons in the parks.'

A letter was sent on to him from his mother, in her eighties and tired of life: 'I am losing my strength fast. Hope I shall not live much longer. Life is a weariness now.' She had been a widow since 1914 and it was her lot to live on well into her nineties. 'A.J.' wrote about her to his wife: 'Poor old thing. I wish now that instead of spending so much on horses and hunting and things I had got her a little place somewhere. It is all so difficult. I hate that street or road where she lives in Norwich. Why couldn't she have had a house in Harleston and shared it with her sister Jane? But then humans are such impossible creatures.' Adding instructions about the disposal of some of the pictures in the Chelsea studio, he wrote:

'The two pretty water-colours are good and I don't want to sell them – the last time I was happy when painting. The sound of the water, the lovely spot and all about it gave me pleasant hours. I used to sit there and paint quietly with the hours fleeting by and I loved it.

This accursed gout upsets all my life. Nobody has gone on longer at such work than I have. I've made more than enough for myself to live on. . . . No more of those jobs. *Never* again. I'm ready to live simply and do as I wish. My brothers have a quieter time than I do.

I detest all the surroundings of Castle House – I do indeed. It's alright [*sic*] on a late night in July with a moon.'

His brother William, the eldest, was making more than a local name as a breeder and judge of Red Poll cattle. Frederick was still at the mill at Mendham. 'A.J.' was annoyed by receiving at Bad Ems a cutting from a Norfolk newspaper that reported a motoring accident in which Fred was concerned. 'More *publicity*,' he complained, severely underlining the word, as if his own reputation was at stake. The next day his temper was bright and cheerful again. 'I've had a lovely time. Took the waters, had a thermal bath, saw Dr Vogler, lunched, then took a boat and rowed up this lovely river to an old village. I sat in the sun in this great landscape', which he considered superior to much English scenery. 'It is all far more delightful than I had ever imagined, far better in many ways than England, which is now too crowded and built over and so *small*.' Then his pleasure in life was darkened by news from home.

'I got your short sad message. It's too sad. I went to my room and wept. I did indeed. Although the dog [Bingy] was devoted to you, he liked me too and I was very fond of him and I shall never forget you holding him up three weeks ago tomorrow when I left in the taxi.

This grief at such a loss is a queer thing. Is it because we can't have him to be fond of and to amuse us any more that we weep? You will miss him on all the little walks. It's perfectly dreadful. Folk weep for *their* losses. It is no loss to the little dog. He's just gone and knows no more, having played his *small* part in a big world.

So in a way we mourn our own loss, because we shall see him no more, hear him bark no more at the gate. Lord, what a shame that these things happen. That dog used to amuse me a lot and in his time what a lot we've done and what stretches of work and struggle I myself have had and Bingy came in and out of it. I shall always remember how he liked to have his face stroked.

Now he is out of it and we must make the best of it and carry on and there it is. You might have had children who might have gone wrong or died even. . . . Don't weep any more.'

The subject was not so easily closed. That same day he wrote again. 'I feel so utterly sad to think I shan't see that dear dog again that I can't keep from tears. I can hardly see to read the paper. It was all because you said there is more room in the car now without him. What a fool I am'; and he recalled the breakfast at Blenheim when the Duke of Marlborough wept at the death of one of his thirty lap-dogs. 'I remember being rather fed up with him. And now there are tears in *my* eyes. Don't mention it to me at Harwich when I land or I shall weep again. Isn't it foolish?' He was moved to make what may have been his only written reference to a far deeper sorrow of the distant past: 'I went through a hundred times worse happening than that and it still stops me dead in what I'm doing when I remember it all. Terrible.'

He enclosed two cuttings from *The Times*, one headed 'Withering U.S. Pastures: Thousands of Cattle Doomed,' the other a letter to the editor from a reader at Kenley, Surrey, who had been called out of bed by the cries of a hedgehog being attacked by badgers – 'only fifteen miles from Piccadilly!' To the news report he attached the comment: 'That drought seems so appalling that it dwarfs small troubles. To think of all those poor patient beasts with no food or water. It's too damned awful.' He was beset also by thoughts of 'that poor little hedge-hog', and scribbled his dismay: '*What* a world!'

In the thermal bath his thoughts 'go on and on about people and things'. He writes of 'damned fool statesmen who live in a world of Press chatter and Parliamentary cynicism', a word he cannot spell, and asks: 'Why doesn't Baldwin come out here for a holiday quietly and see for himself whether these people want war?'

He reverts to his painting life. 'My *best* days have been when painting quiet landscapes and motoring with you and seeing places. I think what good things I could still paint.' He compares his lot with that of the man he saw 'in the largest champagne factory in Germany', who corked 30,000 bottles a day (six exclamation marks). 'I'd rather do thirty thousand words – if I could.'

He quoted, writing to his wife again: 'You said you didn't

think you'd been much of a success as a wife. I should say that you have done better than any artist's wife. Think how you've looked after one thing – the money side.' She had remarked that she would not mind losing money. He asked her: 'What should we do *now* if we did? My sight isn't anything like so good as it was and *well* I know it.' He told her: 'I'm *thankful* for all you've done. Your good influence and sweet kindness have been an endless source of wonder to me. I can't be good but I'm always thinking how natural you are and so kind. B—— and his wife said such *nice* things of you, such *wonderfully* nice things.'

When his wife wrote to tell him how difficult she found it to reconcile herself to the loss of the dog, he replied: 'I feel almost as badly about it as you do. But I argue with myself that it is fate. You must accept these losses. You can alter nothing and must make the best of things. Supposing some *awful* calamity had happened. All our money lost!!! Bingy's departure is all in the law of things. It had to happen. Much worse lies ahead. So try to be happy as you always are.' He changed the subject. 'I know why *The Times* wouldn't publish my letter. It was too much about the good state of people and things over here. Nevermind [*sic*].'

His gout was at last in retreat. 'My feet are right down. I feel *very* well – never better and no exaggeration. That Dr Vogler *knows* about gout and is very kind. I can't imagine being without it. I can now walk a long way.'

The murder of Dollfuss, the diminutive Austrian Chancellor, in July 1934, prompted Munnings to remind his wife and himself that the death of a dog was 'as nothing to the much sadder and more terrible happenings in other people's lives'. He was distressed by the thought of the dead man's wife, 'waiting for him in Italy at some seaside place with their children and then receiving the news that he had been shot down.' He thinks of 'the young fools who did it and who will have to be tried and many shot. What a business – *her* grief must be awful.'

Preparing to leave for home, he asks for a note of the doctor's charges and finds that 'by Jove, Lord Mottistone has paid the bill as well as the one for the hotel and also for a box of cigars for me to smoke!!' He tells his wife how glad he is to have a good home to go to. 'Order some Malvern water, please. On Teusday [*sic*] I'll see you at Harwich, all being well. I'm glad you found my letters welcome. I live in hopes of having you with me for years and that we shan't get too old and that we can always see things alike and go about together.'

A letter from one of the first buyers of his pictures, Thomas Porter, the Norwich builder, by then living in retirement at Lowestoft, brought the reply: 'Are you the man who bought my large picture of trees and the timber waggon? That was a long time ago. Heavens – you paid me in golden sovereigns!' Noting the Lowestoft address, he wrote a reminiscent postscript: 'A great place for the Salvation Army. Blessed preaching hands all along the beach.'[1]

1. 8 January 1935.

CHAPTER 15

Queen Mary Says 'No'

(1)

LOWERING international skies from 1935 onward darkened the outlook for artists everywhere. Like children, they do nothing to provoke the world's larger follies and suffer as much from them. Frost and Reed, who reproduced many of Munnings's pictures as colour prints, were sending him discouraging sales statements. 'It just shows how bad things are,' he wrote on receiving the latest. Economically safer than most of his kind, he might not have been much put out by hearing that Lionel Edwards's prints were more popular than his, even in those difficult times.

'Next year, no extra expenses' was his summarising comment on events. He suggested to his wife that 'this keeping up of establishments' was unwise, that they 'missed much' from doing so, and that they could live more simply elsewhere. 'Dover, for instance – it is A.1. Cliffs, with rows of little houses with balconies, a nice town, restful, with a big harbour.' He was on his way to take a second cure at Bad Ems, accompanied by a Lancashire doctor whom he had met there the previous year, and Dover was for the moment one of his 'V.A.S' (violent attachments), as his wife called those fleeting and frequent enthusiasms of his. Within a day or two he was writing: 'I *must* learn German', because there was 'not a soul to talk to' in the hotel at Bad Ems. 'The older I get, the more I hate leaving you.' He asked her not tell anyone that he was gout-stricken again.

'Alas! all my life I've generally had something wrong and

more and more I feel like taking the years easy and doing what I feel like doing. You'll never guess how I've been passing the time. I'll tell you – reading the 3rd volume of *The Forsyte Saga*. I knew the whole story but to read this part again brings back Galsworthy afresh. What a book!! I take back all I said. In these writings he stands alone. He is wonderful at describing old things, old homes, old memories. Yet he leaves you sad and depressed – all have to pass out. . . .

Well, I can now account for all those quiet periods in your room at night – *The Forsyte Saga*. You're not a bad judge.

Now, to please me, get this book – *The Limestone Tree*, by Joseph Hergesheimer. There are one or two of his books in the house, but, my word, this one is *wonderful*. Do read it. It is like the *Saga*. Old Kentucky, the American war, etc., etc. You'll love it.

Well, to get back to the Forsytes. . . .'

He 'got back to the Forsytes' to the extent of five more closely written pages. 'I tell you, I was so angry with that damned Jolyon and his bloody wife stopping their son Jon from having Fleur that I nearly threw the book down – Galsworthy is annoying there. I don't think a better character of a girl has ever been written – and what a smack in the eye the poor little thing got – how awful. She couldn't believe Jon could let her down. Who could ? I just kept saying *bitch* – bitch – bloody bitch, as I read all the mother was saying. I detest that woman.'

He had new reading excitements to report a day or two later. 'Why I'm really writing again so soon is because I've got another book for you to read and to BUY, *Memories & Vagaries* by Axel Munthe. Our house mustn't be without it. I weep at each story. Do read them. He wrote them long ago when he was young. One is called *Menagerie* and it described each poor animal shut up a prisoner all its life.' His sympathies had been deeply moved.

'What a world it would be if everybody were like Munthe. He says in one page : "Man's right to kill animals is limited to his right of defence and his right of existence. The man of

culture admits his obligations towards animals in compensa-
tion for the servitude he imposes on them. The killing of
animals for mere pleasure is incompatible with the fulfilment
of these obligations.

"Sympathy *extending* beyond the range of *humanity*, that is,
kindness to animals, is one of the last moral qualities acquired
by mankind and the more this sympathy is developed in man
the greater is the distance which separates him from his
primitive state of savagery".'

He was moved to remark in the same long letter: 'We live
wrong. We live for happiness and happiness only comes from
really being kind. Things in life make it difficult to do what we
would. I give it up.' From which point of resignation he was
led to reflect on comments on his work that had lately appeared
in *The Scotsman*: 'When I read the article I thought how *little*
that fellow knows of my methods. He speaks of my being a
virtuoso of the brush, and so on, and not taking care of my
composition. All my life I've sweated blood on painting. It isn't
easy. It may look so to that fellow. All the toil is hidden. As for
design, I'm always, *always*, worrying about it and would like
to send him all my sketches in pencil for a picture. Well, there
it is.'

At home again, purged of the gout, he was beset by the idea
of converting the Old Grammar School at Dedham, with its
sixty-by-forty floor-space, into a studio, a project subsequently
carried through. Having said that he would paint no more
horse pictures, he went to Newmarket and was engrossed in
studies of the start of a classic race, with the jockeys calling
out a chorus of 'No, no, sir!' to the starter as their mounts
pranced in disarray at the gate. There, all over again, he encountered the difficulties of a lifetime. 'Art writers, their minds
urbanised, jeer at my "shiny horses", as they call them. They are
welcome to their Matisse women, to their Braques, Modiglianis
and surrealist horses. . . . There is a certain depth and trans-
parency in the well-groomed coat of a horse – bay, brown or
chestnut. On browns the lights are cooler, greyer, bluer, if you
like; on a bay, less cool; on a chestnut, inclining to pinky-grey.

K

On a well-grown horse in the sun those lights are devastating. The troubles of horse-painting are a hundredfold. I can no more explain these painting problems than I could dart like a chaffinch with a striped wing from one tree to another', or, he might have added, tell why the chaffinch's striped wing was a persisting image of his mental life.

Before leaving Dedham for Newmarket, he sent a pretty compliment to his wife, who was staying at her cottage on Exmoor. 'The daffodils look so well and seem to say: *She* planted us.' He tells her about the little goat that has joined the Dedham household. 'Oh, dear – she is so sweet and comic and absolutely human. But she'll eat *anything*. Now she has started on the rose trees. She's a b——. She picks things out of the carpenter's toolbag. She's quite part of the place now. She shakes her head and dashes about and is very fond of everyone.' The Director of the National Gallery, Kenneth Clark, he said, had invited him to 'do an impression' of the scene in Westminster Abbey at the coronation of King George VI and Queen Elizabeth. 'I said decidedly "No!" I don't want any more of these bloody awful jobs. I'm not happy with them. Terrible.' Sir Kenneth has no recollection of the invitation. He writes: 'I knew Munnings quite well and had a great regard for him, although he associated me with the kind of contemporary art that he disliked. He was very generous in helping young artists and trying to see their merits.'

At Newmarket, he hears about the debilitating effect on a stud groom of being in constant attendance on manifestations of the life-force at a certain time of the year. 'When the season's going full split, darned if it don't get on y'r nerves – nothin' but servin' those blessed mares mornin', noon an' night, week in, week out. It's a terrible business!'

Perhaps himself escaping from the oppressiveness of the stables, he went out on one of his lonely walks. 'I went from field to field, trousers turned up, thinking about this and that, and the sun was warm and the air close.' A path led him to Little Thurlow church.

'In there I beheld the most extravagant and enormous

monument of Elizabethan days. I thought of those folk and
their household and tried to place it all. The Elizabethan
dame, hands in prayer and the bottom end of her so funny,
the frilled petticoats and the little feet sticking out – all gone,
dead long ago, and only this tomb left.

I was tired and my feet wanted rest, so I opened the door
of the old shut-in square pew with high sides and I lay at full
length on the red baize pad so broad and soft. Then I took off
my shoes and gave myself up to meditation and was then
aware of the rain on the roof and it rained and rained and I
lay and thought and thought and realised how short life is
and how soon done.'

(2)

In the heat-wave of August 1935 he was writing to his wife on
notepaper headed 'Manton House, Marlborough, Wilts'. He
had gone there to paint Tiberius, winner of that year's Ascot
Gold Cup race, 'a lovely horse, dark bay brown with strong
quarters'. In his first letter from there he revealed himself as a
creature of habit who experienced 'a funny sinking feeling on
leaving places'. For instance, he wrote, 'leaving Chelsea on my
own I always look round the house to see if all's well and think
did I lock that door or is the gas turned off and go and take
another look.'

He liked the Manton house and training stables and their
setting. 'What a place this is! What downs, what air! The ring
doves and pigeons coo all day and in the evenings round the
house. The boy holding the horse thought that the sound of
their cooing made you feel at rest and contented with life.
Quite right. It does.' He observed that, 'painting and moving
about as I do, I am full of impressions and often think I should
note them down.' In his next letter he acted on that suggestion.

'My walk was a wonder tonight. A long way up a rising
gallop, far, far on. The sun getting lower. I lay down against
a small dry haycock and watched and listened. Such peace
and space. Then on and on and round by a wood and another

rest to watch the sunset. Long curving wisps of dark wraith-like clouds to the left and wisps above getting afire and below streaks of burning gold against *green* slits in the sky. More and more intense. Darker and darker the landscape. Darker the horizontal wisps and torn pieces of cloud. Brighter the afterglow and still deeper and broader the tone of the wide downland and black wood on the top against the light. One or two belated rooks hurrying home. Then plovers in groups passing close to the hollow ground.

Darker and darker. I look to the left – the downs slope towards sombre beech groves surrounding the house below. A sky above of deep intense green and indigo, with a bright half-moon sailing up on high.

And so home. If I live to be 1,000, I'll never forget tonight.'

His wife mentioned in a letter from Withypool on Exmoor that she had met the owner of some of his early paintings. Wondering, in writing, who the owner might be, Munnings was impelled to tell her: 'Lord, what a lot of work I've done from time to time. But I'm going to rest more now. Years fly by. Not many more left.' He recorded his pleasure in the company of 'old Somerville Tattersall, who owns all this', and who had been down for a week-end's stay. 'He is full of reminiscences and stories. Quite the best talker I ever listened to. Delightful. His birthday was yesterday, 72 – and he still sells with the hammer. He left hoping that I'd be here next Friday when he comes.' He wrote again:

'This is Teusday [*sic*] evening. Of course this place is ideal and it seems a pity that the rich firm of Tattersalls is cutting things so fine that one can see the place needs looking after a bit. In the days of Alec Taylor he owned it all and trained and took the money. Now the firm has to pay Lawson and get profits as well for themselves. There are about 70 horses here!

I love the downs. I go out every evening before and after supper. My meals are simple and I have 6 bottles of Contrexeville just done. Walk at night until 9.30. All along

the top big clumps of beech trees and big bushes and the
separate bushes in the dusk take shapes and seem to move.
I never felt better in my life.'

'Farewell to peace,' he wrote the following Saturday. 'I go
this evening. The pigeons are cooing in the trees and the
rooks and jackdaws are talking away. A still, *still* day. Well, it's
been a good week. I'll write you from Norwich.'

He had arranged with a motoring nephew to revisit the
scenes of his childhood in the Waveney Valley, spending a week-
end with his brother Fred at the mill. 'I walked yesterday
afternoon one of the old, old walks we had as boys, to a place
called South Elmham, and home by St Cross. I was glad to be
alone and to think of my life as I sat by the old minster ruins at
Elmham and thought a lot. Then in the evening I paddled the
boat down the river. How curious it all was – and very pretty.'

He visited a number of Suffolk churches with Adrian Bell,
of whose books on farming and rural life he was a keenly
appreciative reader. At Dennington Church he gave an old
woman half-a-crown to wash the face of Lord Bardolf. 'It saddened
me to see how generations of vandals had scratched their
initials on the marble body.' In Stradbroke Church he ascended
the pulpit steps and preached his companion a sermon on life
and art. In Brundish Church he was 'subdued by the silence',
reflecting on the brevity of life. 'We sweat and toil at our art
and then we're gone. What is it all for, Bell?'

(3)

To one of his Norfolk farmer friends, Horace Callaby of
Heacham, he wrote on 24 September 1936: 'I'm going to do a
picture of the late King on the white pony which is now at
Sandringham. Can you put me up some time next week? Please
say nothing of this to anyone because I do not want it known or in
the Press or anything. So, for the Lord's sake, keep it quiet.
You well know they would make a piece of news out of that and
I can't *stand* it. *So mum's the word*. P.S. If you tell anyone of this
I'll shoot you dead.'

Writing to his wife from Heacham the following week, he bade her: 'Never a word', heavily underlined, as if it was a State secret. George V had died that year and Sandringham was mourning him as squire as well as monarch. Munnings referred to his late Majesty in his letters home as 'the poor old King', one of whose shooting suits of homespun tweed he had borrowed, 'spats and all'. The suit and the spats were donned for the portrait by the late King's valet, French, who, Munnings noted, spoke of his dead master as 'the old toff'. One of Munnings's letters was written in the royal saddle-room.

'This room is full of memories – mounted hoofs with all the names of all the horses; racing plates, gilded; portraits of harness, and bits of all sorts. This morning the King's doctor, Sir Frederick Willans, came round and asked me to lunch tomorrow, a nice man. He went to Framlingham and is delighted with the picture. Everyone is. Later, Mr Vanneck, the Chief Constable of Norfolk, came round and he thought it a good one. Mr Howlett, the late King's old confidential valet and Keeper of the Crown Jewels, etc., etc., saw it and shed a tear. This picture is going to make a stir. It's alright [*sic*].

He wrote to remind his wife on 7 October: 'Today, 58 years ago, I wasn't born. Tomorrow, 58 years ago, I was. Today, my last day of my 57th year, I didn't work!' Taking time off, he went for 'a long meandering walk on those stretches of sand' at Brancaster Bay. Lying in 'a hot sheltered spot in the dunes', he listened to the roar of the breakers, 'which has gone on since the world began and will go on until the end of all things'. In the late afternoon, still walking, he was entranced by the cloud pageantry – 'panoramas of gold and purple came and went and the sunset was *superb.*' He was overwhelmed by the splendour, 'almost too much to grasp or absorb. I've tasted a lot of nature's pleasures this year. This was felt even keener than all the rest'. After dinner with the Callaby family that night, his host fell asleep, 'and I made an excellent drawing of him, with his face in utter repose, his small mouth just open.'

The posthumous portrait, 'King George V on his Pony, Jock, at Sandringham', had been commissioned by the Hon. Douglas Tollemache for presentation to the town of Ipswich. It was exhibited at the Royal Academy in 1937 without making the stir that Munnings anticipated. The print publishers, Frost and Reed, wanted to reproduce the picture. To do so they had to obtain Queen Mary's permission. As a preliminary to a formal request, Munnings was commanded to take the picture to Marlborough House. Queen Mary had not seen it. He was accompanied by Stanley Wade, the young director of Frost and Reed who conducted the firm's business with Munnings.

Wade had some difficulty in convincing Munnings that it would be *infra dig* to wear his tweeds and bow-tie and to display the portrait to the Queen on a paint-smeared easel from the Chelsea studio. On the way to Marlborough House 'A.J.' recalled that in his first year as an Academician King George V and Queen Mary, with their sons and daughter, visited a Royal Academy Summer Exhibition before the Private View. By the time they had gone through the first three or four galleries the children were bored and, linking hands, made a barrier to stop their parents from proceeding farther. He told Wade: 'Queen Mary sailed through them like a galleon, refusing to leave until she had seen the last picture in the last gallery.'

Waiting in a small downstairs room at Marlborough House, Munnings remarked to Wade in a low voice: 'I have a feeling that someone is looking at us.' Wade shared his suspicion. 'I had precisely the same feeling.' He then noticed a small aperture in the ceiling.

They were conducted to the upstairs drawing-room, where the picture was placed on the re-varnished easel. Queen Mary inspected it with a critical eye. Having done so she made her pronouncement. 'You have shown the King looking too much the squire and not enough the King. He also has bent shoulders. I do not wish my people to remember him like that.' She would 'on no account' give permission for prints to be made. It was the end of the interview. Munnings had spoken only a word or two. Wade said that he was 'oddly subdued'.

That year he was at Cottesbrooke Hall, Northamptonshire, as

the guest for three weeks of Major and Mrs Reginald Macdonald-Buchanan, to paint the Pytchley hounds, of which his host was joint-master. 'He was in great form,' writes Major Macdonald-Buchanan, 'and I really enjoyed his company at dinner in the evenings'. Naturally, he was much interested in the sporting paintings at Cottesbrooke, one of the great collections. Major Macdonald-Buchanan remembers that 'he spent what seemed to be hours standing on chairs and even ladders with a big magnifying glass, studying details of our Ben Marshall paintings'. He looked closely at every individual figure in the crowd shown in Marshall's 'Sir Joshua Winning the Match Against Filho-da-Puta', a classic of sporting art. Later Munnings gave Major Macdonald-Buchanan advice that led to Constable's great landscape, 'Stratford Mill', being added to the Cottesbrooke Hall collection at the record price, then, of 43,000 guineas. Reading the news headlines of the sale, he was stirred to angry complaint. 'Only its fantastic price – not its fine qualities of paint or achievement of the impossible, its flash of genius – roused the dull minds of Constable's countrymen. A friend gave him £100 for it.'

'Myself – alone,' he noted for the diary which he was constantly intending to keep and never did. 'Went for a long cross-country ramble, downhill and uphill, going through gates and across a brook. Lay awhile on a slope, listening to birds in a state of blissful peace of mind which can only come outdoors in such a spot.' The energetic *raconteur* of the London clubs might have been a dissociated personality.

He painted three Pytchley hounds with the names of Destiny, Proverb and Critical. 'Worked till 12.45, then from 3 till 6 p.m. Tired out. *Why* do I do these pictures? All unnecessary. Once in a lifetime is enough.' Dining alone at Cottesbrooke Hall, he admires the pictures by La Thangue that surround him, recalling it as an event of his early painting life that he met the artist at the Chelsea Arts Club. It was La Thangue of whom Sickert said that 'he painted in the closest and most loving communion with nature'. Munnings reflected again on the perversities of existence in relation to the life of the artist. 'A queer world. Art snobbery. Alas! La Thangue, it will be many

years before you come in again. May your paint last. The one
in the Guildhall, London, is good – painted at Graffham,
Sussex. A boy mowing bracken. A low sun. Pulsing – throbbing
moments of late summer fading to autumn. Moments caught
and set down each afternoon as the light dies.' He supposes that
at Christie's such a picture would fetch very little. 'A crazy
Van Gogh or crude Cezanne is worth far more.'

On 16 June he wrote: 'To end my toiling here: for toiling it
is . . . I long to be out in the sun. At the moment I am all for a
quiet beach, with the smell of the sea, and boats lying about.'
The previous day he had worked many hours on hounds at the
kennels. 'What a stink of boiling flesh – *awful*! Why do I do it?
I'd rather paint these trees.'

(4)

An exhibition of his at the Leicester Galleries, London, in
1938 was a financial success, though he was disappointed because
its centre-piece, a hunting picture which he called 'Why Weren't
You Out Yesterday?' and in which he depicted four of his own
horses, did not sell. What is more, it remained unsold after
exhibition at the Royal Academy that year – 'a warning to me',
Munnings wrote. A warning of what – the fickleness of taste,
the uncertainty of markets, or of waning powers? He left those
questions unanswered and was much relieved when Frost and
Reed, 'consistent buyers of my work and copyrights for many
years', bought the picture and reproduced it with their customary
finished excellence. Their prints had done much to extend his
reputation, though he seemed reluctant to acknowledge it.

Concerning the Leicester Galleries' show, he told his wife
that he was less interested in selling the pictures than in 'getting
lots of folk to know about them – that should be our aim. We
want enough to see it, high, low, rich and poor'. He proposed
to 'keep out of the Private View', saying that he hated it. 'But I
think this will be a useful show.' Having seen the last picture in
its place, he went off for 'a jolly evening' at the Garrick Club
with Oswald Birley, John ('Lamorna') Birch, Fred Elwell, a

fellow-artist with whom he had been on a sketching trip not long before, Maurice Codner, the Dedham portrait-painter who could claim to be one of his few close friends, E. V. Lucas and Seymour Hicks, the two last-named conspicuous in his massive acquaintance rather than intimates. Lucas talked about Charles Lamb. Hicks sat 'staring into his lap, as if he was thinking out a witty saying'.

The exhibition did well. 'We were as free as air.' Munnings left to join his wife at the cottage on Exmoor which had been her hunting retreat for nearly twenty years. There he became 'drunk with riding', thought nothing of hacking forty miles in a leisurely day, coming home to a bath, a meal and a quiet evening with the relish of a happy man. Exmoor took hold of him, as Cornwall had years before, softening his rough edges, moderating his prejudices, dispelling the hatreds that flourished amid the tensions of the town.

> 'I sat in the shadow of an aged thorn in bloom, painting massed white blossoming trees below, casting their shadows on the hillside and their scent all around. Farther below, the gleam of a small stream rippling over stones in the sun, its sweet, silvery music ascending, mingling with the blackbird's song.'

That year, 1938, some of his fellow-Academicians urged him to stand for the presidency in succession to Sir William Llewellyn. It was a position in the art hierarchy to which he had never aspired with the intensity of a wilful ambition. Success for him lay in high achievement rather than in high place. There was advice on the subject from his wife, writing in November:

> 'As far as I can gather, the world is beginning to look down on the R.A. – the way of running it seems out of date and dull. If you became President you could do so much to lift up the dying Academy and make it a live place.
>
> From my own point of view, I hope you won't be President because of the social side. You *must* not let the R.A. down if you take it on. Your clean and pure outlook would greatly influence art schools and help to crush the viper of "modern'

art, the distorted outlook of unbalanced minds and unhealthy brains.

You will admit that I have done nothing to influence you one way or the other until now, when you tell me that at last you have allowed your name to be put down. You have enough money if you only paint 2 *good* pictures a year (and sell all I am dusting now in the studio). You are not rushed into the position, as you have rested (and a *well*-earned rest) since April, and have had time and opportunity (riding and walking alone on Exmoor) to consider it from every point of view.

But consider well: Are you prepared to alter your life, habits, enter into a great position which in 100 years will be *remembered* and spoken of as a great office conducted by a countryman who *saved British art*?

If not, leave it alone. *What thy hand doeth, do it with all thy might.*'

'A.J.', down with an attack of shingles, replied from Chelsea: 'Have just been reading your instructions on taking on the R.A. I shall always treasure that letter. At the moment I feel 1,000 per cent below that level. Very weak. Poor heart. No strength and just ready to agree with anyone about anything. This house is full of you.'

He was at Cliveden again in May 1939 and, as before, was hampered by bad weather which left him vowing yet once more, 'Never again', meaning that he had done with horse painting. 'It reminds me of that bad year in Ireland. No more.' His wife had been able to buy one of Constable's sketchbooks as a present for him, 'something unique which up to now no money could buy'. She thought it fitting that 'this little sketchbook should now be *your* personal property, and *your* fingers turning the leaves. It will go down to posterity with *your* sketchbooks. Often have I thought he may live again in you and your work.' A few days later she was writing: 'I get so annoyed when you are called an "animal painter". Your backgrounds of the horse pictures are often pictures in themselves.'

He decided to relinquish nomination of the presidency of the

Royal Academy for the time being. Reporting rumours of disturbing happenings in Germany, he received from his wife the rebuke: 'Now, dear A.J., do, for goodness sake, be sensible and leave off this war-scare talk.' Aggrieved by what he denounced in print as an 'unrepresentative exhibition' of his work organised by the civic authorities of Bury St Edmunds in August 1939, he withdrew his support and produced his largest crop of press-cutting thus far. 'The show is appalling,' he wrote, adding that he had 'told off the organiser in front of the Mayor'. It made him, he said, 'very, very sick'. A local newspaper recorded that 'until the recent by-election, it was the only exciting event Bury had known for several years'.

(5)

In the first days of September 1939 he was enjoying a spell of landscape painting on the north Norfolk coast, staying at the Ship Inn, Brancaster. One of his subjects was Morston Church, 'a place of repose – a place to dream in'. On his third morning out a sheaf-piled harvest waggon passed slowly along by the churchyard wall. A boy on top of the load called out to him: 'The war's started!'

Munnings wrote afterwards that he went on painting, his emotion of the moment perhaps beyond recollection. Later in the day he chose another subject, the Old Hall at Stiffkey. Its land was being farmed by Henry Williamson, then living through the experiences set out in his *Story of a Norfolk Farm*. Munnings had used up his supply of canvases and was looking round for something to paint on. His exploratory eye noticed a trousers-press in the granary. It contained a rectangle of millboard. He took it and started work again. Shortly afterwards a boy of thirteen, one of Williamson's sons, came and stood silently behind him, watching. Henry Williamson noted the ensuing dialogue.

A.J. (roaring over this shoulder:) 'What the hell are you doing here? Go away, boy!'

Boy: 'That's my father's trouser-press! He wants it!'

A.J.: 'Go away, I tell you! Get out of it! I want to paint this before the light changes!'

Boy (resolutely): 'When Dad comes he'll want to know why I let anyone in the granary, you know. You *took* that, didn't you?'

A.J. (continuing to paint): 'Look at that light – wonderful! Can't you see how *beautiful* it is? What the hell's all this about *trousers*? Go AWAY!'

Writing from the Ship Inn, Brancaster, to his wife: 'I told you there was a possibility of war, but this has been a surprise to us all. What a go!' He left the Norfolk coast unwillingly, prophesying to Henry Williamson that the war would be the end of the country house in England. 'Brancaster was lovely,' he told his wife, the adjective heavily underlined. After a night at Dedham, where he feared to find 'a horde of children' evacuated from London, he hurried to Chelsea to pack up the pictures in the studio for removal to the likelier safety of Castle House. Telling his wife of those arrangements, he wrote: 'There'll be a raid tonight certain.' At Dedham there were potatoes to be dug, apples to be picked. His wife, in Somerset, was not to worry about those and other domestic matters; he was looking after them and she was to stay where she was. 'I expect gas will be dropped all over the place. I haven't been able to get a mask yet – what a go!'

When the pictures arrived by van from Chelsea, he wrote in relief: 'Wonderful! There is now no need for us to bother about them getting "bashed up". I don't think London will suffer at all. I agree with you that war is madness but it doesn't do to say so. It's awful.' His wife repeated her wish to return home despite his insistence that she should remain in the comparative safety of Exmoor. 'You and I are getting old and I want to spend more of my life with you,' she told him. 'Let us now decide to live at Castle House always.' He replied: 'Don't think you're not doing your duty by staying there. You can do nothing else. Cooper [his manservant] and Mrs are all right. They are decent folk. He is 65 and I told him he ought to draw the old-age pension and save it. He said he couldn't bear to go down to the village and draw it each week and be seen'; these would have been less bearable perhaps because it was his Sunday custom to walk out in a tailed morning-coat, striped trousers and a black Homburg hat, 'like a Cabinet minister', Munnings said, 'carrying a silver-mounted ebony stick and smoking a cigar which I would have brought back from a City dinner'.

Munnings wrote that for about fourteen years Cooper 'made our existence possible'. He and his wife had previously 'managed the household' of a canon of Norwich Cathedral. Before the war Cooper had a slogan which Munnings often quoted with amusement to his friends: 'Watch Japan.' Now, he had changed it to the less ominous declaration, 'All's fair in love and war', to which Munnings fell into the habit of adding: 'So Cooper says.' He quoted Cooper's sayings so often that a London newspaper editor 'featured' them in his columns. Pondering all the pictures he had painted in those fourteen years, Munnings wrote generously: 'I could gaze at anyone of them with the thought in mind: "Cooper was at the back of it".'

He dreaded the prospect of evacuee families being installed at Castle House, feeling sure that it would happen. 'We have all the plums bottled. Cooper is on the pears now. I got plenty of sugar yesterday. Also bought 12 square biscuit tins, candles and a paraffin lamp!! Perfect weather, ruined by this mad business. An air-raid warning this morning. Planes going over.'

Evacuees from London arrived in the village, some to return almost at once to the inferno-to-be. 'The women and children are pretty awful. My word, they give the wretched village folk a bad time.' He decided, 'If I get any, I'm shutting up and coming down to you,' urging his wife on Exmoor, 'Hold on to that little place awhile. No one can tell what this business will mean.' He apologises for 'being too busy to write lately', a rare lapse, and a few days later: 'I don't know whether you've got to Withypool yet, Mrs Munnings. Don't you dream of letting that cottage. We look like spending our lives there in the 15th year of the war.'

There were commissioned pictures to be finished in the studio at Castle House, among them one of Lord Astor which was overdue for delivery. Distracted, Munnings took his paint-box along the river path, 'to paint among the willows and lily leaves'. He feared to leave Castle House, 'because swarms of kids might be put in there and there is a lot to see to. I've stuffed the place with pictures.' His studio in the village had been requisitioned as a class-room for evacuee children. In return for his co-operation in that matter, 'old X – saw to it that I had no children at Castle House. My God, I'm lucky.' His wife was still worrying about being away from him. 'I feel I must come back to be *with you*, that I *ought to be*.' He answered: 'Everyone says: Keep there. You are in a good place. Let things develop. It will suddenly end – or get worse. Never know – gas, or anything. Then I'll flee westward. At present it looks as if towns won't be bombed. We won't bomb theirs and they won't bomb ours. *That's* what I think. We shall see. My mother is best off in Norwich. Norwich is safe. You should jolly well feel glad you haven't six kids and no money. We're all going to be taxed heavily – so cheer up.' Meanwhile: 'I'm doing some beautiful work up the river.'

CHAPTER 16

Facing Another War

(1)

'I FORESEE either a quick end to the war or damned nearly starvation. A crime, the way agriculture has been allowed to go. They'll soon be rationing meat.' He went up to London to dine with The Other Club. 'Winston was clapped when he arrived. Lord Gort was given a tremendous send-off to France', as Commander-in-Chief of the British Expeditionary Force. H. G. Wells had a go at the politicians, 'telling them that they didn't think ahead and so on; he foresees great upheavals and Bolshevism in Germany if Hitler is done with. Anyhow, it was a great evening.'

He wishes to forget his sixty-first birthday, 8 October 1939 – 'awful!' There was a cheque from Lord Astor. 'Send it to the bank. How hard I worked for it, and such a lot will be taken!!' He counselled his wife again: 'You can do nothing here. *Nothing at all.* I remembered small toothcomb for cat. Couldn't get one for *love or money*. All sold out to use on evacuee children.'

He helped Cooper with jam-making and with 'melting pork lard from fat and salting and melting butter into jars', preparing for the war shortages which he said would come. Asked by the American owner of Galatea, an Oaks winner, to do a portrait of the mare, he drove to Lambourn in the Berkshire downs, where he found the hillsides covered by flocks of sheep evacuated from East Anglia. Finishing the picture, he went to stay with his wife on Exmoor, intending to return to Dedham for the winter. Instead, he was captivated by the 'boundless moorland' and soon became a familiar figure in that scene, as his wife had been for twenty years. He is still well remembered in those parts.

From one of their Exmoor neighbours, Dudley Down, of Court
Farm, Dunsford, comes the testimony: 'He and his wife were
loved by the whole village and the surrounding district.'

One of his Exmoor friends was F. Willoughby Hancock, of
Wivelscombe, who bought a number of his West Country
landscapes and hunting pictures and always sought his help in
hanging them. Miss Rosemary Hancock sat to Munnings when,
standing at the easel, he recited to her the whole of Gray's *Elegy*.
She remembers that when she moved while posing, he called
out absent-mindedly: 'Whoa, mare!' If the sun went in, he would
go to the window and shout, with upraised fist: 'You bloody
black clouds, you!' No one in the house was allowed to see the
picture until it was finished. At the end of each day's work he
locked it in the linen cupboard and kept the key, regardless of
inconvenience to the household.

While dining one evening, he talked 'with bewildering
brilliance, a verbal firework display' of reminiscence, quotation
and recitation, that kept the Hancock family enthralled. After
the meal, Munnings sat back in his chair, with the remark,
'There, that's something to remember,' as if he had been not
less entertained himself. His talk flowed as freely on horseback
as at table. Rosemary Hancock recalls that too often when they
were out riding together on the moor he would spoil her pleasure
in his conversation by sending her on ahead, so that he could
study her mount's action. On one of their rides she carried a
basket of eggs. Hearing hounds give tongue in the valley, he
warned her: 'There'll be an omelette if they come this way!'

(2)

Apart from his artist's aversion from war as a principle of
life, he did not feel capable in his sixty-second year of more
strenuous forms of activity than those he was accustomed to.
There was no call for his services as in the old war and, except
as a householder and a taxpayer, he was not encouraged to make
any personal contribution to the national effort of 1939-45.

In the summer of 1940 he was invited by J. V. Rank to 'paint
some of his winners', among them Southern Hero, Black Speck

L

and Knight's Armour. Glad no doubt to be professionally occupied again, he went to Wiltshire for several weeks in August and September. Coming in from his first evening walk on the downs, he wrote to his wife:

> Druids Lodge
> Middle Woodford
> Nr Salisbury
> (Undated)

Now fades the glimmering landscape on the sight
When all the air a solemn stillness holds,
Save where the beetle wheels his droning flight
And drowsy tinklings lull the distant folds.

Perhaps a waste of time, Violet dear, for I'm sure you know it. But I've just come in from the very *thing* as written.

A long track of trodden-down grass and wheel marks in the chalk. The track curves away between vast corn stubbles. On either side of it, thick masses of August flowers in late bloom. Farther away, a great curved sweep of dark green tares and more downs and stubbles.

Sky all around to the horizon. The dusk growing, the droning beetles and, best of all, the distant sheep bells, and the cry of peewits. Great stacks standing sentinel against the sky.

I walked away from the sunset and came back facing it - superb; and so still, not a breath of wind. Oh, for a horse to ride all day and no work.

However, I'm doing the *real stuff* and my picture of the horses grows and will be a good one. Lots of others and studies. I shall do well out of this in both ways.

Of all people, J. H. Thomas, late M.P., etc., etc., [railway-men's leader, some time Lord Privy Seal and Dominions Secretary] and his old wife are here. Had to leave their home in Worthing and went to Wales and now bombed out and Rank is putting them up. Rank is a great fellow. Calls me A.J. and we have rare talks. He is what I call a good fellow and a big man. He and old J. H. Thomas talk and cuss all the time.

I'm well – and I've washed brushes *every* night since I saw
you, excepting Sunday!!! Oh, for a little place in these parts.

It's now nearly 10 p.m. I'm all alone, waiting to hear the
bloody German planes come. *Hundreds of searchlights.*

I shall soon be through, but don't hurry me.'

Writing again, 'all looks so lovely here. Life is short, art is
long,' he added a little farther down the page: 'Not many more
years to live, be gad.' He felt he could go on painting happily
at the Rank place, 'only we don't know if the bloody invasion
is on or not'. J. H. Thomas urged him to buy land. 'He is no fool.
He says it will be better to have land, *any* kind of land or property,
than money before this is over. I think he's right.' He delights in
the Wiltshire scene. 'Oh, these downs, miles of 'em,' but their
peace is precarious now: 'Aeroplanes all the time,' as the Battle
of Britain is fought out in the southern skies. His wife writes:
'Oh, Alfred, this war – it makes me quite ill. It is all so senseless
and so unnecessary, so barbaric. People talk of truth, progress,
education, but where has it all led the world? We are
worse than savages because *they* don't profess to be anything
else.'

'Cheer up,' he tells her in reply and describes another evening
walk. 'Nothing could be better. Such a walk. Cornfields and
downs and streams in the valleys. Stonehenge 2½ miles. You
walk up a long chalky, ancient grass track with barrows on either
side – miles of gold wheat and oats – harvest in full swing. J.V.R.
farms 3,000 acres. White carthorses!! A white bull. The Wylie
valley and the Avon too beautiful. What villages. Thatched
cottages, stone built. As I write, 100s of doves are cooing as they
come to drink in the bathing pool on the lawn. I'm *very, very*
glad I came.' His hostess was 'first-rate', underlined; 'kind,
jolly, and has a mind of her own. Wish I'd met them long ago.
Shows how little we know of folk until we meet them'.

He proposed that instead of owning property they should
acquire a caravan – 'it would be the thing', another of V.A.s
(violent attachments) and not pursued further. On 16 September
1940, when the raging air battles reached their climax, he wrote
to his wife: 'I shall come home. Work is now no good with all

this going on. Raids damned serious.' Bombs had fallen near
Druids Lodge, killing sheep and injuring horses.

He had hardly got back to Exmoor when he was notified by
telegram that the army had requisitioned Castle House, as they
had in the 1914–18 war. His recollection of the state the troops had
left it in then filled him with serious misgivings and he caught
the next train for London from Taunton, going straight on to
Colchester for Dedham. That night, 'bombs shook the house,
real good ones'. He filled the principal downstairs rooms with
furniture and bedding, 'piled to the ceilings', had new locks
fitted to the doors and the windows boarded up. In almost
desperate secrecy he and Cooper hid the contents of the wine-
cellar under the floor of the studio in the paddock. He then left
for Exmoor, taking with him Cooper and a groom.

Hearing, soon afterwards, that thieves had driven up in a lorry
to Dedham Church and stripped the lead from the porch roof,
he wrote furiously, in inch-high letters, to R. H. Mottram in
Norwich: 'IF YOU GET THEM, YOU'RE A J.P., GIVE 'EM FORTY
YEARS.'

(3)

On Exmoor, during the war years, some of his most successful
paintings were of the pony herds that roamed the heather far
and wide. Getting sufficiently close to them was often a large
part of the day's work. He rode to their grazing grounds on an
old staghunting horse called Pineapple that had been the mount
of Ernest Bawden, the noted huntsman of the Devon and
Somerset. Often he was compelled to walk miles before setting
up his easel. Many days he was out from morning till dusk,
stalking and painting.

He described the daily strategy: 'This is my plan of battle –
myself, my wife and my groom, Harry Bayfield, go out on three
horses up on to the moor. There we scout and spread out and
ride along the top of the coombs. We peer down and across and,
behold, far away in the distance – there they are, dotted about
feeding and resting, with their foals lying down in the sun. We
ride as near as we can to the ponies without disturbing them.

I dismount with my small box and panels complete. I send the horses home, and there I am, slowly advancing. Thirty-odd ponies – Exmoors mostly – are grouped about, the wind blowing their tails and manes. I'm out with them from 11.30 in the morning until 7 o'clock in the evening. Then I go home on foot.'[1]

His wife watched him one day at a distance take the wrong track, toiling up the stiff climb of a hillside near Cheriton Ridge. Beyond range of her voice, he pressed forward, carrying his paint-box, stool, portable easel and canvases until at the top of the ridge he fell exhausted, losing valuable light as he lay there recovering. There were always the difficulties, which, he said, were realised by so few of those who looked at his or any other painter's landscapes. He found 'a lovely spot' in the marshes near Porlock. When he went back three days later to finish his study of the scene it was blotted out by flood-waters.

There was a day at Bagworthy Water when he forgot his brushes, usually carried in a brown-paper roll. 'A paint-box holds only a miserable handful', and he liked to take twenty or thirty brushes out at a time. He was twelve miles from home. He snapped thin branches from a tree and chewed the ends into fibres. He tied bits of rag on sticks. He experimented with a tiny fir-cone matted with grass. A teazle proved 'most useful'. His picture of Bagworthy Water was painted with those improvised aids. He went back and painted the 'spot' with brushes. Comparing the two pictures, 'they appeared exactly the same'.

The urge to paint what he saw on Exmoor became a voracious appetite. To satisfy it he would take eight or ten canvases out with him and work on all of them, a form of 'mass production' which contributed substantially to the remarkable sales total realised by his later exhibition at the Leicester Galleries in London. Though he continued to find in painting the pure excitement that it had for him in the beginning, behind those moorland excursions of his in 1940-5 was the assurance of a persisting demand for his work from private patrons and the dealers.

Munnings to Mrs Marshall Sisson:

---

1. Undated letter to Collie Knox.

Withypool,
Minehead.
20 November 1943

. . . You ask if I am getting a little damp by the mists. I curse
the rain and then a fine day comes and I see this glorious *free*
country and am not sorry I'm in it. This week I have been at
Wootton Courtney and walking about between there and
Selworthy and Bossington and the sea, and what with the
great oaks and woods and holly trees and stern hills . . . well,
it is a classic piece of country and gave me food for thought
after reading *The Forward March* by Sir Richard Acland, the
late owner of all this landscape, now taken over from him free
gratis by the National Trust!! What possessions!! What rich
farms and great trees and walls and banks. One farm is where
the best barley is always grown and it gets prizes at the
Brewers' Exhibition each year. Last year it got the champion-
ship.

You can't imagine the green smooth knoll crowned with
fantastic hollies and oaks which spring up in the landscape or
the smooth subtle modelling of the fields.

I sat on a stone arch over the Horner water and ate my
lunch to the tune of the stream – copper and gold all around.

I tell you, ma'am, there's no telling what will happen after
the war. Yes, I've read and possess Portsmouth's book
[*Famine in England, 1939*]. Great – he is as one crying in the
wilderness, alas! Nobody cares. Read *The Living Soil* – read it.

CHAPTER 17

President of the Royal Academy

(1)

ON 31 December 1943 Munnings received a letter from an architect member of the Council of the Royal Academy telling him that 'dear Ned', Sir Edwin Lutyens, who had been President since 1938, was 'sinking rapidly ' and that 'the end is a matter of days'. The writer of the letter expressed 'the profound hope' that Munnings would allow himself to be nominated Lutyens's successor. 'It is the painters' turn to be represented.' The election, he pointed out, was an annual affair and if the presidency were found too heavy a burden it could be given up at the end of the year. The writer ventured the opinion, 'I don't believe A.J. can beat A.J.M.', a reference to the likely candidature of Augustus John R.A. A friend of both John and Munnings, who expected John to gain the day, afterwards wrote to tell Munnings. 'John told me some time ago that his refusal to stand last time was probably a mistake.'

Munnings's wife, who had given him advice when the possibility of his nomination had previously arisen, now urged him to stand. 'But think it over well. Remember the tie it will be.' He thought it over. He thought of the responsibility, the burdens, of how it would mean giving up his 'free way of life'. He thought of the ceremonial side, the speech-making, the hand-shaking. He thought also of 'the honour of the post', its constant reminder 'the finest statue in London,' as he called it, that of Sir Joshua Reynolds, the first President, in the courtyard of Burlington House. Presumably he did not think of the expense. He could afford it, without the annual grant made by the Royal Academy to such of its presidents who need supplementary aid.

In turn hoping and fearing to be elected, Munnings travelled to London from Exmoor for 'the day of days', 15 March 1944, standing all the way from Taunton in the corridor of a crowded wartime train. His Chelsea house was 'a dreary, hopeless muddle', from bomb damage. The Arts Club in Dover Street had been badly hit and, as an incident of that occurrence, the charming picture which he had lent to the club, Tissot's '*La Danseuse le Cord*', was destroyed. He was accommodated in Priory Road, St John's Wood, by one of his small number of close friends, Edward Whitney Smith, the sculptor, whose punctilious observance of his duties as an air-raid warden added to Munnings's regard for him.

Munnings was elected President of the Royal Academy in a ballot which gave him twenty-four votes to Augustus John's eleven. The bells of Mendham village church did not ring out for him across the Waveney Valley, but it was the countryman who spoke when, on receiving word of the result, he shouted: 'I feel like riding along Piccadilly on a horse. What a go!' The sense of triumph was short-lived. When Adrian Bury, artist, art historian and poet saw him that afternoon, 'he was almost apologetic for his success, as if he was trying to justify himself'. His mother, staying with her eldest son William at Weybread and receiving the news of Alfred's election by telephone, remarked: 'Tell him that is what I have been expecting.'

That night a heavy air-raid brought London's transport to a standstill. Munnings and Whitney Smith had to walk home to St John's Wood. 'Up Piccadilly, with fires lighting the sky, through Park Lane, along the Edgware Road, passing burning buildings, flooded streets, fire brigades – pictures of hell. A nightmare forgotten in sleep.'

Next day the congratulatory deluge began to fall. 'Hundreds of letters and messages' – no exaggeration – 'to be answered'. A formula had to be invented for much of his large acquaintance as for the well-wishers whom he had never met. He decided on: 'Stacks of letters but thank you for yours.' Responding to friends, he did his best to impart the personal note: 'Thank you very much. What a go!' Numbers of them had anticipated that familiar exclamatory reaction by including it in their messages to him. To those he retorted: 'Bless your good soul – thanks!' Several who were entitled to address him 'Dear Alfred' may have been dismayed to receive acknowledgements beginning 'Dear Sir'. Some of his more personal replies imparted the information that he had hoped that 'Augustus John would have borne the burden.'

(2)

To Mr Justice Hilbery who had written to tell him that he regarded him as the 'greatest living representative of what is our own true native tradition in painting', he made reply: 'How on earth do you think I am to live up to it?'; to Allan Aynesworth, actor: 'What a joy to get your letter. By jove, my lad, we'll meet soon'; to George Belcher, *Punch* artist: 'I have had to get someone to help me through with a typewriter. In spite of so mechanised a device, may these lines convey to you all the delight I feel in getting a wire from the great grey-headed squire of Chiddingfold, Surrey'; to Kent, the groom at the Southcourt Stud, where he had painted so happily and pro-fitably years before: 'My dear old Kent, Thank you so much for your letter. I still have a mare I bred by The Winter King. A beautiful ride. Son-in-Law hocks, dark brown, white hind foot. How I would love to see you again'; to the President of the Society of Old Framlinghamians: 'Many thanks for your letter. I am trying to answer hundreds more. Yours brings back days of yore. Alas! what a long time ago'; to Sir Sydney Cockerell: 'What a kind letter. I wish I could answer it in a worthy manner, for you do me proud, Sir'; to Frank O. Salisbury: 'You touch me to the heart'; to H. B. Craft: 'How well I remember the Newlyn days and your father's pictures and name long, long ago'; to James Woodford: 'It was a great afternoon at the R.A., and the whole lot treated me like a swell'; to W. Crampton Gore: 'How I wish I was still in Dedham, but the Army took it. Soon I'll be back'; to Hanslip Fletcher: 'What a kind letter! If I had all the qualities you speak of I should pass out of this wicked world to a better. I'm full of letters – hundreds'; to Lord Cherwell: 'the Prof.' of Churchill's wartime circle: 'Thank you for your telegram. See you at The Other Club again soon'; to Mrs Dorothea Coxhead: 'I read your letter with tears for the past.'

Art controversies of the old war, and one of the highly individualistic temperaments that they were centred in, were recalled by a telegram which read: 'Delighted. Heartiest congratulations from hopelessly stricken C. R. W. Nevinson'. Brendan Bracken, one of the several successive Ministers of Information, was also 'delighted by this news', and declared in writing: 'I am going to suggest to Winston that if anything should happen to the Poet Laureate that job should also be conferred on you.' From the Director of the National Portrait Gallery, Sir Henry Hake, there came word: 'I am delighted at your election and it will be my duty to summon you to meetings of the Trustees and I hope you will be able to assist.' Munnings answered: 'I shall be delighted to see more of your Gallery. I'm very fond of it.' The Director and Principal Librarian of the British Museum informed him: 'As President of the Royal Academy you are *ex officio* a Trustee of the British Museum.' A privilege of office that he valued above all was membership of the Athenaeum Club under Rule 4 of its constitution, admitting the P.R.A. and the heads of one or two other public bodies connected with the arts.

There was an enthusiastic letter from the Isle of Wight. 'A thousand congratulations from one of your oldest and greatest admirers. I see you now in your quaint civilian costume painting Warrior and me at Smallfoot Wood and, again, on a bright sunny morning right in the middle of the March retreat, painting Antoine of Orleans on his black horse at the Château de Bargemont. . . . What fun we had together. Yours ever, Jack M. [Lord Mottistone]'. Munnings was moved to reply: 'My dear Lord of the Isle, Only you could have written that letter and I thank you from the bottom of my heart.'

An aged aunt wrote from Yoxford, Suffolk: 'Dear President, We heard your name on the wireless. It so set up my ears. 'Tis very wonderful.' He wrote to her: 'Dear Aunt Mary, Thank you for your letter. So glad to see the clear wonderful writing. I wish you everything you want'. Hers was one of many letters that stirred memories of other days. His heart was given a lift of

pleasurable recollection when he picked out the name of Stebbings from the flood of compliments, a tribute from the son of
'the proper, kindly, sprightly country bank manager', George
Stebbings, who had watched over his financial affairs from a
desk at Barclay's branch at Harleston so long ago.

Mrs A. Lovell Taylor of Llandudno recalled herself to him as
'the Miss Crossley who was for some years with Caley and Son',
the Norwich chocolate and mineral-water firm for which he
designed showcards and posters in the late nineties. 'I well
remember you coming into Mr Shaw Tomkins's office with a
picture and he in his jolly manner offering you five shillings for it.
You said: "I think it is worth a little more than that, Mr Tomkins." How delighted he would be to know of your great
success.' Munnings remembered her too, and, thanking her, asked
the not immediately relevant question: 'Wasn't Caley's
bombed?'

Mrs Kate Fassnidge of Uxbridge wrote to Munnings: 'I
expect you wonder who I am. I nursed you as a baby. Our
parents were friends and I often walked over to Mendham Mill.
I have always taken a great interest in your career. I am a
daughter of the late Mr C. Woods (chemist) of Harleston. I am
now an old woman.' Munnings replied: 'My thanks. What early
days you write of and how the name C. Woods, Chemist, of
Harleston, brought back memories of old days. I wish you many
happy years.'

Mrs Constance Villiers-Stuart of King's Lynn addressed him
as 'Dear Mr Mummings' but received the forgiving reply: 'I like
to hear from Norfolk and wish I was there now. I was at Brancaster when all this started.' The headmaster of the City of
Norwich School of Arts and Crafts, Charles W. Hobbis, invoked
the respected name of his predecessor of Munnings's time,
Walter Scott, in sending the School's congratulations. He received the one-line acknowledgment: 'I am more than glad to
hear from you.'

From her Cavendish Hotel in Jermyn Street, London, Rosa
Lewis wrote: 'Many of our American friends who come here
ask me about you – they all seem to know you.' Munnings replied: 'My very dear, dear Rosa, Thank you. I will see you soon.'

The chairman of the Norwich Art Circle, mouthpiece for his council, wrote that 'they feel your accession to so great an honour is the logical goal of your career'.

His election to a prominent place in the established order evoked a mass of good-will that was not only complimentary to him. Chaos had come again. The letters and telegrams and telephone messages, flowing in from all parts of the country, were a salute to the Royal Academy as one of the fixed points in a changing world.

(3)

Gerald Kelly R.A. to Munnings:

at Windsor Castle,
March 16 1944

My dear President, I did not wait to offer you verbally my congratulations because you were surrounded by those who had voted for you and I had a train to catch.

But I do congratulate you on being elected President by so very large a majority which gives you the assurance of solid support among the members of the Royal Academy.

I voted for John. I did so because I wish above all things to see the rising generation of artists reconciled to the Academy; and I felt that John was the candidate most likely to bring about this consummation.

You beat him handsomely, and I accept the situation. It is the easier for me to do since for many years I have greatly admired your paintings, and still do so.

I feel certain that we both love this institution, the Royal Academy, and wish to see its traditions honourably maintained. For my part, that is my sole objective, as it is surely yours.

The more successful the President, the better for the Royal Academy.

In every point that I can, my support, for what little it may be worth, shall be at your service.

If we should differ I may feel obliged to contest the point at issue, but always, let me assure you once more, in what I conceive to be the true interests of the Royal Academy.

Yours very sincerely,

GERALD KELLY

The President to Gerald Kelly:

My dear Kelly, Many thanks for your letter. I had hoped John would have to bear the burden and set me free. Since it has fallen on me, I want you all to be good friends of mine.

You and I will never disagree about things that matter. Art is long, etc.

Yours,

A. J. MUNNINGS

An unexpected sequel to his elevation was 'a very friendly and well-expressed letter' from the President of the Moscow Art Society. It led to the exchange of what Munnings called 'fraternising correspondence', in the course of which he and the Secretary of the Royal Academy were invited to 'several enjoyable luncheons' at the Soviet Embassy. 'There I met young Russians who were full of enthusiasm for Dickens and Thackeray. I talked of Tolstoy and *War and Peace*. How pleasant those meetings were!'

A practical result of them was his advocacy of a Russian and Soviet Art Exhibition at the Royal Academy. The complicated processes of post-war cultural diplomacy between the U.S.S.R. and the West were long in giving effect to the scheme. It matured in 1959.

Many other entertainments were offered him as the new P.R.A. One of them was a dinner of the Omar Khayyam Club, at which he was the guest of honour. Proposing his health, the chairman of the evening, Philip Guedalla, the biographer of Wellington and other figures in history, said: 'I ask you to drink to our distinguished friend, the President of the Royal Academy, to whom, I am told, the horse stands in the same relationship as Lady Hamilton to Romney.'

CHAPTER 18

The Athenaeum's Noisiest Member

(1)

HE had no administrative gift and in the Council Room his presidency of the Royal Academy might have been a disaster but for the diligent and persuasive loyalty of the secretary, Sir Walter Lamb, whose situation was not always eased by his regard for Munnings as a man and an artist. 'Let Lamb do it!' the new President would demand. 'Why do we have so many Council meetings? Are they necessary?' Not even his reverence for Sir Joshua had the power to restrain him within the bounds of protocol when the agenda became tedious.

At some of the meetings he himself had to be called to order by protesting voices round the table, a situation which he accepted with great good humour. 'My dear President, you can't over-ride the Council in this way,' he was reminded by a senior member, who the following day wrote apologising for rudeness which Munnings had provoked. 'I do realise that your method of dealing with us is dictated only by devotion to the honour and glory of the R.A.'

He complained that his fellow-Academicians turned down more than one 'grand idea' of his, but on occasions he achieved spectacular dominion over them. At a General Assembly to elect new members he appeared to be perturbed by the prospect of a majority vote for a candidate whose work he did not favour. Just before the vote was to be taken, he called out: 'Wait a minute! We'll go into the gallery and have another look at the fellow's pictures.' Crossing to the door, he beckoned his colleagues forward with an imperious sweep of the arm. 'Come on, *all* of you,' and, with varying degrees of alacrity, fifty Royal

Academicians trailed in procession behind him at his bidding. It was a demonstration of his power of command that not all who were there have forgotten.

The Royal Academy's business at that time was frequently conducted against the background of air attack. Munnings would sit gazing up at the painted ceiling of the Council Room as Lamb read the minutes. 'There comes the warning cry of sirens. Of what is each of us thinking, as he smokes his cigarette? Lamb goes on reading the minutes. We pretend that we are not thinking of doodle-bugs until we hear one approaching . . .' It passes noisily overhead and within seconds falls on the Regent Palace Hotel a few hundred yards away, with heavy casualties. 'And still Sir Walter goes on reading those endless minutes of the last meeting.'

The flying-bombs ploughed the London sky like roaring atmospheric tractors. The V2 rockets arrived in a silence that was more nerve-racking than the earth-shuddering crash that followed. Munnings spent many of his London nights talking and drinking with his friends and 'trying to forget the calamitous explosions bringing sudden death to people'. His country-nourished nerves were impervious to the stresses. It was his patience that was most sorely tried, the perfectly genuine emotion of the artist who fears to be deprived of the joy of communicating his sensations to others. His brushes were laid aside. There was solace in his pen, in filling pages of Athenaeum Club, Arts Club or Garrick Club notepaper with descriptions of scenes which he would have preferred to paint: beech-tree boles on Hampstead Heath, shadows on a lawn at Temple Fortune Hill, 'as I listen to the birds and watch the almond blossom falling', light on the Thames on a late afternoon. Like many in wartime, he was hungry for æsthetic experience and, while he had never been acutely appreciative of the best in music, he now gratefully went with his friend Codner 'to hear Chopin all the afternoon'.

Gout distracted him again while he was staying with Codner, a desperate attack that compelled him to descend the stairs next morning in a sitting posture, an agony of effort. He was miraculously relieved by a lumbar jab given him by 'a most wonderful doctor'. In twenty minutes he was walking again.

His old friend Whitney Smith, the sculptor, was bombed out of
the house in Priory Road and Munnings wrote of the occurrence
with comical *non sequitur* dismay: 'After all, his are not
stark, droll figures with round knobs for heads.' The war,
which was shattering so much more than material forms, in-
tensified his hatred of 'modern art', to him a nightmarish denial
of the joy that art was meant to bring mankind. The Editor of
The Times felt constrained to remind him in a letter explaining
the non-publication of one from Munnings that 'in the house of
art there are many mansions and some of them are pre-fabs'.
Munnings reacted cholerically. 'The damn' fellow,' he exclaimed, '*likes* that Madonn*er* in Cavendish Square!'[1]

(2)

There were blessed hours of relief from the stresses when he
relaxed with therapeutic contentment amid the glories of
Burlington House. 'The silver was *wonderful*,' he wrote after
lunching there for the first time as President. 'We now have
first-rate chicory and lettuce salads and meat pies and soup for
lunch and lager beer and old sherry if we want it.' The Royal
Academy silver fascinated him. Every piece was a traditional
gift from new members. He never failed to hold his silver plate
to the light to read the name engraved on it, as he went into
dinner in the Assembly Room. 'It might be Sargent or Landseer
or Etty or Sir Joshua himself.'

When Council meetings were appointed for five o'clock,
there was the enjoyable ritual of tea from 'large handsome silver
Georgian teapots, milk-jug and sugar-basin on a large silver
tray'. Relishing the amenities and privileges, 'seated on a
period settee or in one of the Nelson armchairs', he thinks
about the history and traditions 'housed in this noble building',
and he solemnly asks himself: 'Should we not try to live up to
them?'

Memorable lunches and dinners were given in the Assembly
Room where, he was careful to point out to his guests, there was
a Constable landscape insured for £40,000. One of his 'grand

1. By Epstein.

Munnings on the way to 'a spot' on the River Stour.

Lady Munnings at Castle House.

ideas' which his Council colleagues did not reject was a dinner
to those correspondents who had written to *The Times* on the
subject of the Picasso exhibition at the Victoria and Albert
Museum in 1946. His guests included the Prime Minister (Mr
Attlee), the Hon. Sir Cyril Asquith, Sir Malcolm Hilbery, the
Lord Mayor of London, and the King's Private Secretary, Sir
Alan Lascelles, with Sir Giles Gilbert Scott, Professor Richard-
son and other Royal Academicians supporting him.

Munnings would have gone to the stake rather than concur
in the proposition that Picasso was one of the Olympians. He
despised the mumbo-jumbo posturings and incantations of 'the
Picasso crowd', and that painter's name was scathingly invoked from the chair during the dinner. Afterwards one of the
guests, Sir Cyril Asquith, raised a pertinent question in his
letter of thanks to Munnings 'for one of the most delightful
dinners I have had in six years'. Why, he asked, is it 'that in
poetry the exact transcription of a sensation into words is
regarded as admissible, while in *painting* it is regarded as
ninth-rate?'

Another of Munnings's ideas, which were usually associated
with hospitality, was to give a lunch at the Royal Academy to the
editors of the leading national newspapers. The purpose was
their indoctrination with his views on art critics. He made a
speech pointing out that at a time when newspaper managers
were clamouring for more newsprint, some editors – and his
glance round the table was scarcely discriminating – were
printing silly things about silly people, 'and almost nothing
worth-while about art'. He asked why newspapers that encouraged 'the incomprehensible in art' did not 'practice what
they preached and print their news stories upside down and
without punctuation marks'. His emphasised assertion that any
newspaper that 'hired an intelligent writer on art' would be
rewarded by a gratifying rise in circulation was met by merited
if too cynical laughter.

It was all a manœuvre to cover a more subtle intention. With
the arrival of the port Munnings set himself likewise in movement round the table, engaging certain editors in close private
colloquy. That part of the proceedings was recalled by some

M

who were not thus favoured when a well-known art critic resigned from his paper. Those best qualified to comment never doubted that Munnings had helped to bring about that climax in his career.

' "O, blast him. Will nobody do for him?" as Lord Scamperdale said when Sponge collided with him in the hunting field and knocked him and his horse sideways,' Munnings had quoted in a letter to Sir Desmond MacCarthy, literary critic of the *Sunday Times*, writing on 13 September 1946. 'If you could see letters I get from important teaching people who tell me of the nonsense talked by lecturers in the schools and the rotten art education being stuffed into children, you'd weep. Or, perhaps, unlike Chekov's folk, you don't weep ever – you laugh.'

He begged MacCarthy to review a book called *Addled Art*, an attack on the moderns by his friend Lindsay, the Australian artist and critic. 'I sent one to Winston and he's reading it.' He had sent copies to 'Lord Justice Asquith, Lord Brabazon, Lord Crawford, and many more.' The Klee exhibition at the National Gallery provoked him to tell MacCarthy: 'When Charles Morgan went there with me on a Saturday afternoon and saw the crowd – it finished him. The crowds at the Victoria and Albert Museum were terrific, seeing the Picassos!! I don't suppose you went. All commercialism and ramp and these silly small amateur experts are swallowing it.' He ended a long letter: 'For the sake of Lindsay and tradition do review that book. What would de Maupassant have said to all this French art of today?'

(3)

The disarray at the Chelsea studio and the pressure of his Academy duties precluded him from giving much attention to his professional side. As a serious worker, for whom every major subject involved a series of variants, he always had pictures on hand to sell if need be. An exhibition of his work in 1947 yielded the highest returns of his working life, £20,788. It was and may still be a record for a living British artist of our time. Sales totalling £12,000 were reached on the first day.

The exhibition was promoted by Oliver Brown at the Leicester Galleries, London, under the title of 'The English Scene'. Munnings's first one-man show had been held there as far back as 1913, when his prices ranged between £20 and £60. Brown remembered him from those days as 'a sporting-looking fellow from Norwich'.

Sir Desmond MacCarthy wrote to Munnings:

> The Athenaeum,
> Pall Mall,
> 25 November 1947

My dear Munnings, I darted up to London to see your exhibition. I enjoyed it very much and its astonishing *success* sent up my spirits.

I asked X – if he had grasped the significance of those sales – the general significance. He looked blank. 'It means,' I said, 'two things. First, that at last lovers of pictures are asserting their faith that painting is a *representative* art, a principle which no one doubted till lately, and, secondly, that they are beginning to kick against the capture by the theoretical cliques of all the main channels of art criticism, who scare and hypnotise people with incomprehensible jargon (I quoted a few specimen phrases) and spread esoteric snobbishness instead of appreciation.

If your name had been Degas, how 'the critics' would have raved about your skill in recording movement and the gait and gestures of horses.

Many congratulations. I'm afraid the critic of the —— is a *toady*.

> Yours sincerely,
> DESMOND MACCARTHY

The congratulations were as bitter aloes to 'A.J.' The works he had sent to the Leicester Galleries were the fruit of years of labour. Yet the proceeds were treated by the Inland Revenue as income for one year, which meant that his receipts from the exhibition were taxed at 19s. 6d. in the pound. An appeal to the Treasury on his behalf, and on behalf of all one-man shows, met with no response. 'In three days,' he wrote to Nevile Wallis, then art critic of *Punch*, 'they have sold well over £15,000 for Mr Dalton [Chancellor of the Exchequer] to play with.' Increasing his exasperation, the best of the pictures were bought by dealers and re-sold at a profit.

Only a short time before, one of the finest paintings of his Cornish period, 'Zennor Moor', fetched £1,350 at auction in Edinburgh, frustrating the hopes of the director of the Ferens Art Gallery, Hull, who wrote to Munnings: 'I took £300 with me, thinking there was a chance to get it cheaply in the wilds of Scotland, where there would be no one to compete with me. I sat with open mouth as it rocketed up.' The price reached by the Zennor picture prompted P. and D. Colnaghi, the Bond Street fine art dealers, to send him a congratulatory telegram.

Frost and Reed reported better sales of his prints and wanted more of his copyrights, sending him suggestions for pictures they would like to reproduce. He countered testily with one of his own, 'Hounds Feeding', assuring them: 'It will sell in *thousands*.' When the firm responded with no more than moderate interest, he retorted: 'I am too busy to go on advising people who think they know better than the artists.' To another approach from the same quarter he replied: 'I'll find you something. Why the hell don't you do that lovely picture of the two girls in the canoe? A *stunner*, 20 × 24. A blaze of light and, by Jove, art lovers will be all over it. What a picture for you. There's never been such a picture for reproduction. P.S. I've no time to write letters.' His suggestions for reproductions were seldom practical. He persisted in his belief that he knew more about the market than those who specialised in it.

He was at Buckingham Palace that year, 1947, to receive the insignia of a Knight Commander of the Victorian Order, the traditional titular award to Royal Academy presidents. 'I have seen the King,' he wrote to his wife. 'He put on the chain and fixed it all up himself. He was so nice and we talked about all sorts of things and about Sun Chariot and her foal.' They had also discussed 'a very fine Millais picture,

"The Eve of St Agnes". The woman stands in the barred pattern of the moonlight on the floor made through the window.' He did not disclose in his letter that the King had asked him, 'Why is your hand in a sling?' and that he had answered, 'Sprained my wrist, Sir.' It was swollen with gout. Munnings said that he 'didn't like to confess it', though ordinarily for him embarrassment was the least troublesome effect of his ailment.

Invited by the Commander-in-Chief at Portsmouth to lunch in distinguished company on board *Victory*, he accepted and then, as the day drew near, got 'cold feet' about going alone. He rang up a well-known newspaper writer, Collie Knox, with the command: 'You come with me.' Knox protested that he had not been honoured by an invitation. 'I'll see to it,' Munnings said. Knox afterwards described their outing: 'Every inch of that famous vessel was examined. . . . Up and down we went, the President hatless and wearing a very old raincoat . . . and myself hatless – for my head-covering had blown away out to sea – and chilled to the marrow. But there was no escape. Never had I met a more single-minded man than Munnings . . . he had come down to Portsmouth to see over the *Victory*, and nothing would stop him doing the job thoroughly. Until, miserable, wet and sneezing like mad, I cried: "For mercy's sake, let's go home". So we did. Ye gods, what a day!'[1]

(4)

He was taking full advantage of his apostolic membership of the Athenaeum Club and that not only because it offered the comfort of a hot bath, a facility which was beyond the resources of the President's accommodation at the Royal Academy, where a tin hip-bath was still in use. He found more kindred spirits at the Athenaeum than he may have expected; also some who were not so kindred and who could be seen either slumping more deeply in their armchairs when his voice heralded his approach or hurriedly remembering engagements elsewhere. An aged country member, rarely in town, asked his neighbour at dinner

1. From *People of Quality* by Collie Knox: (London: Macdonald & Co. Ltd., 1947).

after hearing Munnings talking loudly several tables away:
'Who brought that ostler fellow into the club?'

Against a small uncongenial minority could be placed a
heavy counter-weight of regard for Munnings and of pleasure
in his company. His foremost affinity in the club was with the
scholarly, domed-headed C. K. Ogden (1889-1957), inventor of
the phonetic system of communication known as Basic English,
of which the Churchill administration bought the copyright for
£20,000 as a contribution to Allied political strategy in the
Far East. In basic American Munnings and Ogden were
'buddies', and that to a point at which it was said that Ogden
looked 'pained and deprived' when Munnings failed to appear.
Someone who knew them both remarked: 'Theirs is like one
of those queer animal friendships that are written about in
Country Life.'

Ogden's entry in *Who's Who* included the note 'bedevilled by
officials, 1944-6'. He collected Chinese bird-cages with
mechanical singing birds in them by which he hoped to entice
rare migrants to his window-sill in Bloomsbury. His rooms were
a fantastic clutter of books. His visitors had to sit on piles of
them because he had left no room for chairs. Disarmingly he
said that he liked Munnings because he was 'pleasantly eccentric'. Pressed for a definition of Munnings's eccentricities, he
said: 'Well, perhaps eccentric is not the right word. Weird,
shall we say? I find him weirdly amusing.' The two dining
together became as fixed a feature of the Athenaeum as the
classical busts in the hall. They always finished with large
brandies and Benedictines mixed; and Ogden apparently never
thought his day complete until he had persuaded 'A.J.' to give
one of his ballads, which might brazenly rhyme 'Sunday' with
'Bungay', but which invariably caught the ear with their fluency
and swing. Meanwhile, Ogden would sit with his chin almost in
his plate, as if secretly dissociating himself from a performance
that not everyone in the room appreciated.

Professor John Mavrogordato, Fellow of Exeter College and
some time Professor of Byzantine and Modern Greek Languages
and Literature at Oxford, always enjoyed Munnings's proximity,
even when it was a matter of overhearing rather than of being

in his circle. 'He had such an infectious pleasure in life, somewhat rare.' The Professor was echoing a comment made by Bernard Berenson to A. W. Rawlinson, a director of Wildenstein's of London. Berenson divided human beings into 'life-givers' and 'life-diminishers'. He had nothing to say about Munnings the artist. Munnings the man he put into the 'life-giving' category.

Professor Mavrogordato was 'never in the least perturbed', as some Athenaeum members were, by Munnings's effusiveness. 'I say!' he was heard to exclaim over a wide area of the dining-room one lunch-time in a tone of the highest esteem: 'What a lovely shape!' Blanc-mange was not on the menu and some of the members may have been puzzled until it was seen that he was referring to a new young Irish waitress standing at his table. If there were fastidious minds that deemed his exclamatory gusto better suited to a saloon bar, maybe there was also an art historian, reflective over his claret, who recognised that 'A.J.' had the exuberant Venetian attitude to beauty of form, as to colour. That he sometimes went to the Athenaeum predisposed to *épater la haute bourgeoisie* was made plain when, after lunching there, he returned to the Royal Academy, telling the head porter: 'I made those old boys jump a few times today!' He had read aloud in the smoke-room 'an old piece of Norfolk rhyming' called 'Ben Bolt'. It was coarse enough to offend tastes not primarily censorious.

Another of the professorial members of the Athenaeum, Thomas Bodkin, some time director of the National Gallery of Ireland and the Barber Institute of Fine Arts at Birmingham, complained that 'Alfred likes to be the centre of attraction and sulks when he isn't'. In that intellectual society it was an emergency which fairly often arose. As insurance against it, he took guests who could be relied on to play their part to his satisfaction, content to be periphery men when circumstances were propitious for him and rallying to him when they were not. His friend Codner, without surrendering his integrity as a person, conducted himself as if he had been specially trained in that role. When a less sagacious guest of Munnings's dared to disagree with a remark made by another member, Munnings warned him sharply: 'Better keep out of this.' The guest, who was more intimately acquainted with accountancy than with the topic under discussion, behaved as if gratified at being rebuked by genius.

Munnings's generosity as a host is well remembered at all his clubs. He had a sound taste in wine and always lavished the best on his guests, whoever they were. Frequently his own intake of drink through a long evening was restricted to a weak whisky and water. Humphrey Brooke, who as Secretary of the Royal Academy was often with him in their ten years' association and friendship, never saw him the worse for drink. Away from his usual centres of conviviality he was capable of long periods of strict moderation. His boisterous humours were the expression of an exuberance of the heart rather than of the vintages. It is a fair assumption that no member of the Athenaeum has been heard to uplift his voice in the hymns of Moody and Sankey within those walls since 'A.J.' passed from the scene.

(4)

'Look, there's the spire!' he exclaimed to his wife, as they travelled by car along the London road towards Norwich on a June day in 1947. Cathedral spires, like the edifices they adorn, are not notably susceptible to the changes and chances of this world; even so, Munnings was excited enough to insist: 'Exactly as it was when I used to ride here on horseback forty years ago! I'll bring it into my speech tomorrow.' He was going to Norwich to receive the freedom of the city.

He was being unusually honoured. It was part of the civic history of Norwich that its freedom was always sparingly bestowed. Not even some of the most distinguished Norwich names had been admitted to the roll of freemen. For the first time, the Lord Mayor told a crowded gathering in St Andrew's Hall, they were recognising 'services to culture' rather than political or military distinction. Munnings, in his seventieth year, was noticeably moved when he was acclaimed by the burgesses of the city of his youth. Returning thanks, he spoke of far-off days when he sat in the same hall poring over examination papers for the Cambridge 'local', or listened to the music of Sir Hubert Parry and Sir Edward Elgar and the voices of Edward Lloyd, Madame Albani, Clara Butt and Plunkett Greene.

He spoke of a particular morning in Tombland Alley where there was an elder-bush in flower and a woman was shaking a door-mat in the sunlight, a vignette of memory so evocatively expressed that it drew applause. The Lord Mayor's brother, Tom D. Copeman, wrote in his diary that night: 'Munnings, who for one dreadful moment lost his notes, gave a wonderful impression of his love for Norwich and of the happy freedom of his early painting days – gorse – commons – village inns – and his amazement at finding himself on the platform in St Andrew's Hall.'

That night he was guest of honour at a dinner of the Norfolk and Norwich branch of the English-speaking Union. He told the company that he had been looking at some of his pictures in the Art Gallery. 'I found them depressing. There isn't anything right with them. The only good picture of mine in that place is 'The Timber Gill' – and I don't know how I did it.' It was the picture of which he had written forty years before: 'I shall never do anything as good again.' The chairman of the dinner, R. H. Mottram, has written: 'He then launched into a long passage of impeccable prose, at first mystifying his listeners; an excerpt from Borrow's description of Norwich in *Lavengro*. It was a terrific feat of memory and, once everyone understood what it was about, highly appreciated.'

The following day he appeared, a delighted apparition from fifty years before, in the bar of the Bush at Costessy, Norwich. He was retracing the footsteps of his youth. When the landlady, Mrs Blogg, asked for his autograph, he wrote:

1907 – 1908 – 1910

In the years above I used to come to this old inn and have glorious times and painted in the garden behind. WHAT DAYS!!

Alfred Munnings,
President of the Royal Academy of Arts.

adding, as if he still could not quite believe it, 'Yesterday, June 20, 1947, I was given the Freedom of the City of Norwich,' underlined.

He went in search of the sandpits in which he had been the happy warrior with the paint-brush in those far-off times. They were now unrecognisable lakes, deepened and widened by gravel digging for air-strips in the war.

He took the opportunity, while he was in Norwich on that visit, to investigate the activities of a forger who had been busy on some of his early studies, painting in caravans and other embellishments typical of his Norfolk period. He needed no reminding that Crome had been similarly victimised in the Norwich of 150 years before. Nor did Munnings forget to register his indignation that the city of his art nativity should recently have tolerated an exhibition of 'modern art' within its walls.

At the jubilee lunch of the Lady Lever Art Gallery, Port Sunlight, in December 1947 he told the 200 guests that 'there are now more experts on art, more teaching art, more folk broadcasting on art, than there are artists'. As a result of those myriad attentions the younger generation of artists, he feared, was being made 'too self-conscious, afraid of what certain types of critic will say about their work'. He urged them to get on with their painting and to pay less heed 'to the many talking about art'.

After the lunch he was told that Lord Derby had asked to see him. Munnings was conducted outside to greet him, a pillowed invalid lying back in a Daimler, 'the lamp of life glimmering but faintly'. Derby took Munnings's hand and held it as they talked about his great racehorse Hyperion, which Munnings had painted. When they said goodbye it was for the last time. Driving home with Charles (now Sir Charles) Wheeler R.A., then President of the Royal Society of British Sculptors, Munnings entertained him with quotations from Surtees – 'not simply extracts; passages long enough to have been chapters from the books. To me, it was an astonishing display of memory'.

(4)

'I'm not quite up to the mark,' he said as he handed over the main part of the task of organising the extremely popular winter exhibition at the Royal Academy in 1946-7, called 'The King's Pictures', to Gerald Kelly R.A. He took the liveliest interest in the exhibition and chronicled the King's remark on visiting it: 'I didn't know I had so many pictures.'

The Chantrey Bequest exhibition at the Royal Academy in 1949 was Munnings's own idea, a gesture of bravado made by him in the course of discussions between representatives of the Tate Gallery and the Royal Academy. He told the Tate Chairman, Sir Jasper Ridley: 'You shall be invited to drink champagne in front of "Amy Robsart"', (by W. F. Yeames R.A., one of the first Chantrey purchases in 1877). The promise was kept. The Chantrey Bequest exhibition, almost an afterthought, was a considerable success.

During succeeding talks at the Tate, where the Chantrey Bequest pictures are housed – too many of them in the basement for Munnings's liking – he was impressed by 'an intelligent and keen young fellow', Humphrey Brooke, Assistant Keeper at the Tate. Brooke's translation in due time to the office of Secretary of the Royal Academy, following Sir Walter Lamb, gave Munnings more satisfaction than some other happenings arising out of his dealings with the Academy. From the time of the Chantrey Bequest exhibition he tended increasingly to regard the Tate, a sugar-magnate's benefaction of the early '90s, as a clearing-house of corrupt ideas in art emanating from Paris. 'What sheep we are,' he protested, 'to be led by a small handful of highbrows.' This was part of a generalising attack which he made on the Tate and its Director as a result of the banishment to its cellars of two lush specimens of Victorian pictorial art, 'A Hopeless Dawn' by Frank Bramley and 'The Health of the Bride' by Stanhope Forbes. 'Fully justify their sojourn in the vaults,' said the *Manchester Guardian*; 'a sad parade of dead reputations', echoed the *Yorkshire Post*.

Feeling betrayed, Munnings rebounded with schoolboyish

delight when the London *Evening News* published an article endorsing the judgment of the Royal Academy in holding the Chantrey Bequest exhibition. 'These Victorian artists looked *outward* with aspiring eyes upon a world of stable values, acknowledged principles, and accepted duties. Good was good and bad was bad. They did not look *inward* upon their fretful minds out of a faithless and codeless world adrift.'[1]

It was meat and drink to Munnings and the *Evening News* Editor's telephone crackled with his appreciation. He begged for reprints. Four thousand were supplied at once and he had them distributed free from the Royal Academy catalogue counter. Nor did he shrink from thrusting copies into the hands of visitors coming up the steps of Burlington House. An attack on the exhibition in *The Spectator* by Harold Nicolson brought the reminder from Munnings that Nicolson had once written that 'Tears, Idle Tears' placed Tennyson beyond dispute in 'the first five' greatest poets. The point may or may not have been worth making; the point of bringing it forward here is that the *tu quoque* was usually the limit of Munnings's mental dexterity in any argument.

Gerald Kelly R.A. to Munnings:

117 Gloucester Place, W.1

8 February 1949

My dear A.J. Oh, how I wish you hadn't this appetite for publicity. I'm shocked at your 'bustling catchpenny tactics'. Alas, alas! I received the copy of *Picture Post* sent with somebody's compliments. Oh! horrible, you were at it again and worse. The same sincerity which is so lovable – yes, but you mention living artists and members of our body. It's not fair. You shouldn't do it. It makes so many of us ashamed. How difficult it is to write, to paint, to criticise and to collect well and wisely!

Yours ever,

GERALD KELLY

---

[1]. *Evening News*, 11 January 1949.

(5)

Munnings's membership of The Other Club gave him easy access to Churchill's ear and an invitation to lunch at Chartwell enabled him to press his intention of securing Academic recognition of Churchill's amateur talent as a painter. That intention was reinforced by an inspection of the garden studio, which he found 'stacked with paintings of open-air themes, more than I have ever seen in any other studio'. The canvases, he noticed, were all of the same size, 30 inches × 25 inches, and he at once saw the explanation, that Churchill's painting motto as in other affairs was Danton's *l'audace, et encore l'audace*, and that his zest could not comfortably express itself on a smaller surface.

It was in no such spirit that Sir Winston finally agreed to submit what he called 'a number of my poor daubs' to the Royal Academy. He told Munnings: 'I don't trust you a yard, Alfred. You'll pass them because they are mine. Unless you treat me as an outsider and put my work in with the rest to go before the Selection Committee, I don't wish to send in.' His unjaded appetite for new satisfactions presumably made his resistance more brittle than it was when, for example, a short time previously he was asked to sanction a one-man show of his pictures. 'I couldn't think of it,' he said. 'They're just sketches,' and dismissed the idea. When, later, it was taken up in another quarter it was a great public success. As for the Royal Academy, it was Munnings who persuaded him to think more favourably of his chances of acceptance there.

In celebration of Churchill's election as Royal Academician extraordinary, Munnings gave a dinner-party for him in the Assembly Room. Afterwards, the guests toured the galleries where the summer exhibition was in progress. By 11.30 Munnings, gouty and tired, slipped away to a settee. At midnight only three of the guests remained, including Sir Winston, then seventy-five. From his resting-place Munnings called out: 'Winston, when the hell are you going home?' The reply was quiet and admonitory. 'I shall go home when I feel like it.'

CHAPTER 19

A Speech that Made History

(1)

Two great wars considerably reduced the scale of the London 'season', so long a commanding fixture of the social calendar. It is certainly not now of high importance in the lives of as many people as it was in the late Victorian years or those of Edward VII's brief reign. The Royal Academy annual banquet remains as one of its surviving great occasions, remarkable in that it is attended only by men and those representative of all the arts and most of the talents. Always held on the Wednesday evening before Private View day, it continues to be reported by the newspapers as an event of the year, while ever since the 1920s the speeches of the chief guests have been regularly broadcast by the B.B.C.

Like the newspaper readers, the listening millions are not infallibly entertained by what is annually relayed to them from the glittering top table at Burlington House, however eminent the names rolled out by the duty announcers. Royal Academy banquet speeches, delivered by spokesmen for the Government, the armed forces and the arts, too often over the years communicated a dullness that was popularly assumed to be a condition of the institution rather than of individuals. It need hardly be said that there have been notable exceptions.

In 1934 the assembled company was startled when Adrian Stokes R.A. interrupted the speech being made by the then Prime Minister, Ramsay MacDonald. It ranked as a sensation in the newsrooms of Fleet Street and made a considerable stir in the world outside. Significantly, in view of subsequent happenings, Munnings kept a London evening paper's report of the

episode and had it framed, as if it was an important souvenir. He
hung it in the room used by the Secretary of the R.A.

The Royal Academy banquet of 1939 was the last to be held
for ten years, the longest lapse, it was said, since the days of
Reynolds. Two years after the end of the Second World War
Sir Winston Churchill, as a newcomer to the Academy, said to
Munnings, who was still President: 'You must start those
famous dinners again.'

Munnings was by then beginning to tire of the presidency,
an indication of the state of his health and of his growing impatience with the more liberal policy being pursued by the
newer members of the Council. The gout attacks were severe,
some of the worst of his life, disabling him for weeks at a time.
The lumbar jab that had brought him relief that he thought
magical in 1945 'did not always act the same'. He fancied that
he had found a remedy in pineapple. Then he dieted strictly on
cheese, carrying little dried bits of it in his pocket and taking them
at intervals like pills.

Churchill's suggestion was reinvigorating. Munnings wrote:
'It stirred something within me.' He resolved to remain in office
one more year and to be instrumental in renewing the long
succession of banquets. He made a pact with the new honorary
Royal Academician that he would 'come and make a speech'.
Churchill agreed, saying: 'Let's have a rag,' drawing on the
vernacular, no doubt, of his past as a young officer of Hussars. 'A
good party – that's the thing,' said Munnings, who, seized with
the idea, impulsively proposed the innovation of a toastmaster
'in full splendour'. Lamb, the Secretary, was not a man of sudden
new enthusiasms. 'We've never had a toastmaster in my thirty
years here,' he said. Munnings declared, 'Well, we're going to
have one this time,' and entered into the project with all the
liveliness that he had shown as the organiser of studio parties
long ago. He was seventy-one.

Speeches by the Archbishop of Canterbury, the Duke of
Gloucester, the Lord Chief Justice, Sir Winston Churchill and
Lord Montgomery, did not confer exceptional distinction on the
Royal Academy banquet of 1949. It was when the toastmaster
announced, 'Pray silence for Sir Alfred Munnings, Knight

Commander of the Victorian Order, President of the Royal Academy,' and Munnings rose to acknowledge the toast to the institution of which he was the head that the occasion changed into a reverberating event.

Dressing for the banquet in the President's private room, he had said to Hubbacks, the resident attendant: 'I'm going to say a few things tonight that some of them won't like.' He had already hinted to one or two of his R.A. colleagues that Churchill privately supported his intention of 'having a go' at the new art trends to which the Academy was opening its portals in those post-war years.

Transgressing rules of taste as well as of form, his was the first presidential speech at an annual banquet to be interrupted by dissenting voices. They were incited by his references to Cézanne, Matisse and Picasso as 'foolish daubers' whose influence had defiled the British tradition. More interruptions came when he spoke no less slightingly of the Arts Council and the Tate Gallery. Two objectors were escorted from the room by uniformed Academy servitors. Recalling the scene, a later President, Sir Albert Richardson, said: 'I could hardly believe that I was at a Royal Academy banquet. Nothing like it had happened there before', nor, it may be added, since.

In the unprecedented situation which he had created Munnings stood staunchly firm: 'I am President and have the right of the Chair'; and he continued to speak with undaunted sincerity if with faltering sensibility and logic. A stormy atmosphere outside matched the tensions within. Raindrops of a heavy passing shower fell on the tables from the glass roof, setting the candle flames spluttering amid the silverware. Munnings seemed not to notice them. 'Violent blows of nothing . . . foolish drolleries shown to the public . . . all this affected juggling . . . highbrows who think they know more about art than those of us who paint the pictures. . . .' As always on that topic, he spoke from the heart, so fully charged with feeling that parts of what he said touched incoherency. Because he mismanaged the word 'innumerable' a number of radio listeners thought that he was drunk. The assumption slandered him. Sir Cecil Wakeley, then President of the Royal College of Surgeons, was with him im-

'The River Box at Thorrington Street, near Stoke-by-Nayland'.

'A Summer Evening: Cliveden'.

mediately after the banquet and still remembers his abstemious-
ness on that occasion. He was in fact recovering from his latest
attack of gout. Sir Cecil had been supplying him with glucose,
then hard to get, as part of the treatment.

Others who heard the speech over the air were offended by his
arrogant petulance; a few by his intellectual brashness, to them
unseemly in the presiding genius of a venerated body. Sacks
full of letters showed that a great majority approved what he
said and the force with which in part he said it. Obviously, many
people experienced an exhilarating mental kinship with one
who, speaking from a place of authority, put into words what they
felt and could not express.

Some of their reactions were telephoned before Churchill,
who followed Munnings in the toast list, sat down. They
heralded the heaviest load of calls that the B.B.C. switchboards
had dealt with for some time. The telephone at the Chelsea
studio rang unceasingly the next day. Uplifted by the immense
public response, he strode through the Academy galleries
exultant in tone and bearing, his jacket pockets stuffed with
telegrams.

A private hearing of the recorded speech was arranged for
him at Broadcasting House. Sitting attentively in a listening-
room, he chuckled with glee, as if every word he had uttered
was a surprise to him. 'Did I say *that?*' he asked continually,
and slapped his thigh with pleasure, saying 'What a go!'

(2)

The newspapers gave the speech priority space, bringing him
cabled approbation from well beyond the British bounds, from
France, Holland, Finland, the United States, South Africa. The
letter-flow grew daily into a flood that did not abate for a month.
Munnings read every letter and printed a representative
selection, for and against, in his reminiscent third volume, *The
Finish.* The Royal Academy had never had such a press in its 186
years, not even during its exciting 'problem picture' phase of
the '90s. A comment from a letter written to him by 'an old
woman of eighty', of Sanderson Road, Newcastle-on-Tyne,

found permanent lodgment in his mind: 'Some people murder people, others murder art.' He received with the same degree of satisfaction a quotation from a novel by Dornford Yates, in which a character is made to say, after visiting an exhibition of modern art: 'This filth is produced by failures and foisted on fools.'

There was the commendation of Lionel Edwards R.I.: 'Well, done, A.J.! I was delighted to see you had a crack at them. The fault is not so much the young artists' as the critics', whose words these foolish youngsters take as gospel.' He was particularly gratified by a letter, signed Jack Shingfield, of the East Anglian Divisional Office of the Transport and General Workers' Union. 'You will doubtless be surprised to receive support from such a quarter. I am sure you have the support of all who want truth, decency and beauty, as against vulgarity, pretence, laziness and licence.' Lord Dunsany wrote to suggest that as a result of the speech, 'sanity's tottering throne will be steadied'.

A communication of another kind brought him a discomfiture that he had not foreseen. It was a sequel to his use of Churchill's name in his derogatory reference to Picasso. Churchill telegraphed a private protest the day after the banquet. Munnings showed it to Hugo Wortham, 'Peterborough' of the *Daily Telegraph*, who disclosed that the telegram had conveyed Churchill's displeasure 'in unmistakable terms'. When Wortham asked Munnings how he would reply, the answer was 'the most defiant snort ever delivered in the direction of Sir Winston'. It was repeated when Munnings heard that several British art-gallery directors had sent an open letter of regret to Matisse and Picasso. He was mildly put out by Churchill's rebuke. Realising that he had offended by giving publicity to what had been a private joke between them, he admitted: 'Maybe I did go too far.'

He had gone further than any other President of the Royal Academy in bringing art controversy into millions of homes where the names of Picasso and Henry Moore had never been heard. As for Sir Winston Churchill's opinion on the main issue, he had stated it personally to the present biographer three years before: 'Modern art,' he said with solemn directness, 'is deluding the people.'[1] Within a few days of the Royal Academy *furore*, a one-time leader of the surrealist movement, Chirico, proclaimed at a luncheon of the Royal Society of British Artists his conviction that 'the practice of camouflaging lack of talent arose from the break with the tradition of good painting'. There was also tangential satisfaction for Munnings in Sir Thomas Beecham's concurrent declaration that 'modern music is not only dead but thrice damned'.

Extravagant as Munnings was in his attitude to the introspective art that roused him to his worst excesses of opinion, he was also extravagantly misunderstood. Behind his agitated, indiscriminate and often ineffectual utterances there were prejudices as firmly rooted in integrity as in tradition. He was intolerant not of every new manifestation in art, but of the shams and falsities associated with some of them and particularly of the pretensions of artists who had never 'served their time', as he so sedulously had, who sought the overnight reputation and fashionable *réclame*. That any artist should aspire to success without seriously studying and working for it was to him a kind of blasphemy, the breaking of a natural law. He loudly approved the dictum of Mencken, the American critic, who said that 'any lout who puts on a smock, and a palette on his thumb can call himself an artist'. Munnings never doubted that 'the easier painting is to a man, the worse his work will be'.

His pocket-books were filled with a myriad drawings of trees, twigs, leaves, clouds, with notes on the anatomy and movement of horses, all lovingly and endlessly studied. Round the walls and on the floors of the studios at Dedham and Chelsea were stacked scores and sometimes hundreds of sketches in oils and water-colours, many repeating the same theme because for him the life of the artist was the longest apprenticeship of all.

He was so inflamed by what he called 'the pretentious rubbish' on view in an art gallery near St James's Square that he visited it a second time, taking with him an Assistant Commissioner of Police. Afterwards, at the Athenaeum, he was heard saying:

1. See: *A Maypole in the Strand* by Reginald Pound (London: Ernest Benn Ltd., 1948).

'He was in full uniform too. Gave that fellow' – the proprietor of
the gallery – 'a shock, I can tell you!'

(3)

'Thank God, I shall not be here next year,' he had brusquely
told his Royal Academy banquet audience. The presidency had
become a burden no longer to be borne. He reiterated his
sentiment that 'to be in London with my heart in the country
is not easy', and gave substance to it by spending more time at
Dedham than he had been able to do for five years. The sight of
a start at the July meeting at Newmarket hardened his resolve
to be free of official trappings and worries. 'To my own profession and purpose – seeing visible beauty; the grouping, the
movement – colour, all dependent on the lighting, the sky.
Orange satin, cerise-and-white, blue-and-yellow, emerald green
– a large field, waiting, waiting, regrouping.' The old passion
was on him again, compelling him to describe in words what
the brush could not transfix.

'. . . . no living soul could write in words or music the songs of
the skylarks, or even the gentle sound of the wind. A thousand
tiny flowers grow on the course, and, pacing slowly ahead,
looking down, one sees myriads of infinitesimal blooms
patterned about as stars in their systems in the sky at night.
Here and there a swarm of tiny blossoms, like heliotrope dust
thrown on the grass. Like the songs above, and the sound of
the wind, the sweet scents of the air are beyond description.'[1]

He scribbled his pleasure on race-cards, where other men
pencilled bets, never an indulgence of his for all that he had
access to 'information' of the coveted kind. Among his letters
are many such cards filled with intimations of the beauty he
perceived in earth and sky. 'Marguerites and pink vetch sway-
in the breeze . . . unceasing song of skylarks . . . yellow coltsfoot
is my particular cushion today . . . wind blowing through tall
seeding grasses, stems as graceful and strong as the spines of
wing feathers shed by rooks.'

1. *The Finish.*

At Dedham that summer he walked often by the river again, experiencing anew the joys denied him by his official life in London. He wrote on a card of invitation to Luton Hoo: 'I was in the meadow adjoining the river and on the sloping bank I lay down. Happier by far than I have been these twenty years. The reason being that I had sought and found the spot I must find at the moment or die. So satisfying were my surroundings that it is impossible to express my feelings. I could only sigh and groan with pleasure. Downstream I could see the roofs and chimneys of Stoke-by-Nayland through the trees. Behind me a row of willows and a large poplar tree which rustled *crisply*, making its own separate sound.'

His 'moment in Arcady,' as he called it, was shattered by a screaming jet aircraft, 'a blasted thing that shook the dust off Dedham church roof', and set his thoughts running on the desecrated English scene that he knew too well: 'cluttered with motorcoaches', deprived of life-giving humus, 'poisoned by artificials', its hedges grubbed up to make way for 'the almighty combine', its horizons tangled 'in the grid', its lanes no longer safe for children to walk in. Rural humanity was changing too. The higglers who drove through the villages of his boyhood with crates of cackling hens were long-distance lorry-drivers now, the white-aproned orange-sellers at Bungay races were dodgem-car 'barkers' at the fair. Village schools were becoming as obsolete as the village pump.

He proudly played his part in little local acts of reclamation; for example, saving the willow-trees by the river between Dedham and Flatford. 'You should see them now, all along the stream – saved for years, the old stems putting out new tops,' gratefully recorded, as if he had been permitted a hand in a miracle. 'Willows, trimly pollarded, give a look of decency and finish to a valley.' He hurled his slings of scorn at the Suffolk Preservation Society. He protested against the choice of pictures for Essex County Council schools. He spat his contempt at the Central Electricity Board's siting of sub-stations and pointed the finger of derision at an agricultural policy that denuded England of sheep. To an East Anglian farmer friend who shared his fears, he penned the lines:

Long after all of us are dead
This teeming population
Will breed and multiply and spread
And end in desolation.

Regardless of their future fate,
They'll go on breeding faster,
Until at last they will create
Their ultimate disaster.

I see them seeking for a crust
With keen and hungry eye;
But you'll be dead and turned to dust,
Thank God! And so shall I.

The more deeply he felt the menace of the twentieth century, the more wilfully he asserted the characteristics he had in common with the eighteenth century, less with the urbane Sir Joshua than with George Morland, who said that he would rather paint dogs than dukes. Walking the pavements of Piccadilly on his rarer visits to town, he still looked as if he had a horse tethered round the corner, his nose beaked over the lemon-yellow muffler, his eye still as alert as a sparrow's. Meeting you unexpectedly, he would lean back to inspect you as if he were appraising a half-finished picture on its easel. Like many artists, he habitually held his left arm as if it bore an invisible palette. The explosive temper, which could make even his victims smile with tolerant regard and some with affection, was touched off by so many aspects of modern life as to seem often theatrical if never insincere. In part, it was due to awareness of his own intellectual limitations, which were severe.

He was still capable of a sensitive curiosity far beyond that of the average mind; and he still used the word 'wonderful' as if it was mint-new in his vocabulary. He could be overcome – it is not an exaggeration – by the beauty of the veining in a stone picked up at random on a walk. He telephoned the editor of the *Evening News*, Guy Schofield, begging him to leave his desk at once to join him at the Arts Club. 'I've something wonderful to show you.' When later in the day Schofield called at the Club, Munnings drew from his pocket-book a dried beech-leaf: 'Just look at it – all those intricate veins – see how the smaller ones run into even more tiny ones! Did you ever see anything like it? Wonderful! And then they tell us there's nothing left in nature to paint!' The living tree could captivate his attention. 'Imagine the perfection of it – all that harmony of green breathing life!' In one such moment of enthusiasm he declared that trees were more important than animals.

(4)

He went back to the Rank racing establishment near Salisbury in September 1949, to paint Prince Regent, his first racehorse portrait since the war. 'What could be better? A haven of rest, lots of horses, a beautiful house to live in', Druid's Lodge, where he had spent part of the fateful summer of 1940. On the first evening of his return visit he took his usual lonely walk, returning in a twilight that made him 'want to write poetry'.

The next morning he was in the grip of a new and terrible attack of gout. 'It is impossible to describe my misery.' He hobbled out to the stables on two sticks and, in obvious distress, forced himself to do preliminary studies of the horses as they were brought out. As the attack progressed, he could not even stand up; moreover, it affected his sight. Bags of hay were brought for him to rest his feet on as he sat in a chair, a painting posture that was altogether hateful to him who had always emulated the heroic stance of Sir Joshua at the easel. Thus a week went by and he had accomplished nothing. 'I suffered the torments of the damned'. He conjectured that 'the mental strain of painting a thoroughbred in the sun, or on a grey day, irritates the whole system', paving the way for an onslaught of his hereditary enemy.

His long specialised experience had never finally subdued his anxieties. 'Painting racehorses drives one to despair, apart from the gout,' he wrote. 'Again and again I have decided to leave it alone, to give up.' The prospect of the visit to Druid's Lodge had renewed his confidence. 'I was ready and fresh to face anything, to paint horses, to ride, to walk on the Downs, to see the rising moon, to get glimpses of the Avon valley.' Instead, he had been laid low, crippled. 'An artist needs to be well to do his best', a modest postscript to days of suffering that, he wrote, had caused him 'the deepest despair'.

Munnings to Nevile Wallis, art critic of *The Observer*:

Castle House,
Dedham, Essex.
13 November '49.

My dear Wallis, I'm glad you're better and now I will, in a few words, try and impress on you the position you hold . . .

By sound writing on art you should attract fresh readers to the paper. Do not hestitate to write sense on pictures.

It stands to reason that if the artists of the past had not painted for the people there would be none to follow on. Only until just lately in art history have these fools appeared who think that they can paint any rubbish and that the public has to be lectured and written into a new way of looking at art. . . . You do know something of English sentiment and painting. Roll it out, sir!!

That picture from the Ashmolean, now at Glasgow, by Holman Hunt is a masterpiece and as brilliant as on the day he finished it. What an achievement compared say with an Ivon Hitchens.

Start on that foolish stuff [modern sculpture] in the Park at Battersea and on the poor stuff now in the Tate – on the rotten colour of the walls there in some of the galleries. See how 'The Lily Pond' by Monet looks blue on pale yellow. Look at the two lovely Tissots on the ghastly *red wall*. Go and say what you think and don't be apologetic.

Room after room is wasted with ordinary rubbish or, rather, silly rubbish. Do, after looking at the P.R.B. [Pre-Raphaelite Brotherhood], go straight into the Courtauld and look at that Cézanne with the curved tree-trunk. After all, what the hell does it say to the man in the street? It is *paint* and the niggling of an incompetent mind. *Experiment* is the curse. The word has been hatched lately and everybody uses it. Turner – if you like to use his name; there are plenty of others; he is not the only one – didn't *Experiment*. He tried to get what he wanted and learned all from those before him with Nature thrown in. Read Burns again, if he is in your library.

Perhaps the most pitiable thing of all is inane vanity satisfied with half achievement, revelling in the fool's supper of worthless praise. Don't encourage the inane vanities. Cross them out and don't go piddling about saying: 'Well, who knows? Perhaps there's something in it!'

False, partial Fame has stood, blaring on her trumpet in the market place, proclaiming now this, now that, as the greatest name in art and, by God, she is still at it and yet how stands the account? Taking reputations at their current worth, their market price, both in amount of recognition and coin, and turning a deaf ear to the din of the mountebank's trumpet, it stands simply thus – the two greatest English names are those of men whose art was formed and whose glory was built in the 18th century, namely, my lad, Reynolds and Gainsborough.

Yours to serve,
ALFRED MUNNINGS

(3)

'I've done. Clear. No more troubles.' He was writing immediately after resigning the presidency in December 1949. Gerald Kelly R.A. reigned at the Royal Academy in his stead: 'my good successor – fresh – strong – full of beans.'

Having stepped down from the official pinnacle of his profession, Munnings set about the technically distracting task of writing his autobiography, which ultimately revealed more about his period than about himself, in several of its aspects a valuable social record. Unlike the masters, Rembrandt and Van Gogh, for example, he had never felt a compulsion to paint a self-portrait, except for one or two jaunty sketches of himself at work. His face did not index tempestuous passions, buffeting reversals of fortune, or lonely moral grandeur. Self-portraits of Munnings at various ages would have recorded too few facial changes to be interesting. His three successive reminiscent volumes, *An Artist's Life*, *The Second Burst* and *The Finish*, disregarding structural form and chronology, are notebooks for an autobiography that he was not equipped to write. 'Lord, keep my pen in some order!' he groaned as he proceeded along his erratic writing course. Effusive, and deficient in emotional discipline, he had not the means to fulfil his purpose of 'forestalling anyone who might tell strange things about me when I am departed'. Discussing the project with Guy Schofield, the Fleet Street editor whose attention and advice he could always command, he confided: 'I cannot tell the truth.'

While never invoking his secret self, he succeeded in recapturing in his books much of the glamour of his career as a successful painter and in communicating the enviable gusto with which it was lived. His imagination unfolded only in the aura of a past in which candlelight gleamed on old port, graciousness abounded, and the sun shone without benefit of science. His surest response was to physically realised experience. It made for readability if for no more than surface truth.

He wrote to Sir Desmond MacCarthy, who had reviewed the first volume of his autobiographical trilogy, *An Artist's Life*: 'What a memory you have! Of course Lutyens was with us when we sang *Julia*,' the ballad Munnings had composed for a Christmas party just before the First World War. He wrote out some of the verses in his letter to MacCarthy:

When the March floods had all done their flooding,
And the meadows with daisies were white;
And the dear little April buds budding
My days were all happy and bright!
Happy and bright with Julia – with Julia – with Julia!
Happy and bright with Julia,
With Julia ages ago. . . .

I go back in life's early pages
Since time has been flying so fast,
To a winter time in the dark ages,
And I think of the long buried past.

The long buried past with Julia – with Julia – with Julia!
The long buried past with Julia,
With Julia ages ago!

He mentioned in the letter: 'The volume I'm finishing may be better. Not sure.'

CHAPTER 20

'Dealers? I Can't Stand Them!'

(1)

IT is commonly and erroneously believed that every Royal Academician has the right to send in six pictures for the annual summer exhibition and that they are necessarily accepted and put on view to the public. The right to submit six pictures is not coupled with a right to assume that they will be hung. The Hanging Committee is free to use its discretion and on occasions has used it. In 1935 Stanley Spencer A.R.A. was surprised and hurt when the Hanging Committee discarded two of his six pictures, one of them a study of St Francis which was afterwards widely shown elsewhere. He promptly resigned from the Academy, trying unsuccessfully to secure the immediate return of his four remaining pictures which had been hung.

On succeeding Munnings in the presidency fourteen years later, Gerald Kelly at once set to work to secure Spencer's reinstatement. It was accomplished at a General Assembly of the Royal Academy on 17 January 1950. Munnings was present and as the vote was unanimous he must have at least technically concurred in it. He had never liked Spencer as man or artist and he had misgivings which he communicated to Kelly, who replied to him on 23 January: 'I don't think Spencer will do the Academy any harm. He is almost uncannily skilful and a lovely craftsman.' More gratifying to Munnings was a remark made during the election proceedings by a prominent Academy member, 'Spencer doesn't paint. He knits,' quoted joyfully by Munnings, as if it was the quintessence of wit.

In May 1950 Spencer's 'The Resurrection: Port Glasgow' was bought by the Chantrey Bequest. Kelly was also active in that

matter. The picture roused Munnings's dislike of Spencer and his
work to passionate hatred of both. He denounced the figures in it
as 'barrel-like human beings, stark, pseudo-comic; hands like
bunches of bananas'. Kelly, who in his letter of January 23 had
asked Munnings to write more often, 'because I am in need of a
few chuckles', also fell under the shadow, his pro-Spencer
attitude displeasing Munnings.

Hardening Munnings's animosity to Spencer was his discovery that Spencer, whose public reputation rested largely on
his preoccupation with religious themes, had done certain
paintings that might be considered pornographic. Munnings
resolved to lay hands on them. They were in the custody of one
of the smaller London art-dealers who had bought them from a
collector. Spencer had never intended them to be circulated,
either privately or otherwise, and it was a mystery to him how
they had passed into other hands. It was the dealer who informed
Munnings of their existence. When Munnings saw them he was
disgusted. He contrived to obtain photographic copies, it is said
by misrepresenting his purpose in borrowing the originals
from the dealer.

According to a well-known artist who is still with us, the
paintings demonstrated the peculiar tensions of Spencer's
private life. Others who saw them thought them of no more
than anatomical interest and in no sense morbidly objectionable.
Spencer's brother Gilbert referred to them as 'the expressions
of one who never hesitated to state clearly every facet of life as
he saw it'.

Determined to expose Spencer, Munnings took the photographic copies of the paintings to show to the then Dean of
Westminster, whose support he hoped to secure for a moral
crusade against Spencer. Members of the Athenaeum have an
arrangement with the United Services Club opposite, whereby
they use the latter club at week-ends. It was there that Munnings
found the Dean, who said that he was surprised less by the
pictures than by Munnings's choice of venue in which to display
them to him. Pursuing Spencer's downfall with the grim intent
of a Cromwellian zealot, Munnings then showed the copies
of the paintings to a police inspector at Newmarket, of all

places, apparently hoping that a prosecution would follow.

There was subsequent private discussion between a prominent member of the Royal Academy and high legal authority in Whitehall. No formal steps were taken and probably none was contemplated. That Munnings could have emerged creditably from the *cause célèbre* which he seemed recklessly bent on provoking was unlikely. His hatred of Spencer was largely temperamental, an antipathy that became enmity when his East Anglian puritanism was involved. His imagination had conceived Spencer's genitalia studies to be not only an affront to the decencies but a degradation of art and the glorious gifts that graced it. He was astonished when Sir Gerald Kelly accused him of 'caddishness' in that he might have brought the Royal Academy into disrepute. For his part, Sir Gerald never doubted that '"A.J.'s" better side easily outweighed his worst'.

The episode was closed when the Council of the Royal Academy, after considering the matter, recorded a minute expressing sympathy with Spencer. From then on Munnings was silent about Spencer, who in due course received a knighthood. He continued to be critical of newly-elected members of the Royal Academy, but of Spencer he spoke no word. The clash between them supplied the theme of a play televised by the B.B.C. in 1960.

(2)

With more time for letter-writing he kept in touch with a residue of friendly correspondents left over from the immense post-banquet mail. One of them was a Canadian cowhand, Harry Backhouse, of the Ranchmen's Club, Calgary, whose pals, he wrote, 'wonder how the hell I come to be corresponding with toffs like you'. From the same quarter Munnings received the possibly unexpected professional comment: 'I'm not such a tremendous admirer of Stubbs. He couldn't make the wind blow and he never put the sunshine into his horses' coats as Ben Marshall did.'

A letter from Churchill, dated 24 September 1950, implied absolution for the lapse in taste of the previous year by addressing

him as 'My dear Alfred'. Sir Winston was pleased to know
that Munnings would paint Colonist II, the racehorse which
had carried his colours first past the post in three successive races
thus far. He hoped that Munnings would allow him 'to pay you
your usual commission', just as he himself expected, he wrote,
to be paid for his books. The letter ended with the hope that
Munnings would be present at the next Other Club dinner, which
was on 26 October. 'I am taking the Chair and will have something to say about the loss we have sustained in the death of our
famous Jan Smuts.' The last time that Smuts had been at a dinner
of The Other Club he had asked Munnings to recite his ballad
of seventeen verses entitled 'The Chef', written after his stay at
Baron Robert de Rothschild's château near Chantilly, thirty
years before:

> My story is sad with an ending bad;
>   Its moral may help to show
> That taking an art too much to heart
>   Will probably lay you low. . . .

Munnings to Sir Winston Churchill:

> Castle House,
> Dedham.
> 30 September 1950

My dear Sir, Of course I got your letter – the most wonderful
letter I ever received in my life – written, I take it, on your
way to see Colonist run at Ascot.

I was there, as I always am, watching you and the horse
after the race, and you spoke to me there, which I shall
remember always.

I saw Colonist start at the first Newmarket October
meeting. Had you looked last Saturday, you would have seen
two figures by the course between the Stands and the five-
furlong post – my wife and self. We had seen the horse pass
close to us on his way out across the Heath, and we had seen
him pass close to us on the return journey, leading the other
two – ears pricking, his wall eye intent on the ultimate end,

galloping on with perfect action. What a horse! What a hind leg, what hocks! I could paint him with my eyes shut.

I do not paint horses with races ahead, or when the late autumn gives them a coat like a bear. He will be a picture in the spring. Never part with him. You might have bought a thousand worse steeds for millions. This one has done you proud.

Until Thursday.

Yours sincerely.

A. J. MUNNINGS

Punctilio was ill-served on that occasion. Churchill inscribed his letter to Munnings as R.A. instead of K.C.V.O., P.P.R.A. (stamped proudly at the head of Munnings's notepaper). Munnings addressed his letter to Churchill: 'The Right Honourable Winston Churchill M.B.E.'

(3)

'No more great sporting pictures,' he told Frost and Reed[1] 'You've had my best. *The best was my wife on the grey*, for which you paid me a mere pittance. I always told you I could not go on. What a bloody firm!' He told Stanley Wade of that firm: 'See *you* writing a book!! Wait for the explosion of *An Artist's Life*! Desmond MacCarthy is reviewing it.' He wrote again the following month: 'Did I but run the print business what quick sales you'd have! However, this has nothing to do with American blunders and Chinamen in Korea. Has it, Sir Wade?'

Letters asking him to paint horses lay unanswered on his desk. He was 'fed up', his own words, 'with working for what will all go in taxes', rationalising his impatience by pretending, aloud, that he did not agree with the way the Government spent the money. 'If they'd do something for the land – yes – yes! But the —'s won't do it because they're a lot of townees and out of sympathy with everything but steel and concrete. Some of them have never seen a green hedge'. Out would come the large coloured silk handkerchief with a flourish of contempt

1. 22 October 1950.

Munnings as President of the Royal Academy.

'The Full River'.

that could be relied on to attract attention when his vituperation did not.

To some it seemed that his self-emphasis grew as his public eminence waned and that he exerted himself with theatrical bonhomie when opportunities came for him to stand again in the limelight. As the chief speaker at a Foyle's literary luncheon in December 1950, he behaved in conformity with the public image of him as a champion of sanity in art, but other Royal Academicians at the top table were not the only guests present who stared into their coffee cups as he held forth on 'the horrors' he had seen at the Tate Gallery the previous day. He had made notes during his visit to the Tate and expanded them into a chapter of invective for his final volume of reminiscences.

On 30 September 1951 he unveiled the L.C.C. plaque at Schomberg House, 82 Pall Mall, where the dying Gainsborough spoke his last memorable words to Reynolds after their bedside reconciliation: 'We are all going to heaven and Van Dyck is of the company.' An irate voice called out from a taxicab hindered by the gathering in the street: 'What on earth's going on here?' Incongruous laughter was raised when a woman was heard explaining, 'It's only Mr Attlee,' as the taxicab moved on.

That autumn Munnings was a guest, with his wife, of Lord and Lady Manvers at Thoresby Park in the Dukeries. 'Nearing Thoresby, our road ran through Sherwood Forest, between groves of ancient oaks – mighty relics of the past, six or eight hundred years old. Life, thought I, is too short to see and know our beloved England. . . .' At the great mansion he had the pleasure of 'discovering' a Hogarth picture, 'Ladies Picking Fruit', 'hanging high in an upstairs passage'. He wrote reflectively: 'Thus do treasures hang unseen, though safe and unborrowed, on the walls of many a large house, whilst owners brave the never-ceasing attacks of taxation – daring to live in a home left them by ancestors!'

Invited to Welbeck Abbey by the Duchess of Portland: 'In a long subterranean gallery were hanging eight huge canvases by Snyders. Forgotten and uncared for, these mighty designs of a famous painter told their story of the Chase in the dim light. . . . Contemplating them, I stood transfixed – filled with sadness and regret that such works were allowed to go into decay.'

In the winter of 1951–2 the Council of the Royal Academy invited him to give two lectures, one on Stubbs, the other on Constable, in the lecture hall of the Royal Institution in Albemarle Street. It was a new kind of challenge to his competence and renown: 'I've never attended a lecture. I know nothing about lecturing'. But no one could have been more eager to acquit himself well in an unaccustomed role. On the subject of the Stubbs lecture he wrote to Humphrey Brooke, whose appointment as the new Secretary of the Royal Academy he wholeheartedly approved: 'It was through old Stubbs that I grasped the idea of the man in a picture *holding the horse*. ALL was taught me by old Stubbs and others.' As the day of the lecture approached: 'Will you ask the great librarian [of the Royal Academy] what he has on Reinagle or Chalon or Barraud or Morland, or others of that ilk? They must be mentioned, if only to chuck my weight about.' There was a message for the President: 'Please thank him for the kind invitation to dinner on the night of the lecture and tell him I'd rather do it on an empty belly.'

Both lectures were a success, the most crowded, it was said, since Marconi spoke in that place in the early 1920s. More than 600 tickets were sold in advance. The lecture hall was packed; there were waiting queues. Munnings told Humphrey Brooke to pour half a bottle of gin into the water carafe. He sipped it throughout the lecture, with no noticeable effect. There is a tradition at the Royal Institution that lecturers walk on to the platform promptly at eight o'clock and leave it promptly at nine. Munnings observed the first part of that old ordinance. He not only flouted the second part of it but set up a record at the Royal Institution by speaking for nearly two hours at his first lecture, on Stubbs, whose name he did not mention until he had reached the end of the officially allotted time. He had touched, meanwhile, on a variety of subjects, including the shortage of studio space in Chelsea. The august exemplar of discursiveness on the lecture platform, Samuel Taylor Coleridge, could not have been more disdainful of his central theme than

Munnings, who then paused, leaned forward on his toes as if searching for a familiar face, and called out, 'Are you awake?' Violet?' to his wife. A roar of laughter was wider assurance and he went on to give a sparkling and instructive discourse on Stubbs.

His second lecture, on Constable, was judged the better performance. Constable himself had lectured from that platform on landscape painting 116 years before. A Suffolk miller's son of their own day saluting the genius of a Suffolk miller's son of the eighteenth century was a thoroughly English equation that drew fervent applause from an audience that may have welcomed also the opportunity of registering its disdain of cosmopolitan art. When it appeared that at last he had come to the end of his discourse, the audience made a general movement to leave, only to be checked by his loud command: 'Stop! Stop – there's one more thing I have to say'; and he kept them listening for a further quarter of an hour. During that time one old gentleman stood transfixed in his place, gazing intently at Munnings, his overcoat only half on.

Nearing sending-in day for the summer exhibition in 1952, Munnings wrote to Brooke: '*Gout, colds*, and the two Academy pictures interfered with finishing other works.' To complete his formal contribution of six pictures, he sought the loan of his 'Gipsy Life' from the Aberdeen Art Gallery: 'It is an honour for one's work to be in such a collection as that at Aberdeen'; and he was annoyed to find that the picture was being hung at the Royal Academy without acknowledgement of its source. 'For fifty years I've shown at the Academy and this is the first time I've borrowed a picture.'

(4)

His hands were beginning to look like those of one who has toiled too long. The mischief was of time as well as of gout; his right forefinger was permanently misshapen. He was worrying greatly about the eye that had borne its double burden for more than half a century. He was painting less and writing

more, encouraged by the demand for his first book, *An Artist's
Life*, with its significant omissions. Not all those who had
shown singular kindnesses to him in the past were happy to be
overlooked in a work commemorating so much fleeting if
more imposing acquaintance. As an author, he was a benefactor
of the printing trade, the bill for re-setting made necessary by
his afterthoughts running into several hundred pounds.

The books increased his correspondence and the demands
made upon him, straining his patience to the point at which
those who had some claim on it were brushed off with those
who had none. 'God Almighty – too many bloody letters,'
was his reply to the landlord of the Magpie at Harleston, one
of his old haunts of conviviality. Asked by the widow of his
first Norwich patron to sign her copy of *The Second Burst*, he
scrawled in reply: 'I have more to do than sign books for people.
Damn the book. I refuse to sign another.' He signed one with a
slight diminution of his irascibility for James Green, then of the
Bond Street Galleries: 'I inscribe this copy to an indescribable
art dealer, a plausible enthusiast. If he ever reads this book he
may discover that it is more difficult to paint a slight sketch than
to sell a world's masterpiece.'

A letter from the secretary of the Ewell Art Group, Surrey,
was more favoured than most. Munnings put it aside to be kept.
It reported that two entries of 'modern stuff' were submitted
for the Group's winter exhibition. 'When we opened, the third
person to pass the pictures was a woman with a child. The child,
on seeing the first of the two "modern horrors", burst into
screams and had to be carried out.' Another correspondent who
struck the right note was the senior English master at a leading
public school. 'I used to be one of those "intellectuals", parlour
Socialist, *New Statesman*, and all that. And I really felt that I
ought to like the hideous works of Henry Moore and all the
rest of the bloody fools. I regret that this state of mind persisted
as late as five years ago, when – on the enticement of a friend – I
took to riding at the age of forty-five. It altered my whole outlook' – a confession that Munnings may have been reckless in
taking at its face value. 'Another good one,' he wrote in the
margin and had copies made and circulated to his Academy

colleagues, whether by permission of the writer of the letter is not recorded.

Munnings to A. Egerton Cooper:

> Castle House,
> Dedham,
> Colchester.
> 29 May 1953

NO MORE of these things for me, my dear fellow [opening an art exhibition in Chelsea]. They interfere with all I try to do. Life is too short and gets shorter each day.

Open it yourself – grand idea! Paint carmine on your nose, sir!

My God! I went out in a car yesterday into Suffolk. Was left at a SPOT at 11.30 and was met again at Kersey Church 4.30.

Arcadia, sir! Buttercups, may trees in full bloom, and a gentle flowing stream meandering on its course, and all the rest.

Damn all openings of shows.

Too old.

God bless.

A. J. MUNNINGS

After seeing a picture that he had long lost sight of, painted by him in Cornwall, he wrote to E. J. Rousuck, Wildenstein's vice-president in New York: 'I was glad to see it (in tempera, Lamorna Brook). Anything from £20 to £40 in those days, just before the 1914 war.' He told Rousuck: 'I have masses of pictures, studies and hundreds of framed drawings both here, at Dedham and in my Chelsea home. But a sale results in no money and no pictures. Clients buy the latter the Government *takes* the first – *all* the money!'[1] He stressed the point again, writing to Rousuck, 7 August 1954: 'At the moment I am not anxious to make too much, as I am against painting for a wastrel Government.' Augustus John had told Rousuck that he preferred Munnings's horses to Stubbs's. Asked why, he replied: 'Better

1. 29 December 1953.

picture quality, groupings better.' It was a valuable 'quote' for a dealer in Munnings's work.

The death of an aged Norwich collector brought a number of early Munnings paintings on the market that year, the prices soaring high above those obtained for the Cotman water-colours in the same sale. He wrote to Rousuck: 'Those early works . . . I have no remembrance of them. They were bought at the sale in Norwich only 10 days ago – and now they are in New York! Amazing!!'

(5)

His relations with the dealers had more of awkwardness than ease in them. To him, the countryman, dealers were part of the vast complicated apparatus of city life which he disdained. He was well aware, but rarely acknowledged the fact, that Wilden-steins had done great things for his reputation and pocket by showing and selling his work in their New York galleries, as a result of which the international prices of his pictures were fixed at a high level.

'Why do you buy from dealers? I can't stand 'em,' he remarked to an American to whom he had just been introduced at Claridge's and who was showing what Munnings took to be purely æsthetic appreciation of his work. It may have been his worst *faux pas*. The American was Stephenson Scott, of the Fifth Avenue firm of Scott and Fowles, who were eminent enough to be Duveen's greatest rivals in the English Old Master market.

His trick of fabricating fancy names for the impresarios of art was intended to steer him comfortably between intimacy and aloofness. The then proprietor of the Bond Street Galleries often opened letters from Munnings beginning 'Dear Viscount Worcester Sauce.' His print adviser and publisher over many years, Stanley Wade of Frost and Reed, Bond Street, was ex-posed to the neutralising effect of 'Dear Sir Wade'. Oliver Brown of the Leicester Galleries was 'All-over' Brown. Many of Munnings's letters to the dealers opened without salutation and read like communiqués.

His habit of painting a subject in a dozen different ways was an asset to the dealers, who usually found buyers for all the pictures he let them have. His begrudging attitude to their function rarely troubled them. They were content to go on telling each other stories of his lurid language and bawdy humour. One of them still makes a point of contrasting his off-hand reception in Munnings's studio with the regal hospitality at Augustus John's.

Not all were prepared to tolerate his unprofessional conduct in disclosing prices and varying contracts. A leading London gallery suspended business with him because of his broken pledge to let them have a picture for which they had a waiting client. For one of his racing-start studies he accepted an offer from an overseas buyer. When the buyer came over to settle and collect, he was told by Munnings that the price had gone up from £350 to £600 as a result of other inquiries received. That figure agreed, he asked for time to enable the picture to be shown at the Royal Academy. When the buyer claimed the picture at the end of the summer exhibition, Munnings announced that he had sold it for £2,000

He could be equally obtuse in small dealings. A dealer who sold a drawing of his at the catalogue price of £50 asked him to sign it for the purchaser. 'In that case,' said Munnings, sitting down to add his signature to the work, 'the price will be £75', nor would he take a penny less. He had just been speaking about the rapacity of the Government and the futility of working at all.

He could still whip himself up into a frenzy over what had happened to him after the Leicester Galleries exhibition in 1947. It was a standing excuse for regarding the dealers as fair game for his temperamental perversities. Yet it was a dealer who wrote: 'I love him for all his good points, which never cease to warm one's heart.'[1]

1. Stanley Wade: *Pictures and Prints* (London: The Fine Art Trade Guild).

CHAPTER 21

Crowds at Burlington House

(1)

BATTLING with his infirmities, Munnings applied himself with extraordinary tenacity to the task of finishing a picture, begun about six years before, which he called 'Moving Up Under Starter's Orders, Newmarket' (Royal Academy, 1954). The canvas was one of the largest he had ever worked on, 48 × 90, demanding from him all his reserves of concentration and strength, a major effort at any time of his life. The picture was acquired for the collection of E. P. Taylor, the Canadian brewery magnate.

At a dinner party arranged at the Athenaeum so that Munnings and Taylor could meet, James Gunn asked Munnings's permission to use the Newmarket picture as a background for the portrait he was painting of Taylor. 'Of course,' said Munnings. Gunn then remarked, casually: 'I find painting a horse much easier than painting a man.' The recollection of another guest at the table, J. Mitchell Chapman, of Santa Monica, California, supplies the *dénouement*: 'That was the end of the dinner party!'

The dealer who had acted between Munnings and Taylor included the copyright in the document of sale. Munnings signed without noticing the clause. When Taylor had the picture reproduced as a Christmas card, Munnings worked himself up into a high state of indignation, threatening legal redress. Shown a copy of the contract with his signature, he shifted the focus of his anger to the quality of the reproduction, which he declared was ruinous to his reputation. After more threats of legal action he calmed down and resorted to his usual form of apology, laughing the matter off.

It was in similar company and in the same place that he ignored the civilities of picture buying and selling by naming the amount he received from the dealer. He apparently hoped to uncover the dealer's profit. In fact, the dealer concerned, one of the most respected in the London art market, had foregone a profit on that particular sale.

One of his last equine pictures, called 'Newmarket Incident: Runaway', was also shown at the summer exhibition of 1954. It was a 40 × 50 study of a racehorse that had broken away from the start, its jockey engaged in a silent, fiercely resolute struggle for control. The scene is an otherwise empty heath under an aloof sky that emphasises the private drama of the combat and the implacable will needed to resolve it. The perspiring brown of the horse, the yellow jacket of the rider, the sweeping green of the turf and the cold blue of the sky, are ingredients in a composition of classical severity that is the more impressive when one realises the conditions in which it was painted. He was seventy-six.

His eye was giving more trouble; the tear-duct was blocked. Rather than face the operation that was proposed, he gave thought to the possibility of submitting himself to a course of faith healing. His doctor found signs of cardiac disturbance. His right hand was no longer a precision instrument. He complained that his left thumb 'went dead' under the weight of his palette, a kind of infirmity he had not known before. Added to it was the indignity of being obliged to sit at his easel. The picture could only have been painted with the intensity of purpose implied in the jockey's handling of the horse; and the effort of completing it was probably a greater charge on 'A.J.'s' physical resources than he knew. Not long after finishing the work, which was reproduced in full colour in *The Connoisseur* for December 1960, he wrote to the purchaser, J. Mitchell Chapman: 'All's well, except that I'm ageing – 77 now – and you may not see me again.' He wrote also to E. J. Rousuck, of Wildensteins, New York: 'I've been under the weather lately – every damned thing and then gout. B. awful.' His right foot, he said, 'feels the size of a horse's thigh'.

He was still capable of sitting up late and 'talking his head off', as his old friend Tom Bodkin put it. 'Alfred was the life and soul of our little dinner party last evening at the Ladies' Annexe [of the Athenaeum Club],' Bodkin reported. 'He talked for an hour and a half – enormously entertaining. Then he slumped, suddenly. Deep furrows appeared on his brow. He seemed to become years older in just those few minutes.' Similar recessions of his vitality were noticed by Mrs Dod Proctor R.A., meeting him during her visits to London from Cornwall in those later years.

His uncertain health states largely explained his lack of interest in a proposal that he should paint Queen Elizabeth II, who, it was intimated, would be willing to sit to him for a horse-back picture. Official sources supplied him with twenty-four photographic studies of Her Majesty. He behaved as if he had privately decided that he could do no more commissioned work but did not wish it to be publicly known. There was also a suggestion that he should paint Foxhunter, the greatest show-jumper of the post-war years. Again Munnings did not stir himself.

(2)

In 1955 an exhibition of his work was the spring attraction at the Russell Cotes Art Gallery, Bournemouth; 'the most fascinating, most completely retrospective' show of its kind ever held there, according to the director, who somewhat ambiguously predicted that 'on free days, when the weather is wet, the exhibition is likely to be crowded.' Its success with the Bournemouth public may have helped to clinch a proposal being considered by the Council of the Royal Academy that a still more comprehensive exhibition of his work should be staged in the Diploma Gallery at Burlington House the following year. No previous President or past-President and only two R.A.s, Frank Brangwyn and Augustus John, had been thus honoured.

There was a firmly rising market in Munnings's work. He was paid £2,000, a dealer's price, for his 'Unsaddling A Winner at Epsom' from the 1955 Royal Academy. Later, it was understood to have been sold to an American buyer for £5,000. The same dealer paid £2,500 for his hunting picture called

'Who is the Lady?'. The proprietor of the Bond Street Galleries told him of his determination, 'no matter how long it takes', to deal in his work 'at the best prices'. Munnings wrote to him concerning a picture painted many years previously at Hackforth Grange in Yorkshire: 'All told in Vol. 2. Do read it and become *intelligent*', heavily underlined.

Receiving letters of protest from members of the public about certain exhibits in that summer's Academy, he wrote to Humphrey Brooke, the Secretary: 'Don't say here's that old bore Munnings again. Keep calm and read the enclosed – just an ordinary letter, one of *scores* expressing the same feeling. You yourself, I know, are a servant of the R.A. For all that, I don't agree that you are a *mere* servant, but a helpful and tactful observer and friend to us all and for us all and, above all, for the Academy itself and its *Traditions*. Letters that I get and things that are said of the R.A. to me personally by ordinary folk who make their yearly visits are upsetting. I would far rather take it easy, let things rip and say, "What does it matter?" and all the rest.'[1]

He was 'glad to hear' that Charles Wheeler [later Sir Charles Wheeler P.R.A.] had resigned from the Arts Council and 'sad to hear' that a director of Sotheby's had said that Picasso was the greatest artist whose work had passed through their auction-rooms. Munnings to Brooke: 'The P.R.A. needn't do all the work he does. BUT a sec. should think of naught else but the R.A.' An exhibition of his work at the MacNicol Gallery in Glasgow that autumn yielded results more gratifying to him as a publicist than as a harassed taxpayer.

Munnings to the Secretary of the Royal Academy:

Castle House,
9 January 1956

Dear Brooke, I was very glad to see your countenance on Saturday. Carry on for the glory of the R.A.

Do please write to Nevile Wallis, *The Observer* man. For he really is intelligent. With someone like yourself to talk with, I believe you could get him more into the *decisively*

1. 3 July 1955.

critical stage against a lot of this rot and *help* on the younger
and better painters who are left out. His notices *are* read,
though often he is inclined to wander on uselessly about the
muck we put up with until readers become *bewildered* and
begin to think there's something in it.

The Laughing Cavalier is one of the high lights of art and
must remain as an uplift; also that astonishing and more than
realistic view of Delft by Vermeer, only a great and gifted
genius could have done it. But where would such as he be
today in the running?

David Astor is a decent fellow. You'd get on with him. He
edits that paper, *The Observer*.

Yours in hopes,

ALFRED THE GREAT

He was ordered into the Ipswich and East Suffolk Hospital
that month as a cardiac asthma patient. Arriving in room 21 of
the private ward wing, he refused to unpack and undress, protesting that there was 'not much' wrong with him. When he
became agitated and announced that he was going home, he
had to be given a soporific injection.

Sister Henrietta Mills still laughs at her remembrance of
him, 'the muffler he *would* wear in bed, his nose plugs, his
language', which had shocked the nurses of Norwich nearly
sixty years before. She appeared in his room one morning with
a white-coated visitor whom Munnings took to be a new doctor.
Indicating that he wanted Munnings to undo his pyjama top,
he somewhat ostentatiously flourished a stethoscope and went
through the motions of a routine chest examination. It was a
joke not to be kept up long. The white-coated visitor's name
was Giles, well-known to readers of the *Daily Express*. He
then disclosed himself as a nephew of 'A.J.'s' old esteemed
manservant Cooper.

Munnings's unpredictable tempers, real and assumed, made
the probationer nurses hesitate before entering his room. He
declined the prescribed salt-free diet, saying 'Give it to the
dogs', which, in defiance of the rules, he had brought into the
ward. He was worrying about the hanging of the Diploma

Gallery exhibition of his works and the doctors decided, after three weeks' treatment, that he would be better off at home. Sister Mills said: 'We all missed him. We had never had anybody like him in Burton Wing before.' Soon he was writing to Humphrey Brooke: 'I'm half dead. My hand is dicky. Took lots of colchicum tablets which have cured my gout'. But the side-effects were unpleasant. He hiccuped for ten days.

Meanwhile Brooke was exerting himself to make the forthcoming Diploma Gallery tribute to Munnings the greatest possible success. At the same time he was busy with arrangements for the annual summer exhibition. Munnings was making heavy weather of both events. Particularly he was fussing about the likely effect of sunlight on his pictures in the Diploma Gallery. His temper was further ruffled by undertones of opposition to his intention of sending in a picture satirising the kind of art he despised.

Amid his preoccupations and irritations he cheerfully lent a hand to a wall-paper exhibition put on at Foyle's Art Gallery, Charing Cross Road, in February 1956. The organiser, representing Wall-Paper Manufacturers Ltd., had no personal claim on his time or attention but Munnings was ready and even eager to help, telephoning his encouragement from Dedham. Asked to choose his 'favourite wall-paper', he picked out a rosebud pattern. It reminded him, he said, of his childhood at the mill.

Concerning the Diploma Gallery exhibition, he wrote to Brooke: '*Please* get the skylights done over with muslin *at once*. The heat will be unbearable in May and June. Please, dear Secretary, don't get hotted up – just give orders and remember my poor old artist's temperament and that I painted them all. . . . You have taken no end of trouble. The R.A. must have poured out money and you can't let this happen – *what a blow*! Not for you but for the artist. Why do we all seek a north light? No painting can stand the sun. It becomes a joke, a skinned piece of paint on the canvas.'

He was compelled now to use a wheeled chair, a manifestation of invalidism that made him feel worse than he really was. It reduced his painting capacity but not the flow of his letters, which in 1956 became voluminous, with the Secretary of the Royal Academy as his chief correspondent. When he heard that James Gunn was to do a television introduction to the exhibition, he wrote to Brooke:

'Tell Gunn from me, all the change and variety is ready if an artist paints from Nature. Nature can give lovelier surprises than all abstractions – do tell him and show him page 329, Vol 2, where I'm writing of 'The Jay's Wing' at Bayonne by Durer. I quote Durer. Do read it to Gunn – 'I know not what beauty is; in truth Art resides in Nature, etc.

He must see it.

Nature has always beaten me, but all I've done that's any good is from Nature.'[1]

Making suggestions for hanging the exhibition, he affirmed: 'Too often have I been accused of using photographs, which, of course, I never have.' He begged that a drawing of 'one of my early loves – the girl playing the piano in Boswell's shop, a place full of antiques and eighteenth century pictures', should be given a place. 'She was a great local soprano singer. Alas, gone with the wind. And do hang old Ted Ellis. We used to go down and drink old port with him on a Saturday morning in amongst the antiques.' Unlike some who reach eminence, Munnings never forgot his day of small things. He urged Brooke to 'make use of the stairs' for a display of his Caley's chocolate posters of long ago. The stairs reminded him, he said, 'of those I had to climb since I was 14 when I began my apprenticeship', and led him to recall also: 'Believe me or not, most of the designs for Caley's, etc., were lithographed on the polished stone by me and the colours on them too, generally 3 or at most 4.' He was depressed by his inability to supervise the hanging of his pictures, ending his letter: 'And here I wish you well. I also wish that I were again vigorous, young and active like you. God bless.'[2] His wife wrote privately to the P.R.A., Sir Albert Richardson: 'Dr Becket has told me that he must be very quiet and *not* get excited. He has already had two set-backs.[3]

1. March 1956.
2. March 1956.
3. 30 March 1956.

(3)

The number of public men who have any magnetism left to assert as they advance into old age is always small. Munnings was one of them. The appearance of his name on framed red-and-green posters spaced along the railings of Burlington House, Piccadilly, and emblazoned on a banner slung over the portico in the courtyards, brought people in large numbers to see the exhibition of his works in the Diploma Gallery from March to June 1956.

The exhibition opened on 10 March. It had already been informally visited by the Queen and the Duke of Edinburgh. Her Majesty, who mentioned her satisfaction in knowing that Munnings would paint her racehorse Aureole, headed the long list of contributors of pictures, with the centre-piece, 'H.M. King George V and Queen Mary Going to Ascot', sent from Windsor Castle. Ranged round the walls of the Diploma Gallery's four salons was a panorama of his working life, from his first Royal Academy picture, 'Stranded' (two children in a boat stuck in the Waveney reeds), dated 1898, to his most recent horse study, painted for his wife in 1955. The walls glowed with the boisterous yellows and blues of his Alton gipsies, the high scarlet of his huntsmen, the multi-coloured silks of his jockeys, the bright green and gold of his summer landscapes. As well as including examples of his early commercial art, the Royal Academy had borrowed from the National Gallery of Canada a selection of his First World War paintings, not seen in England since 1919.

It was like a harvest festival of the kindly fruits of his sixty years of painting, subduing the monumental professionalism of the equestrian set-pieces that had made his name but in which he never found the fulfilment of his best powers. 'Not too many of those commissioned pictures,' he had counselled Brooke, repeating the injunction more forcibly as the selection proceeded.

That was Munnings acknowledging the duality in his life as an artist. Combined in his personality were elements of poetry and opportunism. The sensitive interpreter of nature co-existed with the slick and often naughtily fecund producer of pictures that he never wanted to paint. Not even the most percipient visitor to the Diploma Gallery exhibition could have found an affinity between them and 'The Full River' from the Harris Gallery, Preston; 'The River Box at Thorrington', lent by Mr Brian Till; 'Landscape with Cows', from Ottawa; 'Autumn, Stoke-by-Nayland', lent by the artist; 'Camp at Malbuison', from the National Gallery of Canada; or 'The Frozen River, Flatford', from the Russell-Cotes Art Gallery, Bournemouth. Here was proof that more of his early work demonstrated his best powers than the new and rather slick style, a blending of both sides of his artistic nature, which later became his most widely recognised manner.

The dichotomy was strikingly confirmed in individual pictures. Kindred points of heaven and earth were seen to meet in the background of 'The Bramham Moor Hounds', lent by H.R.H. the Princess Royal, with the local eminence known as Great Alms-cliff rising like a place of pilgrimage in the clouds. 'Morning on the Manton Downs', lent by Viscount Astor, is a picture of more than horses from a famous stable. They are painted against far-ranging low hills that Munnings lovingly described, in a letter to his wife, as 'miles and miles of England'. 'Belvoir Hounds Walking Out In The Park', lent by Major Bouch, is more than half landscape, with middle-distance water reflecting the sky and Belvoir Castle silhouetted on a shadowy skyline.

One hundred and ten of the 309 works catalogued for the exhibition were 'lent by the artist'. Significantly, sixty of those were landscapes that he preferred to keep for his own pleasure. His pure landscapes would of themselves have made a reputation. In form, colour and craftsmanship, those leading characteristics of the English school of painting, the best of them showed Munnings to be in the line of direct succession to the English masters. Contemplating them in the Diploma Gallery, along with the best of the gipsy studies and the Exmoor ponies, one was forced to the provocative conclusion that the highest prices have been paid for the wrong Munnings pictures, that posterity will honour not the facile remembrancer of briefly celebrated horses and the vanishing panoply of the hunt, but the artist who

Munnings in his studio at Castle House.

Munnings in his last years.

painted the immemorial glory of the gorse on the Ringland Hills.

It was a member of the younger school, Anthony Devas, who prepared the introduction to the exhibition catalogue. Suggesting that art students generally would benefit by seeing the Munnings pictures, while doubting that the dons of contemporary art criticism would approve, he wrote: 'So good a chance may not soon recur – and it is a chance which would rescue a new Constable from intellectualism and neurasthenic probings into æsthetics, and fling open before him the door which leads to the real world. For this is the real world – this delighted response to life, this love of simple and ordinary things, and the enormous skill and technical accomplishment displayed in the more elaborate commissioned works – that too is the real world for painters, for that craftsmanship is the backbone of the master-pieces of artists as diverse as Stubbs and Botticelli, Rembrandt and Degas.'

Professional criticism of the exhibition was about equally divided between the favourable and the hostile, with two or three of the younger and hairier critics seizing the chance of revenge on Munnings for his still rankling assault from the presidential chair in 1949. Reading their articles again, one is incited to suggest that art criticism in our time suffers from too much thinking and too little seeing. True insight into Munnings's worth had been vouchsafed eight years earlier by a former director of the Tate Gallery who was a stern and upright judge of art and, incidentally, a painter of merit, D. S. MacColl, who on his deathbed told Humphrey Brooke, 'Munnings was always a fine artist', adding as a codicil to that important testi-mony: 'Give him my love.'

To 'express a little gratitude' to the Royal Academy for the compliment of the Diploma Gallery exhibition, Munnings made a gift of £300 to the Artists' Benevolent Fund, to which he had long been a donor. A small misunderstanding with Brooke over that matter caused him to write: 'My dear Scrambled-egg Secretary, What a pity you missed my point. Cheer up. Sorry I vexed you.'[1] Staying at the Chelsea house, he was persuaded

1. 10 April 1956.

by his wife to go with her to the Church of the Good Shepherd, Lower Sloane Street, where he wept openly during a service in which children took their pets to the altar to be blessed. The following day he sent the church a handsome donation.

The editor of *The Times* was 'a nitwit' because he refused publicity to Munnings's views on art teachers who were 'behaving like puppets manipulated by the Arts Council'. He was writing letters about the 'subversive activities' of that body and of the heads of certain provincial art schools, which he named, declaring that 'not one of them could make a living by painting'.

Sincerity was blunted by perversity; honesty by exasperation. The red fog that suffused his sight after the thorn-prick in his youth had long since become an emotional accessory, distorting his vision and blurring his sensibilities when he was in the grip of tensions generated by 'modern art'. He wrote to Sir Gerald Kelly: 'Nothing can be done. Nobody seems to care. Both the Sunday papers are busy acclaiming things which are *nothing at all to do with art*.'[1] And to Brooke, the Secretary: 'I'd never heard of Lowry. Elwes would have been a far better man. One of his works was *first-rate* last year.'

(4)

Voicing the opinion of several of his Academy colleagues, the President, Sir Albert Richardson, wrote questioning the wisdom of 'A.J.' in submitting his satrical picture for the forthcoming summer exhibition. There was a fear of legal difficulties arising from his portrayal of recognisable persons. He had circulated photographs of his 'little joke', as he preferred to call it, among members of the Council. The 'little joke', somewhat feebly composed on a large canvas, was an attack in paint on those art manifestations that he inflexibly believed were imperilling the traditions and authority of the Royal Academy. It showed Sir John Rothenstein, director of the Tate Gallery, Humphrey Brooke, Professor Mavrogordato, and an anonymous young lady, grouped about a piece of 'contemporary' sculpture on an upright plinth. In the background Professor Bodkin and an

1. 5 May 1956.

unidentifiable figure were seen microscopically examining a less clearly defined sculptural work. On the wall above were three Picasso copies. The posing was artfully expressive: Rothenstein, raptly gazing; Brooke, officially non-committal; Mavrogordato, classically reflective; Bodkin, elegantly professional; the young lady, unaffectedly puzzled. She was Miss Patricia Potter from Selfridge's fur department. Munnings had asked her to wear a pink frock – 'pink is a painter's colour' – and a black picture-hat.

He could claim no artistic merit for the painting. It was a reversion to the crudity of his early efforts as a commercial artist, the advertisements for Waverley bicycles and Bullard's ale. The President tried to dissuade him from sending it in as much for the sake of his reputation as for the good name of the Academy. When Munnings received the President's intimation, he had a relapse. The doctor had to be called.

Munnings to the Secretary of the Royal Academy:

> Castle House,
> Dedham.
> (Undated)

It was the President's extraordinary letter that so upset me and you must give him my very well expressed reply.

> Man with his burning soul
> Has but an hour of breath,
> To build a ship of Truth
> On which his soul may sail –
> Sail on a sea of death –
> For death takes toll of beauty, courage, youth,
> Of all but Truth.

Masefield wrote that in one of his books that he sent me.

> Yours,
> ALFRED

He enclosed the long letter that he had drafted for the President to see, dated 3 April 1956. He drafted an even longer one

the same day to be read to members of the Hanging Committee,
begging them not 'to make a storm over this very ordinary
picture'. He reminded them of the President's 'brilliant thrusts
at the critics, likening them to owls that hoot, bats that cling,
fleas that nip'. He recalled it to the President himself, adding:
'Far more publicity was given to this, and other cracks, than
ever I should get from this very ordinary picture. You have
attacked, in biting phrases, works of modern architects. This
gave many of us hope; now you tremble at a humorous picture,
aimed at modern art and its strongest supporter!' His letter to
the President continued:

> 'In last year's summer exhibition you never used your
> right to criticise a single one of the many atrocities hung in
> Galleries VII and VIII. After the private dinner you gave in
> the Academy, I went round with some of your noble guests,
> who were surprised and disgusted at the drolleries and
> nonsense shown there. Lord Ilchester said it was appalling,
> asking why they were hung. You took no regard of these
> foolish works, and now that I am trying to hit back for tradi-
> tion in paint, as you do in words, you object. For me it is a
> setback that I least expected.'

He deemed it proper to remind the President further that his
election was supported by men who regarded him as a fighter.
'I invited a party of reliable sculptors and painters to dine at
the Club, when as a block we decided to vote for you and get a
move on. I was all for you. Alas, now you seem full of nebulous
fears.' There was an extra flick of the whip for the President.
'A pity I didn't put you in my picture too.' He concluded:

> 'Although the picture is no masterpiece, it will draw the
> public, who will be with us. Excepting for a cultured few,
> no one will know who Sir John R. is or Brooke either. The
> crowd hasn't heard of them.
> Bodkin and Mavrogordato were looking forward to seeing
> themselves on the walls of the R.A. Other members of the
> Athenaeum, who have seen the photograph, as you have,
> reckoned it a good picture with one exception.

After all, Sir, what in God's name is there to fear?'

Members of the Hanging Committee were told in Munnings's letter to them that the picture 'compares poorly with Ruskin Spear's satire called "Abstractions" that was in last year's show.' According to Munnings, 'Spear copied Victor Pasmore's £500 Arts Council purchase now in the Tate!' He further informed the members of the Hanging Committee:

'My first model was an Athenaeum friend, Mavrogordato, Oxford Professor of Greek. My next was the Selfridge girl, whom I was allowed to choose through one of the directors. Afterwards, I gave her that dress and hat. Then came Brooke's figure, scraped out and moved twice. He tired quickly in his pose and took fright at the Barbara Hepworth object.

Sir John's figure was an afterthought, copied from an old *Illustrated*. It contained an article with photographs of the Tate director in the Gallery with a lady called Zsa Zsa. One of these showed him smiling at her side as she cocked her leg up on a reclining monster by Henry Moore. This was the picture I used for the portrait with a lawyer friend posing for me. All three Picassos on the wall were faithfully copied from a book of coloured Picasso pictures.'

He was willing, if doubts persisted in spite of those explanations, to take the further precaution of 'giving Brooke side-whiskers or a beard and to put a moustache on Rothenstein', at the same time insisting that 'the painting can never bring down more abusive criticism than the R.A. receives yearly.' He revealed that he had taken the title for it from 'an excellent Third Leader in *The Times*. It was called "Does The Subject Matter?" and concluded by saying that one day the Tate would again honour its walls with Bramley's '"Hopeless Dawn", etc.'

That *Times* leading article, he declared, had helped him 'to get well again'. He warned the Hanging Committee: 'If we don't make a stand for tradition, a time will come when those who dare to sculpt a beautiful figure or paint a good picture will be liquidated or transported for life.' There was a final injunction:

'One word more from one who has often been on the Hanging Committee and who has tried to paint for 60 years – hang the bottom line as low as you dare. They look better and give the top line a chance. Clever dealers sell a picture placed on a low-seated high-backed chair.

Lastly, kick out all the nonsense. Beware!

I wish you all well.'

CHAPTER 22

Waning Powers, Rising Market

(1)

His gratitude to his fellow-Academicians for the tribute of the Diploma Gallery exhibition did not inhibit him from ostentatiously refusing to attend the Royal Academy banquet in 1956. He told newspapermen: 'I just don't want to go. If you were a painter, how would you like having your work hung next to some of those bits of nonsense they are letting in now? Any amount of good painting doesn't get hung because of that stuff.' Though once again the news-cuttings agencies were kept busy reaping the harvest on his behalf, he could genuinely have pleaded that he was not well enough to go to London. He may also have been misreported, as he was apt to be when in the grip of his most violent prejudice.

The Diploma Gallery exhibition had yielded rewards of greater substance than news-cuttings. He wrote to his old friend 'Tommy' Bouch, the ex-M.F.H. at Ashorne, Warwick: 'Frost and Reed have sold a lot of prints, over a thousand pounds' worth at the show in R.A.'[1] High prices were paid for his racecourse studies. At a Christie's sale his 'Ponies in a Sandpit' made a thousand guineas. For 'The Whip', one of his Royal Academy pictures that year, the Bond Street Galleries paid him £1,200.

The people continued to flock into the Diploma Gallery. It was Munnings who also 'stole the show' at the adjacent summer exhibition of the R.A., when its doors opened in the first week of May. His lampoon on modern art entitled 'Does The Subject Matter?' had been hung, inconspicuously, in Gallery IV. Its

1. 5 May 1956.

partial eclipse did not prevent it from becoming the season's most talked-of picture, justifying Munnings's hopes if not confounding the fears of the President and others who thought it unworthy of both the artist and the institution.

Those who considered that 'Does The Subject Matter?' should not have been hung at all were not necessarily devotees of the newer schools of art thought and practice. Munnings always had admirers who trembled for his reputation. Some passed the picture by as a bad joke. Others thought it a good joke and stayed to laugh at Bodkin's elegantly poised right foot, the comically caricatured Picassos, the resigned eye of the artist's dog Toby, painted in as a whimsical afterthought. To the catalogue entry he had appended the lines:

> And why not purchased for the State?
> The State, alas, had come too late.
> Because the subject's so profound
> 'Twas sold for twenty thousand pound!

In the original version he had written 'Tate'. Official scruples led to its being altered to 'State', a substitution which he did not fail to advertise verbally to all and sundry in hearing radius when he was well enough to visit the show – 'the worst I've seen in my fifty-seven years as an exhibitor here.' Standing before the exhibits of some of the new men, he spluttered: 'Young brutes!' – precisely the kind of thing that was said about the post-Impressionists in their day. A picture by John Bratby brought on the over-excitement which the doctors had warned him against. 'Lumps of squeezed paint – still soft – you can pull chunks off it. *Craftsmanship!*' he shouted with a whole battery of exclamation marks in his voice.

The Times and other newspapers produced a surprise for him on 11 May 1956, by recording the continuing existence of 'Shrimp', his gipsy-boy model of the Swainsthorpe days whom he had not seen since they travelled the Norfolk byways with the caravan and the string of horses. 'What a go!' he exclaimed, reading the news. 'I must send him a present. I thought he'd been killed in an air-raid.' That fate had nearly befallen one of the most memorable of his Romany models, Elizabeth Loveday, the splendid Junoesque figure driving the pony and cart in his 'Gipsies Arriving on Epsom Downs for the Derby Week'. She was maimed in an air-raid on Bristol.

None of his pictures in the Diploma Gallery exhibition was officially for sale. Several were sold privately: 'Under Starter's Orders', £1,200; 'Study of a Start', £700; 'Coming off the Heath', £1,000. He wrote out a contract note for the proprietor of the Bond Street Galleries: 'Agreement between a poor starving artist and a half-dead dealer. . .'

He was making the most and perhaps too much of a blessed remission from the gout by driving daily to Newmarket to make new studies of the starts, a subject with an unfailing attraction for his artist's eye and one that was popular with the dealers. He had been granted a rare favour by the Clerk of the Course, the right to drive to the starting-gate, to make sketches there of the kaleidoscopic scene of horses and riders assembling for the climacteric moment. Returning to Dedham immediately after the last race, he would work solidly into the early hours of the following morning to finish sketches begun on the course. If he had not mastered his disabilities, he was defying them with remarkable resilience and spirit.

One night, after a day at Newmarket, he drove to London for an evening at the Athenaeum with Ogden and other friends. One of them remembers him rising from the table at 12.30 a.m., after seeing that the label on the last bottle of champagne was autographed by everyone present as a memento for Gedge, the wine butler. 'I must get a move on,' he said briskly. 'It's Newmarket again for me in the morning.' He was back at the starting-gate in time for the first race. He was seventy-eight.

Soon he had to admit that he had been 'overdoing it'. On his next visit to the races he saw the starts but did not get out of the car. 'I saw 40 horses at one start yesterday. BUT no notes – no painting,' he wrote to tell Sir Gerald Kelly in an invalid's hand. 'Studio a menace to my decaying wits, with thousands of *unfinished pictures*. Blast the painting – all too difficult. Easier to look at the lovely elder trees in bloom that we pass as we take our 42 miles drive through remote and little used roads in the heart of West Suffolk.'[1]

(2)

The Diploma Gallery exhibition had ended. Many of the pictures were being sent to Wolverhampton for exhibition at the Art Gallery. 'I wish you much success at Wolverhampton,' Kelly wrote. 'You know you are a very lucky man. At your great age, and I am the same, you seem to have unimpaired vitality and you go on painting and there is no better occupation.'[2] 'O that you could televise the ones you like at Wolverhampton!' Munnings replied, recalling Kelly's great public success in that medium. 'You would draw all the Midlands there.'

That autumn he worried Humphrey Brooke about the teaching in the Royal Academy schools, where he fancied that tradition and truth (both words given capitals and heavily underlined) were being jeopardised by the new race of art teachers. Elections to the Royal Academy continued to rouse his suspicion. He prepared an elaborate statement of his views for the Secretary to read to a General Assembly of Academicians and Associates. It was given the 'fair hearing' for which he pleaded. Brooke was able to tell him that, while there were strongly divergent opinions, 'the meeting expressed none but the warmest sentiments to you personally – admiration for your art and affectionate respect for all you stand for. There was abolutely no doubt about this.'

'Three nights in London have finished me off,' he wrote to Brooke on 12 October 1956 from Chelsea Park Gardens. 'The bloody noise of the road drill is in the King's Road. Back again to Dedham.' From Dedham he wrote: 'My studio in Chelsea is full of framed works which I could now sell and be wealthy on. But the damned Income Tax man waits to grab anything one dares to make over and above, etc., etc. What a curse!!' Hearing from Bodkin in Dublin that Noël Coward's latest play, 'on modern art and critics' – *Nude With Violin* – 'is

1. 5 July 1956.
2. 10 July 1956.

:op-hole,' he remarked: 'I hope Sir John Rothenstein will go
to the first night when it comes to London.'

(3)

In December 1956 yet another exhibition of his work was
put on in London, at the Bond Street Galleries, from which the
proprietor, James Green, wrote to him on 3 December: 'I need
not tell you how thrilled I am at the honour you have done me
in holding this exhibition at my humble gallery. Nothing that
I can say here would really convey to you how much it means
to us all.' It consisted of 180 pictures and drawings, nearly all
of them minor works that had lain unheeded in his studios for
many years. Twenty of them were catalogued as 'boyhood
drawings', pencil sketches and water-colours of knights in
armour and Red Indians of his juvenile imagination at the mill.
He threw back his head and laughed when he was told that they
were being bought for fifteen guineas apiece as if they were
treasure-trove. Of the two or three important works that he had
sent, his painting of the Queen's horse Aureole was the most
conspicuous. Its price was £1,500 and Munnings gave the
money to the fund being raised for the purchase of Gainsborough's birthplace at Sudbury, Suffolk. Another picture of
Aureole with two other horses from Boyd-Rochfort's stables at
Newmarket was sold for £1,000, which sum he handed to the
Hungarian Relief Fund. Red tabs, denoting sales, soon appeared
on practically every picture and drawing. One of the purchasers
was a Canadian woman admirer of his work who crossed the
Atlantic specially to see the exhibition.

He went to the Royal Academy on 11 December to take part
in the election of a new President. Gout was on him again but
he was in a fighting mood, determined to throw his full weight
in support of Charles Wheeler R.A., the sculptor whose
figures on the Bank of England and statuary in Trafalgar Square
were already London heirlooms. Also in the running was
James Fitton R.A., who said he had no wish to emulate the Old
Masters but desired 'to paint London and Manchester as they
are today'. Munnings did not hide his sympathies and made

some explosive references to Fitton which were widely quoted in the Press.

The three previous Presidents had been controversial figures in the history of the Royal Academy: Munnings, the scourge of the modernists; Kelly, whose verbal felicities as well as his amusing indiscretions had made him a television personality overnight; and Richardson, champion of eighteenth-century values who ordered the electric light to be switched off at Council meetings and candles lighted in its place. Wheeler, a firmly undemonstrative, peace-making man, was the first sculptor to become President. When Munnings joined in the congratulatory toast it was seen that he held his glass aloft in a deformed right hand. He wrote to Brooke three days later: 'I rang up Fitton and begged him to forgive and to say that I was very sorry. He too was noble and said: "We'll have a drink when next we meet".'[1]

(4)

Munnings did not think it anomalous, as some people did, that he should sponsor the proposed exhibition of Russian and Soviet art at the Royal Academy and at the same time contribute generously to the fund for succouring the victims of Soviet tyranny in Hungary. When *The Times* published a letter from him advocating the exhibition,[2] the *Daily Worker* commented on it the next day under the heading: 'Sir Alfred's Good Sense.' *Komsomolskaya Pravda* endorsed 'the letter of Sir Alfred Munnings'. The London *News Chronicle* saw in it a further instance of his 'readiness to start a controversy'.

He was delighted by the number of greetings cards sent to him that Christmas – 'more than ever before', and many from people he had never met. There was the discordant note that his appeal for money to buy Gainsborough's house had gone largely ignored. 'Just over £2,000 subscribed,' he wrote to the *Daily Mail* art critic, Pierre Jeannerat, 'and £1,500 of it mine!!!! What a country!! One of the world's artists too.' He wrote again: 'If only the *Daily Mail* took the matter up – my dear soul, the

1. 14 December 1956.
2. 2 January 1957.

amount would roll up in a week or two. Cannot you closet your self with the Editor and put the thing to him?'[1]

Driving out with the art critic to see the Gainsborough birth-place at Sudbury, he was roused to indignation by the sight of village children being taken by bus to a central urban school, 'where they lose the love and knowledge of the land and its ways and become garage-minded'. He recalled, as a comment on rural labour conditions, that the Clerk of the Course at New-market had told him that he was 'trying to breed a new strain of cattle that wouldn't need feeding at the week-ends'. Munnings roared anew at the joke. 'How can you be a countryman and have your week-ends off?'

As soon as they had set foot in the fine Perpendicular Gothic church at Long Melford, his voice was uplifted in fresh denuncia-tion. 'What damned fools they were to fill this lovely nave with these ghastly wooden benches! Clear the lot out, I say! Put in rush chairs', a stirring of the memory perhaps from his sacri-legious adventure with the rebel priests of Cornwall. At Gainsborough's house in Sudbury the walls re-echoed his respect for the master: 'a genius far beyond our comprehension,' he had written, 'a genius born of our English climate, landscape and temperament.' He told Jeannerat: 'One of the greatest artists of all time! Think of it – £160,000 from America for his "Blue Boy"! And here are we, scraping round for a few pounds to save his birthplace! Doesn't *any* high-up in Fleet Street care about art?' He had earlier confided to Jeannerat that, being childless, he had made 'a considerable bequest' to the Royal Academy in his will. It appeared that he had since revoked that intention. 'What's the good? Look at the stuff they're letting in now.'

The London *Evening News* reported that 'a private connois-seur' had given £5,500 for his 'Unsaddling at Cheltenham', 'one of the highest prices ever paid for a picture by a living British artist'. At Sotheby's, a picture that he had painted of a coachman 'on the box' in 1909 and sold then to the Mayor of Preston for £25 was bought by the Wildenstein Gallery for 580 guineas. Such figures looked well in print, a good advertisement for the Munnings market. It was an excuse to write a letter to

3. 22 Februray 1957.

the *Daily Telegraph* complaining of 'income tax which stays all incentive and leaves us cursing'. Off-setting his bad humour was a news story of an exhibition in Baltimore of so-called paintings by a chimpanzee named Betsy. Some of them were selling at forty dollars each. A fourth leader in *The Times* suggested that 'the exhibition had its bright side for Sir Alfred Munnings, in whose after-dinner oratory Betsy seems destined to play a useful part'.

Unfortunately, that cheerful postulate was no longer warrantable. The days of Munnings's after-dinner speaking, indeed of dining out, were over. He had now virtually abandoned London, finding the world there at last too much with him.

(5)

'Are we doomed for ever to accept and endure this infernal distracting noise that drowns all the sounds of the sea, the wind in the trees, the songs of the birds?' he asked in another letter to the *Daily Telegraph*, 3 March 1957. He told how 'yesterday, a mild day of sunshine', he had gone in search of 'the peace and quiet of a once unspoilt part of Suffolk.' He did not find it. 'The peace I sought was utterly destroyed by the roar of jet planes. The more perfect the day, the louder the din!'

'Look!' he exploded, talking to a member of the staff of the *East Anglian Magazine*. 'Look what they've done to the countryside! Roads like bloody race-tracks, factories everywhere, miles of council houses all looking alike.' He raised his voice to demand: 'What can we do against the power of industry, the power of the Press, and all this blackguardedly business of living only for a passing sensation without any regard for the consequence of our actions?'

'Blast these pictures and all the letters I get,' he wrote to Frost and Reed, of Bond Street, on 19 March, 1957. The following day his old Athenaeum companion C. K. Ogden died. Receiving the news, Munnings fell back in his chair, saying to his wife: 'I can never go to the Club again,' and there were to be few more opportunities for him to do so. Further mournful remembrance was evoked by a local newspaper announcement that paintings by him belonging to the family of 'the late Mr Shaw Tomkins, of Norwich', his friend and patron of the Art School years who had died in 1933, were being sold at auction in Norwich that week. Though the works were all of his student period, the sale was attended by dealers from many parts of the country. Violet Munnings wrote to tell the proprietor of the Bond Street Galleries: 'He is frightfully nervy. Mrs Raeburn[1] is so good with him, walks, motors, reads to him in the evening.'

Receiving an invitation to a function in London, he answered: 'I would love to be at the dinner. But I have to be careful at last and go *slow*.'[2] There were tentative plans for a show of his work in New York. Knoedler's, the dealers there, were said to be 'showing enthusiasm' and were proposing to send a representative to London for discussions. Nothing came of the scheme. Munnings wrote to Green, of the Bond Street Galleries, in a trembling hand: 'My dear Marquis de Filet Steak, When you come over and take a painting that has given me infinite trouble – and EXPENSE – I like to be paid for it. Please send cheque to the artist who created it, £300. Then I'll think over other matters. In the meantime, eat less.'[3] The cheque was already in the post. Munnings to Green: 'Dear Lord Worcester Sauce, Cheque £300 to hand for a painting of a lad on a horse which nobody today could do. The snow, the light – the pose of the lad – all done at my stables on Exmoor in the last *damned* war. . . . Well, what's the use of painting? See last Monday's *Times*. Miles on Picasso and his show at Arles. God help us.'[4]

When Green wrote to him for his birthday, 8 October, he answered: 'My dear Picture Dealer & Seller, I wish folk would forget birthdays. Besides, we're always a year too much. Being born in 1878, I was not 1 year old until 1879. Work that out, please.' His deepest prejudice was immune from the weakening processes of time. 'How disgraceful,' he wrote to Humphrey Brooke on 18 December 1957, 'that the Tate is asking for

1. Widow of H. R. Macbeth-Raeburn R.A. (1860-1947). Herself a painter, she acted as Munnings's studio assistant.
2. 13 April 1957.
3. 30 July 1957.
4. 31 July 1957.

£100,000, because to get the latest Braque or Matisse they must pay £25,000. There should be a *hell* of a row about it.' He wrote to the President of the Royal Academy[1] on 31 March 1958:

> '. . . Only a line from one who has been through it. Take the advice of a painter and past P.R.A. Remind the committee that it is best to make the *bottom line* not more than 3 or 4 inches above the dado. Kelly used to put it up 8 inches – all *wrong*. Pictures look *far better* at that lower level and the ones above have a chance too. Do make the Hanging Committee see this with my love and good wishes.
>
> Now your troubles begin.
>
> When I got the election list with that fellow X——'s name down, I gave up all hope for the R.A. All going along the *wrong* path.'

The gathering shadows were deepened by the death that year of Gedge, the wine butler at the Athenaeum, whose ministrations had enhanced the pleasures of his membership and whom he mourned as if he had been one of his intimates of that place. He had not been to the club since Ogden died. The passing of Gedge confirmed him in that heavy-hearted resolve. His grief at the death of both those men of different degrees showed the sensitive, tender side of his nature. It was hidden from much of his town acquaintance. He was always at his best in the country, where his truest sympathies had been formed.

Spending his time there now, he occasionally rode out among the familiar scenes of the Stour valley, acknowledging the salutes of passers-by with a lift of his riding whip. The high spirits of other times, when he had neighbours in to dinner and played tricks on those who fancied themselves judges of wine, had evaporated. The weather of nearly eighty years was going from his face. He still had his good head of hair, with the boyishly high parting, and if his clothes hung more loosely on him, he had not lost the old jauntiness of manner that had always made him seem poised for any light-hearted adventure.

When he felt well enough, he drove into Colchester to visit

1. Sir Charles Wheeler.

bookshops or to talk with his wine-merchant. He also liked to buy shrimps, which he would eat out of the bag on the way home, throwing the tails out of the car window. One day, his wife being out, he asked a London dealer, who had come down by appointment, to go with him. Before leaving the house he counted the cash in his pocket. It amounted to a few shillings. He went to the bookshelf and took down a volume of Dickens, flicking through it until he found what he was looking for – a five-pound note. His wink to the dealer suggested that it was a well-tried emergency device.

'My fervour is fast abating. It is for you to carry the lance and tilt it now.' He was writing to Guy Schofield, at the *Yorkshire Post*, after the opening of the summer exhibition of 1958. 'Slip up to town one day yourself and write a *stinger*. Let them know that one paper at least speaks its mind on this frightful letting down of Tradition on the walls of the Academy. . . . Be like Captain Marryat who wrote *Midshipman Easy* and lay it on. *Blast* the critics.'

Four of his Royal Academy pictures that year were bought for £5,850 by a London bookmaker who, at the close of the summer show, sent them to Sotheby's, where they made £10,600. Rage empurpled Munnings's face. 'This man walked into the Academy and bought the four pictures before anyone else had a chance. It's not playing the game!' His anger was not appeased by a reminder that he was one of the few living artists whose work made 'news' in the auction-room. At the same time the proprietor of the Bond Street Galleries had to tell him that 'business has been so bad that I am sorry to tell you it is almost negligible'. To set against that pessimistic disclosure there was the fact that an American woman visiting London was so determined to own a Munnings picture that she paid £500 at sight for a small painting that he had done years before of his wife's fawn Pekinese.

A brief blaze of publicity resulted from the B.B.C. television programme in which he was the central personality during Derby week 1958. In a studio set 'mocked up' to suggest his study fireside at Castle House, he declaimed some of his ballads lately published in a collected edition.[1] The viewers were not

1. *Ballads and Poems* (Museum Press 1958).

Q

to know that after he had faded from their screens he gave a remarkable off-stage display of his mental virtuosity to the workers in the studio.

Normally the camera-crews of television are keen to leave at the end of a day's work in the studios. Christopher Doll, the producer of the programme in which Munnings appeared, says that for once they stayed on, so beguiling was his talk. He spoke about his painting life. He recalled famous contemporaries. He quoted impressively from Shakespeare and Surtees. He aired his opinions in lines of his invention:

> If you want to be reviewed
> By *The Times* with promptitude
> You do a monster nude
> To weigh a ton;
> With a belly to protrude
> Of genetic magnitude,
> And have it crude and rude
> And half begun!

His audience of a younger generation, enlarged by the electricians and other technical hands, fell completely under his spell. Inadvertently, a microphone had been left open, relaying his uncensored utterances to the young women of the control room. They were equally captivated. He held the attention of them all for ninety minutes, an impromptu entertainment that is still talked about by those who were on duty that night in the Hammersmith studios of B.B.C. television.

(6)

Munnings to Humphrey Brooke, 7 July 1958: 'I'm unable to deal with correspondence. Off colour. Right hand still swollen and painful. I *cannot* do it.' Despite the disavowal he wrote letters that were printed in *The Times* and the *Daily Telegraph* on topics that were never far from his thoughts, the menaced beauty of England and the unforeseen effects of scientific progress. To the *Daily Telegraph*: 'Long ago, acorns were planted along hedgerows. Nothing of the kind happens now, and when all the oaks and elms and woodlands are gone ours will be a base scene indeed, with ever-increasing rows of ugly bungalows stretching from one spill-over town to another. But we "couldn't care less".' And to *The Times*: 'Atomic tests may not be the sole cause of disastrous weather. Surely part blame must be laid on the continual rending of the atmosphere by fast and faster jet planes that shatter our nerves, leaving vast vacuums and volleyings of air-filling thunder in their wake. All this cleavage of air, miles above, with burstings of the sound barrier, must cause atmospheric disturbances.' His letter was given in full:

'The vicar here tells me that in spite of cleaning and sweeping of floors and seats layers of dust fall in the fine church after the passing of jets. Last week, at Stoke-by-Nayland, I stood entranced and wondering at the miracle of the swift, *silent* flight of hundreds of swallows feeding their young beneath the wide overhanging eaves of Tudor almshouses behind the tall church tower. . . . Then came the murderous deafening din of man-made noise of jet planes. The very ground shook. As senseless as sputniks and rockets to the moon, thought I, hearing others miles above bursting the sound barrier.

The like of Gray, Wordsworth, Keats and Burns could never exist today. The mind of the scientist establishes a fact which the mind of the artist guessed at long before.'

Jet noise distracted him beyond endurance, a constantly renewed annoyance, overheating his temper, wearing his nerves. Shaking his fist at the overhead turmoil, he easily persuaded himself that the arch-conspirators against the ancestral peace of East Anglia were the American jet flyers. They were the fallen angels of his cosmos. It was they who dispersed the goodwill that he had cherished ever since his exciting and profitable painting trip to the United States thirty-five years earlier.

In August 1958 Humphrey Brooke rang up Munnings at Castle House, asking to be allowed to bring over an American husband and wife from Virginia who particularly wished to meet him. Receiving permission, Brooke drove them to Dedham. As they walked up the drive to Castle House, a jet aircraft went over, shaking the tree-tops. Munnings met them on the doorstep with a hostile glare. Before Brooke could introduce his friends, Munnings said in a temper: 'I hate all bloody Americans.' There was an extremely awkward silence. He then beckoned them in and from that moment was so courteous and considerate a host that the Americans wrote afterwards to Brooke to tell him that meeting Munnings was the highlight of their English visit.

He had asked that his personal appreciation of a painting in the exhibition of Russian and Soviet Art at the Royal Academy should be conveyed to the artist, Kubrinsky, in Moscow. 'I'm glad that my appreciation got there,' he wrote to Brooke on 4 March 1959. 'All I wanted.' It proved to be the last of his many letters to the Secretary. In it he referred to 'a fantastic speech' by the Prime Minister, Harold Macmillan. 'He has no soul. He boasts of England as a land of industrialism, etc., etc.' It was the *cri de coeur* of a swimmer against the tide whose strength is fast failing.

'The Prime Minister doesn't see that the soil of England is killed, that nothing is left. London sprawls to Coventry and Northampton, to Chelmsford, to Brighton and Dover. The end will be *noise* – NOISE – speed – lack of water and a grossly over-populated country. It won't bear thinking about.'

Brooke was with him at Castle House at the end of April 1959. Both his hands were bound up in flannel. He was hardly able to move. 'He told me,' said Brooke, 'that as he would never paint again he wished he were dead.' It was to be their last meeting. In spite of his sufferings he insisted on getting up from his chair to pour Brooke a glass of sherry, a supreme effort which touched Brooke deeply. Almost his last remark before saying good-bye was a chiding one: 'Ah, you're a Lowry man.' The next day he telephoned to Brooke at the Royal Academy, apologising for having been 'such poor company'.

His cardiac state worsened. At Castle House, during the last weeks, he passed many of his hours staring into space, apparently seeing nothing. Now that he could no longer paint, life for him

was bereft of meaning. Now and again he would tug in anger
at a long, untidily knotted length of string that led from his
bed to the window, on the sill of which he had fixed a wooden
clapper to scare the jackdaws.

On 16 July 1959, two directors of a leading Bond Street
gallery went to Castle House in the hope of seeing him. They
heard his voice raised vituperatively in his bedroom, but he was
not well enough to receive them. In the early hours of the
following morning his wife was wakened by the nurse hurrying
in from his room with the news: 'He's gone!' He had died in his
sleep in his eighty-first year.

(5)

For the last time his name blazed in the headlines, a typo-
graphical ovation. It testified to as wide an esteem for Munnings
the unapologetic Englishman as for Munnings the artist.
Summaries of his career and reviews of his work filled many
columns in the newspapers. While the obituarists differed in
their judgments of his painting achievements, there was agreement that his personality contained ingredients of genius and
that it ensured him a place in many of the memoirs of his time.
Those who thought they were conferring the laurels of lasting
fame on him by evoking such masters of equine portraiture as
Stubbs and Ben Marshall may have been less acute than those
who saw his reputation resting finally on his contribution to the
long and honourable tradition of English landscape painting.

There was the overflowing memorial service at St James's
Church, Piccadilly, on 23 July 1959, at which his latest successor
in the venerable presidential chair at Burlington House across
the way, Sir Charles Wheeler, recalled 'his boundless enthusiasm, which at times split Sir Joshua's mantle at the seams'.
Reminded of that unremitting zest and ardent temper, there
were those who, besides his old friends and colleagues, left the
church feeling that a vital force had gone from their lives. Among
the many artists present was the towering figure of Augustus
John o.m., who had travelled from his Hampshire home that
hot summer's day to add his tribute of regard. He wore a straw

hat which he had daubed with black paint to suit the occasion.

The last act of official remembrance and farewell was the dedication, on 3 June 1960, of a memorial tablet placed next to that of John Constable in the crypt of St Paul's Cathedral, where his ashes had been laid. Munnings had never asserted a claim to such eminence of propinquity in life or death. Justice in concord with sentiment had decreed it. Beneath his carved profile are lines by the Poet Laureate:

> O friend, how very lovely are the things,
> The English things, you helped us to perceive.

Index